Eighteenth-Century Disse
Cambridge Platonism

Eighteenth-Century Dissent and Cambridge Platonism identifies an ethically and politically engaged philosophy of religion in eighteenth-century Rational Dissent, particularly in the work of Richard Price (1723–1791), and in the radical thought of Mary Wollstonecraft. It traces their ethico-political account of reason, natural theology and human freedom back to seventeenth century Cambridge Platonism and thereby shows how popular histories of the philosophy of religion in modernity have been over-determined both by analytic philosophy of religion and by its critics. The eighteenth century has typically been portrayed as an age of reason, defined as a project of rationalism, liberalism and increasing secularisation, leading inevitably to nihilism and the collapse of modernity. Within this narrative, the Rational Dissenters have been accused of being the culmination of eighteenth-century rationalism in Britain, epitomising the philosophy of modernity. This book challenges this reading of history by highlighting the importance of teleology, deiformity, the immutability of goodness and the divinity of reason within the tradition of Rational Dissent, and it demonstrates that the philosophy and ethics of both Price and Wollstonecraft are profoundly theological. Price's philosophy of political liberty and Wollstonecraft's feminism, both grounded in a Platonic conception of freedom, are perfectionist and radical rather than liberal. This has important implications for understanding the political nature of eighteenth-century philosophical theology: these thinkers represent not so much a shaking off of religion by secular rationality but a challenge to religious and political hegemony. By distinguishing Price and Wollstonecraft from other forms of rationalism, including deism and Socinianism, this book takes issue with the popular division of eighteenth-century philosophy into rationalistic and empirical strands and, through considering the legacy of Cambridge Platonism, draws attention to an alternative philosophy of religion that lies between both empiricism and discursive inference.

Louise Hickman is Senior Lecturer in Philosophy and Ethics at Newman University, Birmingham, UK.

Routledge Studies in the Philosophy of Religion

For a full list of titles in this series, please visit www.routledge.com

Eighteenth-Century Dissent and Cambridge Platonism

Reconceiving the Philosophy of Religion

Louise Hickman

Routledge
Taylor & Francis Group

LONDON AND NEW YORK

First published 2017
by Routledge

2 Park Square, Milton Park, Abingdon, Oxfordshire OX14 4RN
52 Vanderbilt Avenue, New York, NY 10017

Routledge is an imprint of the Taylor & Francis Group, an informa business

First issued in paperback 2020

British Library Cataloguing-in-Publication Data
A catalogue record for this book is available from the British Library

Library of Congress Cataloging-in-Publication Data
Names: Hickman, Louise, author.
Title: Eighteenth-century dissent and Cambridge Platonism :
  reconceiving the philosophy of religion / by Louise Hickman.
Description: 1 [edition]. | New York : Routledge, 2017. | Series:
  Routledge studies in the philosophy of religion ; 16 | Includes
  bibliographical references and index.
Identifiers: LCCN 2017000541 | ISBN 9781138652415 (hardback :
  alk. paper)
Subjects: LCSH: Dissenters, Religious—England—History—18th
  century. | Cambridge Platonists. | England—Church history—18th
  century. | Religion—Philosophy.
Classification: LCC BX5203.3 .H53 2017 | DDC 210.942/09033—dc23
LC record available at https://lccn.loc.gov/2017000541

ISBN: 978-1-138-65241-5 (hbk)
ISBN: 978-0-367-59511-1 (pbk)

Typeset in Sabon
by Apex CoVantage, LLC

Contents

Acknowledgements

In writing this book, I have become indebted to many people. I first explored my interests in Cambridge Platonism and Rational Dissent in my PhD work supervised by Douglas Hedley to whom I am immensely grateful, not least for instilling in me an appreciation for the history of philosophy and for the Cambridge Platonists but also for ongoing support spanning many years. I would also like to thank Sarah Hutton and Michael Langford for their roles in fostering my research in this field while it was still in its early stages.

Sincere thanks are due to Russell Re Manning for all his editorial help, general encouragement and comments on early versions of the manuscript. I am also extremely grateful to the anonymous reviewers of the manuscript who provided valuable suggestions for improvement and to Roger Trigg who read the whole thing and who has been a considerable source of support for many years. The shortcomings that remain are, of course, entirely my own.

Thanks are also due to Andrew Weckenmann at Routledge for his patience as the final manuscript has taken shape and to the Research Committee at Newman University for funding several weeks' research leave in 2014–15. I would like to acknowledge the editors of *Enlightenment and Dissent* and the *International Journal of the Classical Tradition* for permission to reproduce material first published in articles in their journals. An earlier version of Chapter 2 appears as 'Godliness and Godlikeness: Cambridge Platonism in Richard Price's Religious Rationalism', *Enlightenment and Dissent* 24 (2008), pp. 1–23 and an original version of Chapter 5 appears as 'Casting out Hagar and Her Children: Richard Price, Platonism and the Origins of American Independence', *International Journal of the Classical Tradition* 18 (2011), pp. 393–414.

I am indebted to many scholars who have made cherished conversation partners. Thank you to Tom Hunt, Chris Langley, David Leech and David McLoughlin for stimulating exchanges at various stages of this project. Friends and family sustained me throughout the writing of this book, and without them, I simply could not have kept going. I am deeply grateful to Helen Bardy, Liz Bates, Daniel Davies, Liz Gulliford, Margaret Holland, Alex Mold, Rachel and Alex Moore, Noelle Plack, Merav Rosenfeld-Hadad,

Richard Sanders, Sally Sheward, Gemma Simmonds and Chris Southgate, who have nurtured me in innumerable ways through good company, wonderful cooking, sound advice and practical support. I also owe a special debt of gratitude to Gaynor Pollard for countless hours of intellectual conversation and treasured companionship. Finally, my parents, Judith and Paul, have given me unceasing encouragement, friendship and care, often having more faith in me than I had in myself. I dedicate this book to them, with love.

Preface

Philosophers ask questions and try to answer them. What is often neglected, however, is the fact that the questions considered worth asking, the answers thought worthy of acceptance and the philosophical problems deemed to be in need of a solution have been forged in history and in the re-reading of history. When it comes to the past, the history of philosophical questions, terminology and methods is frequently regarded as inconsequential to the arguments and conclusions forming the mainstay of the discipline.[1] As a result, many philosophers have come to be characterised by a discernible reluctance to study the history of philosophical thought. Philosophers of religion too – particularly those in the analytic tradition – are often no different. The backstory of a given religious claim often doesn't seem to matter much when debating its logical possibility or rational justification, or whether it is the best possible explanation for a given set of observations.[2]

It is the argument of this book, however, that the history of the philosophy of religion is indispensable to its practice. Philosophers, including philosophers of religion, are not ahistorical creatures in their search for wisdom. Furthermore, the study of this past is not only essential for understanding the present and why it is we ask the questions we do but also for imagining new futures. Pamela Sue Anderson is right to lament an excessive concern for the justification of knowledge which has come to typify the philosophy of religion and which causes the neglect of other more ethically important questions. These include questions about the context of our knowledge, what it is, who possesses it and how it is acquired.[3] The history of philosophy, I suggest, has a vital role to play in helping us pursue these alternative questions, and without it, we cannot hope to answer them. It can accomplish this task, I argue, because when the philosophy of religion of the past is examined and contextualised, it reveals very different concerns and questions from those commonly assumed.

The central subjects of this book are the eighteenth-century English Rational Dissenters, but its scope also takes in some of the seventeenth-century divines who preceded them: the thinkers most often called the Cambridge Platonists. It is an important characteristic of their thought that philosophy and theology cannot readily be distinguished. They point us towards a conception of reason that is at once both deeply theological, deeply ethical and inherently political. Their primary concern is with truth conceived of as inseparable from goodness, resulting in a philosophy of religion that is profoundly and consciously political. With this study of history comes an imperative: to conceive of the philosophy of religion and natural theology in ways other than those typically proposed by Anglo-American philosophers of religion. In short, through its study of the history of philosophy, this book aims to remind contemporary philosophers of religion of the ethico-political roots of the discipline – a fact that analytical philosophers of religion are often inclined to forget.

Grace Jantzen asks us to think about

> what a difference it would have made to the history of modernity if the Philosophy of Religion had taken as its emphasis and aim a yearning for beauty and goodness, and fostering their discernment, rather than the justification of a list of beliefs about [God].[4]

It is the argument of this book that much seventeenth- and eighteenth-century philosophy of religion, especially its natural theology, was in fact stirred by just such a longing. It is hoped that by drawing attention to this fact, this book will encourage philosophers of religion to heed Jantzen's call to restore ethical concerns once again to the very centre of the discipline. This is not to defend the logic of the arguments themselves, as they are deeply flawed. Rather, the study of the history of philosophy presented here is meant to direct us towards the urgent demand, clearly apparent in seventeenth and eighteenth natural theology, to re-orientate our present reality in response to an ethical cosmos and towards a philosophy of religion centred not principally on the demand to justify propositional beliefs, but on the perennial Platonic question that should be at the core of any philosophy of religion: 'How should I live?'

Notes

1 Nick Trakakis, *The End of Philosophy of Religion* (London: Continuum, 2008), 32.
2 See, for example, Jake Chandler and Victoria S. Harrison, eds., *Probability in the Philosophy of Religion* (Oxford: Oxford University Press, 2012); Chad Meister, *Philosophy of Religion* (Basingstoke: Palgrave Macmillan, 2014); Corey Miller and Paul Gould, eds., *Is Faith in God Reasonable? Debates in Philosophy, Science, and Rhetoric* (London: Routledge, 2014).
3 Pamela Sue Anderson, "An Epistemological-Ethical Approach," in *Feminist Philosophy of Religion: Critical Readings*, ed. Pamela Sue Anderson and Beverley Clack (London: Routledge, 2004), 92.
4 Grace M. Jantzen, "Feminist Philosophy of Religion: Open Discussion with Pamela Anderson," *Feminist Theology* 26 (2001): 106.

Introduction

Natural theology has had bad press. Commonly understood as referring to knowledge about God that can be ascertained through reason independently of revelation, it has come to be seen largely in terms of arguments for God's existence. The term tends to conjure up images of the likes of William Paley and Samuel Clarke together with other evidentially inclined usual suspects from the eighteenth century: ghosts from the past who laboured to present arguments for God's existence that are now regarded as well and truly defeated. Branded in retrospect the heyday of natural theology, this particular century has been formative in shaping how the nature of philosophy of religion is conceived today. When the philosophy of religion is debated or taught to students in the Anglo-American world in the form of arguments for God's existence and analysis of the concept of God – with the primary purpose of justifying propositional belief in God – it owes much to a particular historical conception of what the philosophy of religion has, in the past, been about. Swinburne, for example, is confident that 'what has worried ordinary men [sic] down the centuries is whether the evidence of human experience shows that the claim [that God exists] is true or that it is false,' and he concludes from this that justifying belief by rational argument is 'perhaps the most important of all deep issues which stir the human mind.'[1] It is widely assumed, therefore, that the rational defence of theism, belief in a God who cares for the world, was principally concerned with epistemic justification.

Analytic philosophy of religion and its reading of history

Given the historical assumption outlined earlier, it seems unproblematic to suggest that arguments about Paley's infamous timepiece (part of his famous – or notorious – 'design' argument) or Clarke's necessarily existing eternal being can be lifted out of their context and vetted purely according to coherence and the rational laws of logic. Surely, all they were doing was trying to put forward rational arguments immune to reasoned doubt. If so, they can be subject to the rigours of today's rational analysis and quickly dismissed. Either the history of these arguments is deemed insignificant or

the arguments themselves are thought to have been intended by their proponents as detachable from their context, a 'pure philosophy,' rational and logical in the service of the justification of belief.

Such assumptions about the nature and purpose of these historical arguments in natural theology do much to reinforce the aims and objectives of analytic philosophy of religion. In the analytic method, philosophers aim to write in sentences that can be analysed formally valuing above everything else the virtues of clarity, precision and logical coherence. The model is scientific. Myth and metaphor are eschewed, and conceptual analysis is treated (as far as possible) as the legitimate source of evidence.[2] This analytic way of thinking has become the dominant feature of Anglo-American philosophy of religion. As Richard Swinburne puts it, 'the goal is now metaphysical: to give a correct account of what are the ultimate constituents of the world and how they interact.'[3] For analytic philosophy of religion, what determines whether an account is indeed 'correct' very much depends on mathematical and scientific criteria.

The philosophy of religion thus takes on a scientific epistemology and an aspiration for objectivity. Notwithstanding more recent attempts to broaden the scope of the discipline – with, for example, analytic theology – a cursory glance at popular anthologies in philosophy of religion (for example, Paul Copan and Chad Meister's *Philosophy of Religion: Classic and Contemporary Issues,* 2008 or Michael C. Rea and Louis Pojman's *Philosophy of Religion: An Anthology,* 2015) further confirms that questions about the nature and existence of God, and the justification of religious belief, are no less dominant now than they were forty years ago.[4] A concern with the justification of propositional religious truth claims and their rational analysis has consequently turned epistemology into the beating heart of this discipline. By utilising the analytic model, philosophical theism has been turned into 'the programme of giving a clear coherent account of the nature of God . . . and providing cogent arguments for the existence of such a God.'[5] The philosophy of religion has thus become characterised by the clarification of the concept of God, arguments for the coherence or incoherence of this theistic concept, arguments for or against God's existence (natural theology) and analysis of the nature of belief (including miracles and religious experience).

The ethical task of the history of the philosophy of religion

The above assumptions need to be challenged, however, and for this task, history is indispensable. Richard Rorty, J.B. Schneewind, Quentin Skinner and others have done much to remind analytic philosophers that they need to be more self-conscious about their place in the historical philosophical conversation.[6] When historical ideas are considered, there tends to be little regard to the social, political and ethical background of the philosophical and theological debate. The contexts of the arguments are often not considered important, with energy spent elsewhere evaluating ideas abstracted from their background. It is the argument of this book that when the arguments of the seventeenth- and eighteenth-century English philosophers of religion are contextualised, a different vision of the discipline emerges. The heyday of natural theology was certainly not what it is usually assumed to be. A closer study of the history of philosophy uncovers a philosophy of religion that was motivated by ethical and political concerns, and a natural theology that rested on a commitment to a world replete with inherent value.

The following chapters bring to light the main concerns of some noteworthy but often overlooked seventeenth- and eighteenth-century philosophers of religion. They focus on two figures most usually categorised as part of the eighteenth-century intellectual movement called Rational Dissent: Richard Price (1723–1791) and Joseph Priestley (1733–1804). The term Rational Dissent, defined in more detail in Chapter 1, covers a diverse group of thinkers (often labelled heterodox) who were committed to the harmony of faith and reason. They were Nonconformist in that they did not conform to the Anglican Book of Common Prayer or Thirty-Nine Articles. Unlike many other Nonconformist groups, they were notable for their rejection of Calvinism, including its theology of double predestination, the depravity of reason and the necessity of spiritual regeneration (the theology that belief does not come from us but from spiritual renewal bestowed by God).[7] Rational Dissent was a complex phenomenon and cannot always be distinguished easily from the Anglican tradition it dissented from, or from others who were outside the Anglican Communion and who also sought a more conciliatory relationship between faith and reason, including many Presbyterians and Congregationalists. By the mid-eighteenth-century, Rational Dissent was best known for its rationalism and political radicalism, and it exerted considerable political clout. Price and Priestley are of importance for this study because they are situated historically at the heart of what has been called the 'Enlightenment' and the origin of the 'secular age.'

Chapter 1 unpacks the dominant narratives of the Enlightenment and outlines the case for paying more attention to Rational Dissent. The leading narratives within philosophical and theological circles depict the history of this era as one in which theology commandeers the tools of secular philosophy through the pursuit of rationalistic natural theology and the epistemological justification of religious truth claims in order to shore up religious belief against the onslaught of an advancing atheism; that is, it concerns itself with the justification of belief. A history has emerged that is characterised by homogeneity in which the theism of this Enlightenment period is depicted as taking a particular turn during this time towards a new scientific methodology grounded in a secular form of rationalism rather than in revelation. In its revision of this historical narrative, Chapter 1 argues that Enlightenment was a multifaceted complex affair.

A study of the Rational Dissenters adds to the difficulties of charting a move within heterodox circles from theology to philosophy in any straightforward sense, thereby challenging the opposition that is often presupposed in popular narratives between theology and secular philosophy. These popular narratives tend to view Rational Dissenting rationality as somewhat deistic in that it is believed to promote a vision of reason as something that can attain knowledge entirely independently of revelation. Deism typically refers to those who believe in a deity but not one that cares for the world or reveals itself. Given this lack of revelation and any account of grace, deism inevitably embraces a view of reason that puts all theological truth within the grasp of human reason. However, as Chapter 1 argues, Rational Dissent was profoundly opposed to a deistic account of reason and was grounded in the principle of *sola scriptura*, a principle with its origins in Martin Luther's Reformation theology acknowledging scripture alone as the source of authority and revelation. The examination of the Rational Dissenting conception of reason in this chapter shows that it was in fact forged to a significant extent by its opposition to ecclesial hegemony and by a debate about scriptural exegesis.

Central to the argument of this chapter, and the book as a whole, is the case that the rationality of Rational Dissent can trace important roots back to Anglican Latitudinarianism, a phenomenon that borrows heavily from the thought of the Cambridge Platonists. The term 'Cambridge Platonism' is often used to refer to a number of seventeenth-century Anglican divines and their associates, so-called for their connections to the University of Cambridge and for their intellectual leanings towards the tradition of Platonic philosophy. They promoted the harmony of faith and reason and promoted a broad and tolerant Church. Those within the Anglican Communion, who were sympathetic to their theology and ecclesiology in the decades that followed and into the eighteenth century, were known as Latitudinarian. Tracing the intellectual debts between Rational Dissent and Latitudinarianism, including Cambridge Platonism, helps to resist the temptation to view eighteenth-century heterodox thinkers as figures who imported rationalism into theology in order to judge its truth claims, or to see these figures, especially later on in that millennium, as smuggling into England the dangerous machinations of the *philosophes*, those French materialist public intellectuals of the Enlightenment, including Diderot, d'Holbach and Voltaire, who believed in the supremacy of reason over claims to revelation. This chapter, therefore, makes the case for the complexities of Rational Dissenting thought and its context.

When philosophers of religion adopt the mainstream narratives of Enlightenment outlined in Chapter 1, the result is a model of the enterprise that tends to be implicitly conservative in political orientation. By turning away from socio-political and ethical concerns, philosophy of religion has a tendency to maintain the status quo. Focusing on the ideas devoid of context makes the philosophical and theological ideas under question look a-political, while at the same time hiding the (unavoidable) ethical and political nature of these ideas. Closer attention to historical context unveils a conception of reason and the philosophy of religion proposed by the Rational Dissenters and Latitudinarians that was at once both deeply theological, deeply ethical and inherently political: a feature shared with the earlier Cambridge Platonists.

This is the argument of Chapters 2 and 3. In the eighteenth century, tensions between High Church and Low, and between Rational Dissent and the Anglican establishment, played an important role in determining the nature and shape of reason and rationality. Chapter 2 concentrates on the conception of reason proposed by Richard Price, and it examines the incorporation into his theology of some of the central ideas of the seventeenth-century Cambridge Platonist Ralph Cudworth, who is often credited with coining the term 'philosophy of religion.' It will be argued that through his uptake of this philosophical theology, and through his reading of Plato's own thought, Platonism played an essential role in forming Price's account of human nature and God. Price's conceptions of mind and matter contrast sharply with Joseph Priestley's, thus demonstrating the different traditions of thought alive within Rational Dissent.

Chapter 3 makes the case that the rationalistic approach of the Latitudinarians and Rational Dissenters can only be understood as part of their repudiation of voluntarism, (the belief that will is supreme over reason, and that God's will determines truth and goodness) in its Hobbesian, Calvinist and establishment-authoritarian forms. In the eighteenth century, tensions between High Church and Low, and between Rational Dissent and the Anglican establishment, played an important role in determining the nature and shape of reason and rationality. Paying due attention to the context accentuates the political nature of philosophical theology in England during the long eighteenth century and highlights how it emerged as a means to challenge hegemonic power.

This has important implications for natural theology. Given the prevailing understanding of eighteenth-century natural theology within analytic circles, it tends to be viewed as an a-political and ethically neutral enterprise. The assumptions made by Swinburne are typical and they sideline ethical and political concerns as unimportant to analytic philosophy of religion or even as completely alien to its goals and objectives. Natural theology, conceived of as the formulation of arguments for God's existence, has thus come to be dominated by a concern to justify metaphysical beliefs through their subjection to the examination of reason. Questions about what we can have knowledge of, and how we justify religious belief, have basked in this limelight and have subsequently eclipsed most other concerns.

The narrowness inherent in the analytic nature of the philosophy of religion has resulted in what Schellenberg calls a lack of curiosity (which should be central to the aims of any genuine philosophy) because it usually omits any consideration of what religion actually *is* or any real engagement with other forms of religion.[8] In other words, most philosophers of religion are reduced to offering apologetics for their own tradition. If beliefs are assumed before they are justified, the enterprise of philosophy of religion can do little more than beg the question, which makes Pamela Sue Anderson right when she warns that its arguments have become worryingly circular. If philosophy is to live up to its name as the love of wisdom and if it is to examine the question 'how should I live?,' it will have to be more than the 'the skill of nit-picking'[9] which a narrow focus and use of scientific methodology has too often encouraged. To address this problem, philosophers of religion need to bring back together the ethical and the epistemic and to connect with the real-world problems that confront people's everyday lives.[10] What this calls for, above all else, is an approach that is able to counter the abstract nature of the analytical method by appreciating the need for philosophy to be culturally and politically situated, and one that attempts a reintegration of the philosophy of religion with ethics.

With a reconsideration of the historical context of the English natural theologians, new possibilities come to the fore. This book does not desire to make a case that the natural theology of the eighteenth century as normally understood should be defended. In a post-Kant and post-Darwin world, Paley, Clarke and others of their ilk do not have much of a leg to stand on if what they are trying to do is infer God's existence from apparent design or the logical impossibility of something being produced out of nothing. In place of this, when it comes to natural theology, what should be sought instead is something substantially reimagined.

The seeds of this reimagining, Chapter 4 argues, can be found in the thought of the Cambridge Platonists and some of their later sympathisers. A reconceived natural theology should be envisaged as having two main aims: a commitment to the reality of truth and goodness and the capacity to reflect critically on our models of self, nature and divinity. Such a natural theology is akin to the second of two types of natural theology identified by Pamela Sue Anderson. The first is an analytic variety, narrow in scope, arguing from the features of the natural world to the nature and existence of God. It is very much part of the analytic tradition of philosophy of religion described earlier. The second type is much broader and encompasses critical philosophical reflection on how we as human beings live our lives and how we relate to the non-human cosmos. In this broader type, natural theology is concerned with questions about the nature of all living things, together with the concepts that human beings apply to nature, to other beings, to our own selves and to the divine.[11] There is also room here to think critically about what has hereto been taken as universal and neutral, and to make space for alternative ways of theologising.

Chapter 4 thus identifies a historical precedent for this broader type of natural theology, which, if overlooked, results in an impoverished view of the discipline that curtails its scope and makes it much harder to imagine its revitalisation. For the philosophers discussed in this chapter, engaging in natural theology was itself a political act. The arguments for God's existence were primarily about a commitment to the reality of ethical value and the rejection of relativism in all its perceived forms, including atheistic materialism but also High Church Anglicanism. Biblical hermeneutics and debates about truth, power and conformity to the established Anglican Church shaped disputes about the nature and scope of reason and its relationship to revelation. The complexities of Rational Dissent therefore uncover a tradition of natural theology that is very different from the concerns associated most often with eighteenth century astro-, moral and physico-theology. Much more was at stake than amassing evidence in a scientific manner to assess propositional claims about God's existence.[12] This chapter, therefore, points towards the validity of more recent attempts to revise natural theology in terms of a much broader enterprise that reflects critically on our models of the nature of human life and our relationship to the world around us.[13] This task is vital for helping to reimagine the philosophy of religion as an inherently ethical and political enterprise.

Chapter 5 pursues the political applications of Richard Price's Platonic idea of reason. He published several controversial political pamphlets in the late eighteenth century about the American rebels and the French Revolution in which he championed the cause of liberty. His political philosophy offers a theological perfectionism with politically radical implications. This further interrupts the attempt to distinguish a secular anti-theological materialistic radicalism from more moderate theologically informed defence of the *ancien régime*.

Finally, Chapter 6 traces the development of the ideas of deiformity (becoming like God) and a divinised cosmos in the thought of Mary Wollstonecraft. Wollstonecraft and Price became friends early on in her life, and she had noteworthy connections with the wider community of Rational Dissent. Her earlier works, it is argued here, propose a conception of reason and freedom that have a distinctly Pricean-Platonic hue. Deiformity and perfectionism galvanised her feminism and political philosophy, which was underpinned by the ongoing search for truth combined with an awareness of epistemic fallibility. Reason for her, as for the Latitudinarians and Rational Dissenters, is the power to discern truth. She takes natural theology in a radical direction, however, developing a panentheistic idea of God (that all is part of God) by reimagining the attributes of God and providence to arrive at a contemplative theology of nature.

Through its discussion of Mary Wollstonecraft, Rational Dissent, Latitudinarianism and Cambridge Platonism, this book establishes that any historical narrative based on the assumption that philosophy of religion was born of an alien invasion of philosophy into theology is substantially flawed. It thus serves a corrective to the prevailing understanding of the philosophy of religion, which sees the enterprise, including natural theology, as a-ethical and a-political. Furthermore, the assumption that the philosophy of religion was born of a secular reason somehow infecting theology has a tendency to hide important philosophical and theological questions, not least those concerning the relationship between reason and revelation, Biblical hermeneutics and the nature of power.

The vision presented here of natural theology as an ethical and political discipline is essential for the task of reimagining natural theology today. Pamela Sue Anderson alerts us to the importance of going beyond questions of justification in the attempt to revision the philosophy of religion and of considering in their stead questions about the content of what is known (what?), the acquisition of knowledge (how?), the context (when?) and the possessor (who?) of knowledge.[14] This brings us straight away to a reflection on ethical, social and political issues. If energies are concentrated solely on assessing the rationality and justification of belief in the light of abstract rational criteria, including coherence and simplicity, the inevitable result is an ignoring of questions of justice and the ethical nature of truth. Jantzen's *Becoming Divine* (1999) therefore remains an astute challenge to the obsession with epistemology that has come to signify the philosophy of religion. If Anderson's questions are to be answered properly, then a study of the history of philosophy that has, as Garrett reminds us, set so many of the terms, questions, methods and answers of our own philosophy today,[15] must be a central concern. How its history is understood and interpreted determines how contemporary theological and philosophical problems are understood, and even more importantly shapes what counts as a valid philosophical 'problem' or 'question' in the first place. The normative and historical are inextricably interwoven.[16] Engaging with the history of the philosophy it has inherited is thus an absolute imperative for the philosophy of religion: it is necessary for imagining – or reimagining – what the nature and scope of the discipline should be.

This volume does not deny a trend towards secularism and scientific methodology in the wider eighteenth century or the fact that the Rational Dissenters should be included as part of an Enlightenment that was radical in its implications and progressive. Joseph Priestley and the other Rational Dissenters who followed David Hartley certainly extolled the virtues of a rational religion and turned theology more fully towards a scientific and empirical method. The alternative and more Platonic model of reason and natural theology present in Price, however, points instead towards a broader understanding of natural theology, which focuses the attention onto inner attitudes and orientation, seeing truth as something to be strived for, while affirming the primacy of the ethical.

This more ethically orientated type of philosophy of religion does not require abandoning a commitment to reason. As Harriet Harris argues, critical reasoning has a crucial role in overcoming falsehoods and distortion, and working towards truer beliefs. What is necessary is, as she puts it, the recovery of 'holding our reasoning to moral account.'[17] The contextualising work done here in this book provides a historical precedent for the contemporary models of natural theology that maintain a commitment to reason while also drawing our attention to the imaginative ways we see the world, and the ethical import of these ways of seeing. Mark Wynn, for example, presents such a model when he challenges the view of religious knowledge as scientific inference and refuses any conception of belief as devoid of practical consequences. His *God and Goodness: A Natural Theological Perspective* (1999) shows how the argument from design can be grounded in an evaluative stance towards the world, and his later work opens up the possibility of the importance of aesthetic contemplation of the material in seeking knowledge of the divine.[18] Stephen R. L. Clark, John Cottingham and Douglas Hedley all propose a Platonised natural theology in which a reductionist, materialistic account of the world is contrasted with their Platonised vision of a nature full of beauty and goodness, infused with value beyond that with which humans furnish it in the name of utility. All three embrace an idea of truth that is in principle discoverable but not via the tools of analytic analysis in any straightforward way. Instead, the imaginative contemplation of nature plays a critical role for all three thinkers. This underscores the fact that our models of the world are implicitly ethical, allowing for a commitment, opposed to all philosophies of an Epicurean inclination, to beauty and goodness having real existence.

This book draws attention to some historical precursors for these models of philosophy of religion that bring together rational reflection with the struggle to discern beauty and goodness. In doing this, it highlights how the history of the philosophy of religion in modernity has been over-determined by both the dominant form of analytic philosophy of religion and its critics. If the emergence of modern philosophy of religion is examined in its context, we are directed towards the inescapable ethical and political nature of the philosophy of religion. Closer attention to the philosophy of religion of the seventeenth and eighteenth centuries and its philosophising about reason in turn supports a move towards the second broader type of natural theology outlined earlier: a natural theology that refuses to be divorced from the political and that makes ethical concerns a priority. The re-reading of the history of philosophy presented in the following chapters makes for crucial groundwork, therefore, for the re-imagination of the philosophy of religion.

Notes

1 Richard Swinburne, *The Existence of God*, Revised (Oxford: Clarendon, 1991), 1.
2 Michael C. Rea, "Introduction," in *Analytic Theology: New Essays in the Philosophy of Theology*, ed. Oliver D. Crisp and Michael C. Rea (Oxford: Oxford University Press, 2009), 5–6. I follow Rea's account of both the method and ambitions of analytic philosophy.
3 Richard Swinburne, "The Value and Christian Roots of Analytical Philosophy of Religion," in *Faith and Philosophical Analysis: The Impact of Analytical Philosophy on the Philosophy of Religion*, ed. Harriet A. Harris and Christopher J. Insole (Aldershot: Ashgate, 2005), 35.
4 Paul Copan and Chad Meister, eds., *Philosophy of Religion: Classic and Contemporary Issues* (Oxford: Blackwell, 2008); See also e.g. John L. Schellenberg, "Imagining the Future: How Scepticism Can Renew Philosophy of Religion," in *Contemporary Practice and Method in the Philosophy of Religion: New Essays*,

ed. David Cheetham and Rolfe King (London: Continuum, 2008), 15–31; For another important attempt to extend the scope of analytic philosophy of religion, see Yujin Nagasawa, *Scientific Approaches to the Philosophy of Religion* (Basingstoke: Palgrave Macmillan, 2012); Tyron Goldschmidt, ed., *The Puzzle of Existence: Why Is There Something Rather Than Nothing?* (London: Routledge, 2013); William J. Wainwright, ed., *The Oxford Handbook of Philosophy of Religion* (Oxford: Oxford University Press, 2008); Michael C. Rea and Louis Pojman, eds., *Philosophy of Religion: An Anthology*, 7th ed. (Stamford: Cengage, 2015) This anthology is much broader in scope but the attributes of God and arguments for God's existence are still of central importance; More recent contributions like Zain Ali, *Faith, Philosophy and the Reflective Muslim* (Basingstoke: Palgrave Macmillan, 2013) have further affirmed the centrality of the justification of belief in God. Ali acknowledges the ambiguity of the evidence but argues first and foremost for the entitlement to believe.

5 Richard Swinburne, "Philosophical Theism," in *Philosophy of Religion in the 21st Century*, ed. D. Z. Phillips and Timothy Tessin (Basingstoke: Palgrave Macmillan, 2001), 3, 5.

6 See esp. Richard Rorty, J. B. Schneewind, and Quentin Skinner, "Introduction," in *Philosophy in History: Essays on the Historiography of Philosophy*, ed. Richard Rorty, J. B. Schneewind, and Quentin Skinner (Cambridge: Cambridge University Press, 1984), 12; Nick Trakakis, *The End of Philosophy of Religion* (London: Continuum, 2008), 32.

7 Knud Haakonssen, "Enlightened Dissent: An Introduction," in *Enlightenment and Religion: Rational Dissent in Eighteenth-Century Britain*, ed. Knud Haakonssen (Cambridge: Cambridge University Press, 1996), 4.

8 William Lane Craig, "Objections So Bad I Couldn't Have Made Them Up (or, the World's 10 Worst Objections to the Kalam Cosmological Argument," in *Come Let Us Reason: New Essays in Christian Apologetics*, ed. Paul Copan and William Lane Craig (Nashville: B&H Publishing Group, 2012), 51–65; Schellenberg, "Imagining the Future," 21.

9 Robert Solomon, *The Joy of Philosophy: Thinking Thin versus the Passionate Life* (Oxford: Oxford University Press, 1999), 8.

10 Pamela Sue Anderson, *A Feminist Philosophy of Religion* (Oxford: Blackwell, 1998), 17; Victoria S. Harrison, "What's the Use of Philosophy of Religion?" in *God, Goodness and Philosophy*, ed. Harriet A. Harris (Farnham: Ashgate, 2011), 29–43.

11 Pamela Sue Anderson, "Feminist Perspectives on Natural Theology," in *The Oxford Handbook of Natural Theology*, ed. Russell Re-Manning, John Hedley Brooke, and Fraser Watts (Oxford: Oxford University Press, 2013), 354–5.

12 When these arguments are discussed, they are often taken out of context – e.g. David Baggett and Jerry L. Walls, *Good God: The Theistic Foundations of Morality* (Oxford: Oxford University Press, 2011); C. Stephen Evans, *Natural Signs and Knowledge of God: A New Look at Theistic Arguments* (Oxford: Oxford University Press, 2010).

13 See, e.g., Anderson, "Feminist Perspectives."

14 Pamela Sue Anderson, "An Epistemological-Ethical Approach," in *Feminist Philosophy of Religion: Critical Readings*, ed. Pamela Sue Anderson and Beverley Clack (London: Routledge, 2004), 92.

15 Don Garrett, "Philosophy and History in the History of Modern Philosophy," in *The Future for Philosophy*, ed. Brian Leiter (Oxford: Clarendon, 2004), 45.

16 Douglas Hedley, "Should Divinity Overcome Metaphysics? Reflections on John Milbank's Theology beyond Secular Reason and Confessions of a Cambridge Platonist," *The Journal of Religion* 80, no. 2 (2000): 275; Wayne J. Hankey

and Douglas Hedley, "Introduction," in *Deconstructing Radical Orthodoxy: Postmodern Theology, Rhetoric and Truth*, ed. Wayne J. Hankey and Douglas Hedley (Aldershot: Ashgate, 2005), xiii–xviii.
17 Harriet A. Harris, "Struggling for Truth," *Feminist Theology* 28 (2001): 40, 45.
18 Mark R. Wynn, *Faith and Place: An Essay in Embodied Religious Epistemology* (Oxford: Oxford University Press, 2009).

1 Enlightenments, the philosophy of religion and the history of philosophy

Most analytic philosophers of religion pay scant attention to the history of their discipline, although many see some level of continuity between their own aims and those of their predecessors, even if the methods need drastically revamping. Richard Swinburne, for example, describes a rapid expansion of a new publicly acceptable atheism in the eighteenth century, which made it an imperative to justify the core claims of religious belief. Swinburne locates himself firmly in the tradition of inductive arguments for God's existence, which flourished in the eighteenth century and, as he sees it, reached their peak in William Paley's *Natural Theology* (1802). The subsequent abandonment of natural theology after Hume and Kant had their say was, in his view, a mistake. What he sees as part of the long and glorious past of using the 'best available secular criteria to clarify and justify religious claims' should, he thinks, have a long and industrious future.[1]

Other notable contemporary thinkers who link their philosophies of religion to the eighteenth century include William Rowe who notes an influence from the methods of Samuel Clarke and William Wainwright whose thought has been shaped by Jonathan Edwards.[2] There are many others. Wainwright is representative in seeing himself as engaged in the task of using analytic techniques to recover insights of earlier thinkers in order to apply them to contemporary problems. The assumption that there is continuity between the aims and objectives of eighteenth-century and contemporary philosophy of religion is widely shared – both by those who would promote natural theology and those who would reject it.

The eighteenth century is particularly significant. It is commonly accepted that the philosophy of religion in its current form originated with the criticisms levelled at religion during the European Enlightenment.[3] This is of critical importance because the historical precedent gives analytic philosophy of religion a substantive part of its legitimacy. The justification of belief against the atheist unbeliever is confirmed as the primary purpose of the discipline and religious claims are consolidated as propositions of fact to be judged objectively through the methods of science. This particular reading of history interprets the natural theology of the seventeenth and eighteenth centuries as primarily reactive, emerging in opposition to a growing atheism.

Natural theology is then interpreted as the attempt to claim that a proof of theism can be achieved through reason or empirical evidence independently of any faith conviction, thereby achieving a significant degree of certainty.

Furthermore, the same reading of history is adopted by philosophy of religion's keenest theologically minded despisers. The aims and objectives of the philosophy of religion have been scorned for being part of a 'soulless, aggressive, nonchalant and nihilistic' materialism, worse than just redundant but violent and damaging, not only in their effects but also in their very nature as a product of secularism.[4] A product, that is, that took shape with the Enlightenment in the eighteenth century. Disdained for being inherently nihilistic in the way it buys into the secular *episteme*, the ideology of abstraction is regarded by some Christian theologians as a 'post-Christian paganism,' a 'refusal' of Christianity and an anti-Christian invention.[5] On this view, anti-philosophy and the end of metaphysics is a 'supreme opportunity' for religion, giving it a chance to break free from the ideals – seen as false idols – that underpin the modern philosophy of religion.

Both those on the defence and those on the attack adopted the same reading of history. The philosophy of religion is understood as a child of the Enlightenment using secular scientific ways of arguing for the purpose of justifying belief. What underpins this narrative is a particular understanding of Enlightenment, either as one project of secularisation or as a movement that contains a secular materialistic programme from which the philosophy of religion in its current form appeared. Determining what this Enlightenment might have been in the past becomes, therefore, essential for imagining the nature of philosophy of religion in the future.

Enlightenments and their projects: how enlightenment has been defined

The first use of the term 'Enlightenment' is usually attributed to Kant and tends to refer to Western European thought from 1688 to the French Revolution in 1789, and it is typically seen to advance a commitment to human reason as an objective source of knowledge, a faith in the empiricism of the new science and a rejection of religious tradition, scholasticism, faith-based religious claims and the social-political establishment. It often tends to be viewed as an anti-theological, secular movement that gives rise to a distinctly a-theological conception of reason substantially different from what came before.

This understanding of it and of the philosophy of religion to which it is believed to give rise has much to do with Peter Gay's long-dominant construal of the Enlightenment as a singular 'project' in the shape of a unified trend towards a secular world view. His *The Enlightenment: An Interpretation* (1967) depicted the Enlightenment as a largely uniform anti-Christian movement, and this portrayal had a long-lasting impact for decades afterwards.[6] Gay's Enlightenment was distinctly French: an age in which the anti-clerical *philosophes* overthrew the ecclesiastical establishment, culminating in the French Revolution. On this reading, the Enlightenment is a tradition of thought characterised by reason's usurping of religion and overcoming of a revelation usually conceived of as a- or anti- rational.

Despite its now widespread rejection by historians of philosophy, the 'one-project' account has been formative for theological conceptions of how the Enlightenment should be understood. Colin Gunton's suggestion that 'the Enlightenment's programme' is one that seeks 'to replace God with the individual as the source of all authority'[7] is typical. Alister McGrath tells us that the movement called 'The Enlightenment' asserted the omnipotence of human reason, with the result that 'ethics since the Enlightenment has sought to distance itself from theology.'[8] This understanding of an inherently secular Enlightenment implicitly sets up some sort of antipathy between reason and faith, with substantial ramifications for how the relationship between theology and philosophy is conceived.

The one-project account has been promoted recently for the purpose of extolling secular reason over and above the theological. For Anthony Pagden, the Enlightenment was a movement that marginalised theology in opening up the potential for scientific knowledge, undermining the claim to one source of knowledge or one source of authority. Pagden's ultimate goal is to promote this particular vision of the project by advancing Baron d'Holbach's assertion that it is up to every enlightened being to 'attack at their source the prejudices of which the human race has been so long the victim.'[9] Theology should be ousted. The only possible just society, he believes, is a secular one. The interpretation of the Enlightenment as one project, therefore, has proved useful both for those wishing to expunge rational thought of all religion and for those wishing to promote more theological ways of thinking conceived of as anti-rational. It also does much to encourage the assumption that if the philosophy of religion originated during the European Enlightenment, it must be a discipline at odds with theology or at least one that utilises a very different secular method.

This view of the Enlightenment has been subject to a considerable amount of criticism in recent years with the result that a much deeper appreciation for the theological underpinnings of Enlightenment thought has emerged. It has become preferable to speak of several 'enlightenments' rather than one and the clear-cut distinction between a secular Enlightenment and premodern religion has been challenged.[10] Jonathan Israel has recently done much to argue that it was theological debate that lay at the centre of the early Enlightenment, and it was not anti-religious in nature.[11] In addition to his work, a number of other important historical narratives have reflected greater sensitivity towards the theological roots of Enlightenment thought, most notably Charles Taylor's *A Secular Age* (2007) and Michael Buckley's *At the Origins of Modern Atheism* (1987). Buckley acknowledges the strongest intellectual forces at this time were not those rejecting belief but those promoting a new form of faith.[12]

Although the homogenous account of Enlightenment has been considerably revised, there are still assumptions embedded in the revisionist histories about the anti-theological nature of the more radical forms of reason and faith that emerged out of the Enlightenment. Buckley himself depicts an account of faith that sees it undergoing a metamorphosis because of its flirtation with the methods of science and the search for abstract objective rationality. For Buckley, what makes religious thought enlightened is that it is fundamentally opposed to the theology of pre-modernity. This is the same reasoning that lies behind Alasdair MacIntyre's use of the term 'Enlightenment project.' For MacIntyre, the originators of Enlightenment thought may have been deeply theological, but the result was a secularised reason sharply at odds with previous theological ways of thinking. MacIntyre has it that ethics became concerned with the project of justifying morality: a project that before was totally inconceivable and unnecessary. In summary, 'the thinkers of the Enlightenment set out to replace what they took to be discredited traditional and superstitious forms of morality by a kind of secular morality that would be entitled to secure the assent of any rational person.'[13]

There is a suggestion here, as with many other recent interpretations, that the Enlightenment took what was essentially a wrong turn, resulting in a form of rationality that ended up justifying conservatism. Although this account of Enlightenment acknowledges its religious character, especially in its early days, it still promotes a narrative in which – in the words of Eagleton – faith is opposed to reason. This is illustrated, he thinks, through the actions of the 'zealots of reason' who aim to reconcile religion with a new, secular form of rationality.[14] These more complex accounts still assume a fundamental incompatibility between the values of the Enlightenment and those of religious faith. The new 'rational religion' that arose with the Enlightenment becomes something inherently inimical to faith. There is much more nuance in these histories than in the work of Gay, but Enlightenment is still viewed as something largely homogenous, characterised by the refutation of religious belief.

On these readings, belief comes to be seen at the time of Enlightenment as either something irrational or as something private, resulting in a focus on propositional beliefs, the privatisation of religion and the 'intellectualisation' of thought.[15] What is believed to unite the scientists and philosophers of Enlightenment is their conviction that the laws determining physical and human nature are 'few, simple, clear, and verifiable by discursive reason and science.'[16] The dominant view in recent intellectual history is thus that by the mid to late eighteenth century, theology and philosophy had 'gone the way of Enlightenment rationalism,' the main feature of which has been defined by Isaiah Berlin as the application of science to human affairs.[17] Philosophy is, in this view, converted into a natural science, thus leaving it innately secular and fundamentally opposed to theological thinking. As Israel sees it, trends towards secularisation, tolerance, equality, democracy, individual freedom and liberty of expression were powerfully impelled by a 'philosophy' that rejected transcendent values and had no need of theology.[18]

This history presents the theologians of the eighteenth century as facing a difficult choice. One response to the predicament of the new rationalism was to take the road that showed religious belief is reasonable; hence, the philosophy of religion (as a distinct discipline) emerged during the Enlightenment.[19] Another was the refusal of modernity and its values, which presented itself in the traditions of fideism and the rejection of natural theology. This emerges today in both anti-philosophical postmodern approaches and in fundamentalisms. Theologians who favour the refusal of modernity have drawn justification from this history for their anti-philosophical and anti-liberal standpoints. If the Enlightenment is read as a commitment to the fully universal, the clearly comprehensible and the exhaustibly justifiable, it becomes easier to dismiss it as leaving us with nothing but emptiness as it tries to fill the gulf 'with modes of purely human self-assertion.'[20]

Nihilism has thus come to be seen as the inevitable legacy of modernity. Any appeal to supposedly objective reason, or universal value, is, on this view, inherently secular. The dichotomy is then further entrenched between the secular and the Christian, which makes the Enlightenment anti-Christian by its very nature. As James Smith puts it, 'the critique of the Enlightenment project now calls for a critique of modernist theology that manifests across the range of liberal and conservative options.' The 'core of modernity' for Smith is the Enlightenment, defined in homogenous terms as a 'prejudice against prejudice,' with the most dangerous prejudice being that of religion. This singular project of Enlightenment is still unfolding, visibly apparent in the political drive to cordon off the secular as 'a zone decontaminated of the prejudices of determinate religious influence.'[21] The secular is thus set firmly against the religious: modernity both then and now is deemed utterly incompatible with the truly theological.

Despite, therefore, the increased nuances of more recent interpretations of the 'Enlightenment' period, a vision of a largely homogenous Enlightenment still prevails in which reason is defined in secular terms and the philosophical is uncoupled from the theological. It is just such a reading of history that lies behind both a substantial amount of anti-philosophical theology and analytic philosophy of religion's self-understanding. The choice for theology that arises as a result of this is stark: either theology should buy into the tools of secular reason (an option embraced by many philosophers of religion but dismissed by its critics as an 'invasion' of Christian theology launched by scientific rationalism) or the entire enterprise of the philosophy of religion should be abandoned altogether.

Muddying the waters: heterodoxy, England and enlightenment

There is something not quite right about the above picture, however. Jonathan Israel's work has drawn attention to some of the shortcomings of postmodern understandings of the Enlightenment, particularly those offered by MacIntyre and Taylor. Their overreliance on a small number of supposed 'enlightened' thinkers (John Locke is one example) whose enlightened characteristics are deeply questionable – largely on account of their social conservatism – results in an overly simplified account.[22] Israel's work alerts his readers to the sheer breadth of Enlightenment thought and this is something that should be taken much more seriously than it currently is by both theologians and philosophers. A reading such as MacIntyre's becomes difficult to sustain given due consideration of some of the Enlightenment thinkers most often overlooked.

For his part, Israel proposes a distinction between what he calls a 'moderate' Enlightenment and a much more 'radical' one. The moderates are depicted as concerned to defend the *ancien régime* and its model of ecclesiastic authority, resulting in a conservative form of Enlightenment, which he sharply distinguishes from an atheist and much more politically radical Enlightenment. The two forms of Enlightenment, Israel insists, were poles apart by the latter part of the eighteenth century, not least because they rested on diametrically opposed metaphysics. One-substance monism, with its roots in the theology of Benedict Spinoza, refused any distinction between matter and spirit and is associated with the radical form of Enlightenment and contrasted with the two-substance dualism (upheld by Locke and others) of the moderate Enlightenment. This monism asserted that only one infinite substance (nature or God) exists and thereby conflated God and nature, body and mind, invoking reason as the sole guide in life and rejecting the tradition made sacrosanct by the moderates. Whereas, 'for the moderate mainstream,' states Israel,

> reason is immaterial and inherent in God, a divinely given gift to man, and one that raises him above the rest. In radical thought, by contrast, man is merely an animal among others with no specially privileged status in the universe.[23]

Israel's reading of history shows the impossibility of depicting Enlightenment as a project and associating it predominantly with figures such as Locke and Voltaire. His work is valuable not least for encouraging the consideration of eighteenth-century figures, particularly from the Continent, making the case for a more contextualised history of philosophy.

When it comes to England, Israel posits an English heterodoxy in the form of Christian-Unitarianism (which embraced a theology of God as one person and thus denied the divinity of Christ), which was closely allied to the atheist radical Enlightenment in its proclamation of reason as the sole guide to knowledge, together with its both monism and materialism. He associates it with various thinkers including Joseph Priestley, Richard Price, Thomas Paine and the radical thought of Mary Wollstonecraft. Furthermore, the radical Enlightenment of which these thinkers were a part is depicted as an 'anti-theological' enterprise.[24] Despite the many differences, therefore, there are similarities between Israel, Buckley, MacIntyre and the other thinkers discussed earlier in that they understand the philosophical radicals of the

Enlightenment as inaugurating a new form of reason – one that was substantially different from a more theologically informed reason that came before.

This reading finds support in other treatments of eighteenth-century English thought. Various historians have attested to the importance of England during the Enlightenment period and some important parallels can be made between Israel's thought and J.C.D. Clark's heresy-radicalism thesis.[25] This thesis proposes that radicalism originated with theologically heterodox ideas, and on this account, the radical challenges to orthodox ideas have theological roots, albeit in unorthodox, heretical theology (which makes this very different from Gay's one-project account). By doing this, a direct link is assumed, particularly in England, between theological heterodoxy and political radicalism. Michael Buckley's narrative about the advent of modern atheism follows a similar line. For Buckley, religious heterodoxy is crucial to the story of Enlightenment. As he sees it, heterodoxy gives rise to Enlightenment theism and to the challenge of confessional religion. Philosophical reflection ceased to be the preamble to faith and became instead the truest religion. Crucially, it is at this time that Buckley notes a change in the nature and purpose of philosophical reflection. A fracture develops between philosophy and faith; one that widens into a gulf that sees a philosophy act as the arbitrator of faith. Natural theology ceases to be a part of metaphysics and is instead derived by common-sense or ordinary philosophic maxims from astronomy, comparative religion, mechanics and biology. The theologians had, he suggests, by the end of the eighteenth century 'become philosophers,' and the dispute between Christianity and atheism had become purely philosophical.[26] This, Buckley states, constitutes a world to which theology has little to say.

In this reading, heterodoxy is made crucial because Christology, the doctrine of Christ, is made pivotal for understanding why this changing conception of philosophy occurred. According to Buckley, Christology was no longer needed to ground Samuel Clarke's religious arguments after his attack on the Athanasian Creed and its doctrine of the eternally proceeding uncreated nature of the Son, of one *ousia* or essence with the Father. Clarke sparked a move towards a focus on the moral life in place of a commitment to Christ that Buckley views as characteristic of the modern form of theism that then gave rise to modern atheism: 'The reality and message of Jesus did not support any assent to the existence of God' and 'the Enlightenment agreed that Jesus was a Jewish ethical preacher, still illuminating a world in which tradition and Church had distorted his beliefs and maxims beyond recognition by any except . . . the *philosophes*.'[27] This was when the philosophically minded theologians of the time bracketed religion in order to defend it: 'The god of these theologians is Christian in the absence of Christ and religious in the absence of religious experience.'[28] Buckley is suggesting that reflection on the nature of Christ is no longer necessary for reflection about the nature and existence of God. Philosophy then becomes theology's judge, jury and, ultimately, executioner. There is heavy investment made in a connection between heterodoxy and the advent of philosophy of religion in its modern form as a discipline that utilises the tools of secular reason.

Heterodoxy, therefore, has become crucial for an understanding of Enlightenment and for appreciating a new or changed conception of reason not apparent before and distinctly anti-theological. Furthermore, a link has been made between Rational Dissent and deism: the theology that a creator god exists, does not care for the world or have any providential interaction with it and reason is the source of all knowledge about the divine. Charles Taylor in particular gives the Rational Dissenters an important place in modelling what he calls Providential Deism. This is an intermediate stage of humanism that views the world as designed by God in an anthropocentric way, thereby affirming the primacy of impersonal order – whereby God relates to human beings through the established order of things – and promoting the idea of a true original natural religion that has become corrupted and which needs to be rediscovered. The Rational Dissenters, Taylor argues, give momentum to this shift through their rationalizing of ethics, downplaying of Christology and move towards a more deistic concept of the divine. In this slide towards Unitarianism, he detects a growing emphasis on the immanence of the impersonal cosmic, social and moral orders.[29] The result is a 'new deism' that puts issues of God's existence outside of the horizon of the religious life of prayer, faith and hope. This consideration of English thought in the eighteenth century makes for a far more subtle and preferable reading of history than the one-project account of Enlightenment promoted by Gay and others, but like theirs, it still posits something new and anti-theological inaugurated by the Enlightenment, associating it with heterodoxy. The assumption that is more or less implicit is that the heterodox philosophy is at odds with faith and contributes to its downfall.

The Rational Dissenters should be paid considerable attention because English eighteenth-century religious thought cannot be properly understood without them.[30] However, none of the narratives outlined earlier pay close enough attention to the complexities of Rational Dissenting thought, and this has considerable implications for how theology and philosophy are conceived. When it comes to eighteenth-century England, Israel's narrative is not a good fit. This is why, despite the fact that Israel is invaluable for encouraging more appreciation for the Continental thinkers, England is worth another look. The reasons for this are essential to consider because they have significance beyond historical study. They require that the dichotomising of the theology and philosophy that forms the mainstay of the other narratives discussed earlier be rethought. It is not so easy to distinguish between a radical Enlightenment, which waged a 'relentless war' on 'theological ways of viewing the world,' from a theologically informed moderate Enlightenment.[31] In turn, it becomes more difficult to separate a clearly secular reason from more theological ways of thinking. There are important ramifications both for the way analytical philosophy sees itself and how its critics respond to it.

The theology of Rational Dissent: challenging the narratives

As Knud Haakonssen warns, it is tempting to see Rational Dissent 'as a Trojan horse full of continental-style *philosophes* ready to burst upon the English *ancien régime*' climaxing with the appearance of Priestley, Price, Paine and Godwin.[32] Such a temptation certainly seems to underpin the narratives outlined earlier. Heterodox dissent is aligned with a Continental *philosophe*-driven Enlightenment, and the heterodoxy of the eighteenth-century radicals is viewed as responsible for accelerating the process of secularisation. The more modest thesis that 'divinity and transcendent principle were banished from social, political, and economic life'[33] by the radicals is extended to hold heterodox Christology responsible for shaping an Enlightenment rationalist theism that leads directly to modern secularism and atheism. Israel's distinction between moderate and radical Enlightenments adds significant weight to this reading.

A deeper consideration of Rational Dissenting thought suggests, however, that this reading needs revision. As Justin Champion points out, the religious thought of the heterodox has tended to be marginalised,[34] and this is a notable characteristic of the treatments of Rational Dissent outlined earlier. There is a tendency to give Rational Dissent a prominent place in the eighteenth-century slide towards atheism, with a focus on the neglect of Christology and the promotion of a rationality that sounds distinctly deistic in the way it is believed to usurp faith and use reason as the sole guide both in human life and in knowledge of the divine. If deism is defined in Samuel Clarke's terms as the belief that reason can attain knowledge of God with no need of revelation,[35] the Rational Dissenters have long been assumed to give rational knowledge primacy over revealed knowledge in much the same way.

When the theology of the Rational Dissenters is given due prominence, however, the result is a very different understanding of the relationship between faith and reason. Theirs was not the philosophy of the *philosophes* or the deists. One important step in appreciating this is to recognise how highly the principle of *sola scriptura* (that the scriptures are the only revelatory authority) figured in Rational Dissenting thought. This suggests a very different attitude to reason than that adopted by deism, and it is important to keep the two distinct. In so doing, an important challenge is raised against the suggestion that the philosophical rationality of the eighteenth century is necessarily inherently alien to theology. The theology of Rational Dissent also draws attention to the important links between Rational Dissent, other English Nonconformists and Anglican Latitudinarianism. This lays the groundwork for appreciating the ethico-political nature of eighteenth-century concepts of reason and natural theology in the chapters that follow. What was of most importance for the eighteenth-century thinkers under consideration in this book wasn't the justification of God's existence per se but questions about power, authority, Biblical interpretation, and, above all, the defence of the reality of ethical value.

Rational Dissent, sola scriptura and authority of tradition

It is not difficult to see why Rational Dissent might be thought of as some kind of subversive Trojan horse. One of the earliest uses of the term 'Rational Dissent' was by the orthodox Soame Jenyns, who bemoaned the fact that, as he saw it, the Rational Dissenters had 'arbitrarily expunged out of their Bibles every thing, which appears to them contradictory to reason, that is to their own reason, or in other words, every thing which they cannot understand.'[36] The prioritising of reason in place of faith quickly came to be taken as a Rational Dissenting motif.

In fact, however, the Rational Dissenters would not recognise themselves in Jenyns's forthright description. This must be taken seriously, as the more contemporary treatments of Rational Dissent outlined earlier adopt a similar misunderstanding. The religion of Rational Dissent was actually a religion of revelation based on the authority of the Bible. Their arguments against Trinitarianism (the doctrine that God's nature is triune, the three persons of Father, Son and Holy Spirit in one) were grounded first and foremost on a commitment not to the principle of reason but to the principle of *sola scriptura* – a doctrine that they saw as incompatible with accepting uncritically the theology of the established church hierarchy or pre-formulated creed.[37] It was their adherence to a scriptural religion that determined the shape of Rational Dissenting rationalism, together with the refusal to oppose scripture and reason. What is often taken for the absence of a commitment to the scriptural Jesus is actually its centrality. This fact challenges the inevitability of Enlightenment reason as an anti-theological product of the *philosophes*, and it disputes the narrative of a modern secular scientific philosophy of religion that came into being at odds with theology. To appreciate this fully, it is necessary to understand the origins of Rational Dissent.

Historically, Protestant Dissent in England originates from the Restoration of Charles II in 1660 and the Act of Uniformity passed in May of 1662. The Restoration of the Stuart monarchy in 1660 brought the end of England's brief fling with republicanism, and it was followed for the next couple of years by a state-imposed policy of uniformity. This took the form of a variety of Acts, known collectively as the Clarendon Code, which attempted to restore the settlement that had existed before 1641 through enforcing the norm of Anglicanism. There was very little room in these Acts for toleration. The Corporation Act of 1661 required all holders of public office to take the Anglican sacrament with the result that even those Presbyterians who were relatively moderate were forced into a position of dissent from the establishment. The 1662 Act of Uniformity demanded all ministers assent to the entire content of the daily offices from the revised Book of Common Prayer and that they receive Episcopal ordination.[38] This mandate for conformity confirmed the bishops of the Church of England and the courts as part of the British establishment. Refusal to conform to these acts resulted in thousands of clergy, university dons and schoolmasters being forced from their positions. The term 'Nonconformist' was thus given to all of those who were separated from the established church after 1662 by virtue of the fact that they would not give assent to everything in the Prayer Book.

The Act of Uniformity created a very disparate group of people, defined chiefly by what they would not conform to, principally the Book of Common Prayer but also the Thirty-Nine Articles of the Church of England that had been passed by Convocation in 1571. These Nonconformists became the first of the English Dissenters (by the end of the seventeenth century the term 'dissent' became more common), and they included Congregationalists, Quakers, Baptists and Presbyterians. Many of these groups could not accept the episcopacy of the Restoration Church and sought to worship in ways other than that prescribed by this established church. They could not, therefore, accept the Act of Uniformity and found themselves at the sharp end of the Clarendon Code. Two more Acts followed as part of this Code. In 1664, the Conventicle Act made Dissenting preaching a criminal offence by forbidding religious assemblies of more than five people, enforced by the threat of fines for attendance at Nonconformist services. The Five Mile Act meanwhile outlawed Dissenting clergy from coming within five miles of their former congregations. Estimates of the proportion of the English population who belonged to some sort of Nonconformist Protestant sect have been put as high as 10 percent with another 5 percent estimated to be Roman Catholic.[39]

These various legal codes made for an Anglican establishment characterised by what was effectively suppression by the state of any Nonconforming parties. Later on, the Test Act of 1673 made it compulsory for anyone taking up any civil or military office to make a declaration against transubstantiation (the belief, held by Roman Catholics, that the substance of the bread and wine in the Eucharist become the substance of the body and blood of Christ, rejected in the twenty-eighth Article) and to receive the Anglican sacrament within three months of taking up office. Britain at this time was effectively a monarchical state buttressed by persecution and a theologically orthodox and hierarchical Church.[40]

True to the old adage, however, a common enemy did much to unite the factions. The adversary came in the form of James II's Catholicity, and it did much to sooth tensions between Anglicans and non-Catholic Dissenters. James's second Declaration of Indulgence had intended to divide Anglicans and Dissenters, but the united Protestant response against it stopped it from being effective.[41] There was even an attempt to resolve the differences between Anglicans and Dissenters in a revised liturgy. After the Glorious Revolution in 1688, which saw James II flee and William and Mary take the throne, the religious settlement that followed attempted to pass two bills, one for toleration and another for the comprehension or inclusion of Dissenters in a broader liturgy. The Toleration Act was passed in 1689, and it guaranteed those Dissenters who were Trinitarian the right to worship. Their freedom was limited, however. They could only worship if their meeting places were registered and on condition that they rejected transubstantiation and took the oaths of allegiance and supremacy. Ministers meanwhile still had to subscribe to thirty-six of the Thirty-Nine Articles of the Church of England. The Comprehension Bill met with less success. Many within the Anglican Church and many who were politically Tory resolutely opposed it, and as a result, it was never passed.[42] Tensions evidently simmered under the surface and, as Gibson puts it, the newly found relative harmony was short-lived after the Catholic threat receded.[43] Furthermore, the Toleration Act suspended, but did not rescind, the acts of the Clarendon Code. It loomed in the wings with the last remaining acts still on the books until the early nineteenth century when the Test and Corporation Acts were finally abolished in 1828.

From 1660 until the early decades of the nineteenth century, therefore, the Anglican establishment, or what is sometimes termed the *ancien régime*, dominated the English political and religious scene. The 'long eighteenth century' was a period of Anglican dominance, but this was put under increasing amounts of pressure from the discontent of dissent that bubbled beneath the surface. The Toleration Act might have allowed greater freedom for some Dissenters but not all were included in its scope. Roman Catholics, non-Trinitarians and deists were explicitly excluded, and these Dissenters had no freedom to serve in government or to attend university.

The lack of political power and social inequality felt by those who dissented was compounded by a notable reluctance to accept the Toleration Act by significant factions of the Anglican Church. A significant number of Anglicans were flatly opposed to granting toleration to anyone who would not subscribe to the Articles of the Church of England. As a result, in the first decades of the eighteenth century, Dissenting interests were continually under attack. The Occasional Conformity Act of 1711 attempted to stop Dissenters taking office by making them take the Anglican sacrament, and the Schism Act of 1714 prevented ministerial training for Dissenters. Although these acts were repealed in 1719, the Dissenters made no other advances until the Dissenters' Relief Act of 1779.[44]

Persecution, whether actual or merely just perceived, remained a real threat for a considerable span of time. Although throughout the eighteenth-century Dissenters were not particularly restricted by the Test and Corporation Acts, suspended as they were by the Toleration Act, they still faced significant inequality in the eyes of the law (especially when it came to education, registration of births and marriages and compulsory support of the parish, system) and this resulted in what Bradley calls a 'symbolic and psychological exclusion.'[45] There was tangible dislike in the established community of any Dissenter taking up office, and it by and large made this blatantly clear. There was also a marked reluctance to extend the Toleration Act to those outside its protection.[46] Gradually, as the eighteenth century wore on, however, the Toleration Act was accepted, and they faced less overt opposition. When 1779 brought the Relief Act, it finally exempted schoolteachers and ministers from having to subscribe to the Thirty-Nine Articles. Many Dissenters, however, were understandably disappointed that it wasn't far wider in scope.[47]

The term Rational Dissent is most commonly used to refer to what became, during the mid- to late eighteenth century, increasingly rationalist and heretical versions of Presbyterianism.[48] Although Presbyterian theology was essentially Calvinistic, with the denomination so-called for its belief that the true form of church government is revealed in the scriptures, a growing number of Presbyterians from the early to mid-eighteenth century onwards, moved away from Calvinism and Trinitarianism, and came to hold a belief in the harmony of faith and reason. Such believers made up the majority of the Rational Dissenters. Knud Haakonssen thus defines the primary feature of Rational Dissent as a Nonconformism that rejected Calvinism and promoted a positive account of human reason.[49] By definition, the Rational Dissenters were Nonconformists, but they were distinct from Calvinist, Roman Catholic and other Trinitarian Nonconformists because of their divergent theologies of God and Christ, and their account of human reason. During their own time, the Rational Dissenters were often equated with intellectual Unitarianism, a view that has persisted to the present day, but such narrow definitions, as Haakonssen points out, do a disservice to the complexity of eighteenth-century Dissenting thought. In fact, not all of those who might be included under the umbrella of Rational Dissent were outside the Anglican Communion, and their attitudes to rationality were far more diverse than is commonly realised.

From the mid-eighteenth century, as their numbers increased before a steep decline at the end of the century, the two most important Rational Dissenting figures were Richard Price and Joseph Priestley.[50] Neither man was Presbyterian, however, but Congregationalist in upbringing. Congregationalism was Calvinist and extolled the authority of scriptures, but both Priestley and Price rejected their Calvinist inheritance at a relatively young age to become theologically heterodox. These two thinkers encapsulate the Rational Dissenting commitment to the primacy of scripture, freedom of conscience, rationalism and movement towards political radicalism: characteristics that have come to define Rational Dissent. As stated earlier, these characteristics are most often associated with materialism and deism, as well as a new form of philosophical reasoning which moves away from a theology of revelation towards a much more scientific rationalism. Such an interpretation does not, however, do justice to the primacy of revelation in their theology.

The commitment to *sola scriptura* underpins Priestley's theology. He had a Calvinist family background, and the commitment to the Bible as the word of God remained steadfast throughout his life. In 1751, Priestley became the first student to enrol at the Dissenting Academy at Daventry, and while there, Priestley himself tells us, he became an Arian, accepting a 'qualified' doctrine of atonement, regarding Christ as a mediator and advocate.'[51] Originating with Arius (c.250–336), Arianism denied that the Son of God was generated from the essence of the Father, declaring instead that he was called into being by God's will. It presents a hierarchical model of the Trinity, and its Christology necessarily demands a revised account of the more mainstream views of atonement. All theologies of atonement propose that Christ atoned in some way for human sin by his death on the cross. A Christ figure not fully, or 'essentially,' divine cannot redeem human nature on the cross either through satisfying the honour of God or through acting as a substitute for human nature, however. Orthodox accounts of salvation are marked by a commitment to Christ as fully human to take on human sin but fully divine in order to redeem and atone. Priestley's Arian Christology, therefore, required that he modify his account of atonement and salvation to one that did not require a story of salvation history that culminates in the atoning action of the God-man Jesus. Jesus acts instead, on his view, as an exemplary model for human beings to follow. This move to Arianism occurred after what seemed to him 'a fair and impartial study of the scriptures,' which refused to take on trust 'subscribed creeds and confessions of faith.'[52] He was certainly right to be alert to the fact that no one model of atonement can be read out of the scriptural texts without dispute. It is not faith and reason that are deemed at odds by Priestley, therefore, but scriptural faith and a theology prescribed by tradition. When he came to abandon Trinitarianism, it was not on account of a rational argument but because Christ's full humanness was the only doctrine deemed properly scriptural. Priestley's early Arianism was Biblically inspired.

After leaving Daventry, Priestley taught at the academy in Warrington and then became a minister in Leeds. During this time, he rejected the doctrine of atonement completely and become an anti-Trinitarian. Socinianism is usually credited with leading Priestley to abandon his Arianism. Popular with the freethinkers and anti-Trinitarians of the time, particularly in Continental Europe, Socinianism was characterised by its rejection of anything and everything that was in conflict with reason. Borrowing from the anti-Trinitarianism of Michael Servetus (c.1511–1553) and his nephew Fausto Sozzini (1539–1604), both from Siena, its rationalism subjected all scripture and revelation to the scrutiny of reason, and it aspired to replace the authority of New Testament revelation with the authority of reason. The role of Socinianism in the development of Priestley's rejection of Arianism is often overplayed, however. Mills informs us that Priestley was on good terms with a number of Socinians while he remained an Arian, and Priestley himself tells us he was 'indisposed' to Socinianism until at least the late 1760s.[53] Priestley's rejection of Arianism was most likely primarily motivated instead by the study of the scriptures together with the Biblical criticism of Nathaniel Lardner, the son of an independent minister who had argued against Samuel Clarke's subordinationalist Christology on the grounds of its scriptural inaccuracy.[54] Whereas Clarke denied the Athanasian doctrine that Christ is the same essence as the Father, he still insisted there was no time when the

Son did not exist. Lardner, however, denied any scriptural warrant for a belief in any part of Jesus pre-existing his earthly life. Lardner had an enviable reputation as an expert in Biblical and patristic studies, and his work is a demonstration of the unshakeable commitment to the Bible as the first and most fundamental rule of faith. Lardner had also taken it upon himself to defend the historical foundations of Christianity from the arguments of the freethinkers, including John Toland (1670–1722) and Matthew Tindal (1657–1733).

Priestley's scriptural studies saw him engage in the task of perusing 'the whole of the Old and New Testament' in an attempt to study the relevant verses with regard to the doctrine of atonement. What he found, he says, was that the doctrine 'had no countenance *either* from scripture or reason.' He pursued the same path in theologising about providence, too, and 'search the Scriptures' became his refrain.[55] The belief that Trinitarianism was mistaken was one reached after prolonged and diligent studying of the Biblical texts. After Lardner's death in 1768, his continuing study of the scriptures together with a careful study of Lardner's own work changed his mind about Arianism. In assessing his change of heart, he is quite adamant that the conversion to 'what is called Socinianism' occurred on the basis of scriptural study.[56] Scripture and reason are not opposed, therefore: quite the contrary. He does not reject the scriptures because of Socinianism but rather comes to adopt Socinianism on the basis of the study of scripture.[57] The difference is important. Priestley is searching for a more sophisticated hermeneutic of *sola scriptura* than one that claims the scriptures can be read in an unproblematic way without interpretation, or one that claims the legitimacy of individual subjective interpretation.

This was a commitment shared by his Rational Dissenting contemporary Richard Price. Although less well known today than Priestley, Price made substantial contributions during his lifetime to the study of mathematics and finance, moral philosophy and theology, and he was actively involved in politics. Although the *Review of the Principal Questions in Morals* published in 1758 was his only book on moral philosophy, it was immensely popular during his lifetime and merited three editions. Much of his theology is contained in two volumes of his sermons, delivered during the course of his ministry at Newington Green where he became a preacher in the Presbyterian chapel, also in 1758. Newington Green was a community of Rational Dissenters, home to several wealthy families who were Latitudinarian in religion and Whig in politics. A weekly supper club on the Green facilitated the exchange of ideas, and it included James Burgh (best known for his *Political Disquisitions* (1774) but also author of *The Dignity of Human Nature* (1794)) and Ralph Thoresby (the rector at Stoke Newington).[58] Price remained there in a ministerial capacity until 1783 when his wife died, whereupon he moved to Hackney and continued his ministry until he died in 1791.

Price's theology was thoroughly Biblical. He was born into a family of Dissenters in Glamorgan in the parish of Llangeinor. His grandfather had followed the Welsh educationalist Samuel Jones out of the Anglican Church when he was ejected after the Act of Uniformity and had helped Jones to set up Dissenting meeting places at Brynllywarch and Cildeudy together with a Dissenting Academy at Brynllywarch.[59] It was at this academy that Price's father and uncle were educated, and when it moved to Talgarth, Price became a student there. His father was a strict high Calvinist, embracing a theology to which Price had an unremitting adverse reaction. Price's entire philosophy and theology and the centrality it gives to ethical virtue took shape through a conscious rejection of the Calvinist doctrine of double predestination: those not among the number elected to salvation are predestined to eternal damnation.

Before Talgarth, Price had briefly attended a Dissenting school in Pentwyn. He did not last long there on account of his father's alarm at the school's liberal attitude towards anti-Trinitarian theology. Apparently, his father became so angry on finding him reading Samuel Clarke that he threw the work into the fire.[60] He was too late to stop a formative influence, however, and it is likely Clarke's theology did much to shape Price's Christological views. Whether Clarke himself was an Arian, as is often speculated, is not clear, but it was the way *The Scripture Doctrine of the Trinity* (1712) argued that was so significant rather than the Christological conclusions it drew. By appealing to Biblical authority while also extolling the virtues of human reason for its interpretation, Clarke proposed a radically new form of Biblical criticism, utilising reason rather than confidence in Church tradition.

The early eighteenth century faced a pressing question about Biblical hermeneutics. Those who rejected Clarke's apparent Arian tendencies were faced with two unsavoury options. The right to private judgement could be dismissed, but this would be too much like popery for many. The other option was the road of 'enthusiasm.' This was a form of religion that was spirit led, granting authority to personal individual inspiration. Those who were called enthusiasts appealed to the inspiration of the spirit and believed God spoke directly to them, thereby claiming absolute certainty in their convictions. How could the enthusiasts distinguish between divine truth and their own flawed constructions of truth, however? This was the all-important question. Without some sort of independent reason, the task seemed impossible. Although ambiguous, Clarke's own theology of the Trinity (in contradiction to the *homoousion* one essence Athanasian doctrine) was certainly interpreted as Arian in the following decades, and it had significant influence on the rationalist nature of Dissenting thought throughout the rest of the eighteenth century.

Clarke made a deep impression on Price who soon came to abandon Trinitarianism in favour of what he saw as a more accurate scriptural belief in the absolute unity of God, when he became a lifelong Arian. His conversion was not, however, due to a belief in the supremacy of reason over revelation. Revelation, he was adamant, was primary. Price rejected Socinianism just as much as he rejected Trinitarianism. He flatly refused this method of judging revelation. The Socinians and deists were wrong, he insisted, to dispute the scriptures as the revelation of God. As he saw it, revelation was a given and reason did not have the authority to determine its truth.

His reading of the scriptures consequently gave him a much higher Christology than the Socinians. He asserted the pre-existence of Christ and acknowledged a role for Christ in creation, granting him the role of saviour and giver of eternal life through his death on the cross. The reason for the shape of his Christology is that atonement and the pre-existence and 'Deity of Christ' are doctrines, he insisted, clearly laid down in the scriptures.[61] Thus the scriptures determine Price's theology. Their authority is higher than that of reason, and, consequently, he rejects what he calls a 'dangerous tendency' of Socinianism towards deism and to scepticism about the Bible. Scripture is prior to reason and reason *cannot* be used to judge it: 'What we object to,' he states is first determining 'from Reason what is truth,' and second trying to 'explain the scripture by it, and make it speak the same language.'[62] Whereas revelation *is* truth, reason can only hope to try to help discover what that truth is. Reason's role is evidently interpretative. Reason is, he asserts, important for religion, but its chief province with regard to revelation is not to judge it but to 'examine that Revelation, and ascertain what it teaches.'[63] Furthermore, Price argues that one cannot use reason to defeat the arguments of the Socinians because this of course would be conceding their argument that reason has primacy. Revelation is 'peculiar' and therefore should not be subject to the same type of interrogation as other truth claims.

The Trinitarians, as Price sees it, do not commit the mistake of subjecting scripture to the interrogation of reason but they do, as the Socinians did, distort the Biblical message. His dispute with them is one of Biblical interpretation. The problem with the Trinity is not that it goes against reason, but that it is not, so far as he could see, scriptural. The Gospel assures us, he insists, of the resurrection of the dead, divine forgiveness and divine reward and punishment, but the evidence that it gives for the Trinity and for the major doctrines of Calvinism (the imputing of original sin and the salvation of only the elect) is found wanting. From where he was standing, if the weight of tradition is removed from a Biblical hermeneutic, the scriptural verses point decidedly towards Arianism and away from Trinitarianism. His monotheism, to which he gives the name 'Unitarianism,' is he thinks far closer to the Gospel narratives themselves.[64]

As with Samuel Clark before him, Price's dispute with Trinitarian orthodoxy was therefore substantially about scriptural hermeneutics and the role in this of the individual, and the authority of tradition. His theology, inherited from his Dissenting background, was grounded in a commitment to the principle of *sola scriptura*, which rejected tradition as being of any interpretative worth but which also denied unaided reason the authority to determine revealed truth. The belief in one God, Price thought, does not have any necessary connection with Socinianism or deism. He took both scripture and reason in harmony together as supporting the truth of his Arian Christology. The debate about Christology turns out to be a dispute about what exactly orthodoxy *is* and how it is determined.

Some of the notable differences between Price and Priestley are explored further in later chapters, but for now, it should be noted that theologically, the principal thing that united them was a commitment to determining scriptural doctrines as carefully as possible.[65] This came to be characteristic of Rational Dissenting thought, and it shaped an emphasis on personal study of the Bible that attempted to take into account, among other things, the history and social contexts of the verses and the ambiguity of their interpretation. This means the debate between the Rational Dissenters and their more orthodox critics centred on Biblical hermeneutics and the question about what constituted an arbitrary interpretation of scripture. Throughout the eighteenth century, Anglicanism was characterised by notable tensions regarding the authority of tradition. Tradition was defined as the faith set down by the Apostles and Greek Fathers (sometimes with the addition of the Latin Fathers), and it was held in balance with both scripture and reason. Gradually, as the eighteenth century progressed, these three pillars of Anglicanism came under greater strain and either reason or tradition came to take precedence.[66] The Rational Dissenters rejected the authority of tradition outright and were particularly at odds with those Anglicans who gave it increasing authority. Priestley, for example, rebuffs the Anglican George Horne, noted for his defence of the authority of tradition:

> With respect to several of your arguments from *the Scriptures*, (on which, as you reject all arguments from *reason*, you justly lay so much stress) instead of giving us the plain words of Scripture, you give your own arbitrary construction of it.[67]

Priestley wanted to know why those who rejected reason could be so confident in their interpretation: what exactly distinguishes the authority of tradition from human interest? This was the crux of the Rational Dissenting dispute with orthodoxy. It was ultimately one about power, authority, tradition and Biblical interpretation.

Michael Buckley is right when he claims that history should aid theological reflection. He asks how it was that the issue of Christianity versus atheism became purely philosophical, suggesting that the theistic moderns tried to fix a common basis for rational discussion that left out any appeal to the witness of Christ and through which religion 'entrusted itself to philosophy.'[68] The Rational Dissenters, however, show us that the move away from Trinitarianism must trace its roots back to the principle of the primacy of scripture and debates about its interpretation. Christ was not evacuated from the Christology of Rational Dissent simply because their theology entrusted itself to an alien philosophy (particularly not to that of the deists or the *philosophes*). Rather, Christology remained at the centre of Rational Dissenting theology. The 'lower' forms of Christology were no less grounded in scripture and in faith than 'higher' more 'orthodox' forms. What was really at stake was not simply a debate between atheism and theism but a question about the role of tradition and established ecclesial authority in scriptural exegesis. In this, Price and Priestley were united in their rejection of established ecclesiology and a commitment to *sola scriptura*.

'The candle of the lord': Anglican Latitudinarianism and the Cambridge Platonists

The rejection of tradition as a hermeneutical tool in interpreting scripture was not unique to Rational Dissent: B. W. Young identifies it as an important element within the Church of England too. By the mid-eighteenth century, he suggests, a rational theology based on *sola scriptura* became increasingly vocal against an orthodoxy that appealed to tradition.[69] Tensions within the established church over this issue became increasingly apparent. The Anglican David Hartley, for example, wondered, 'How can a Person be properly qualified to study the Word of God, and to search out its Meaning, who finds himself previously confined to interpret it in a particular Manner?'[70] Those who shared Hartley's opinion ventured that the scriptures were sufficient, which meant subscription (forcing people to believe among other things various Articles of faith and a particular theology of the Trinity) came to be seen as unproductive at best and persecution at worst. An increasingly vocal case was made that theological beliefs about Christology should be left instead to individual conscience.

Hartley was one of a group of Anglican divines known as Latitudinarians. The Latitudinarians were characterised by their call for toleration of a broad range of interpretation when it came to the Thirty-Nine Articles, for their affirmation of reason against both the enthusiasts and the 'mysteries of religion' (perceived by them as alien Catholic imports) and for their rejection of ecclesiastical authoritarianism.[71] It was the Latitudinarian concept of reason and its role in religious discernment that should be recognised as essential for shaping Rational Dissenting accounts of rationality. Whereas Rational Dissenting ecclesiology was close in its non-hierarchical polity to Presbyterianism, it was, as Philp says, much closer to Anglican Latitudinarianism in terms of its temperament and its concern to cultivate a faith that sought a harmony of reason and revelation.[72] In the tradition of Rational Dissent, *sola scriptura* was joined to an ecclesiology that refused any theology of the mystical body of Christ or Biblical hermeneutic based on reverence for tradition. This prioritising of scripture found a perfect match in a Latitudinarian account of rationality that extolled freedom of conscience and endorsed a theology of the divine light within.

Latitudinarianism itself took shape amidst disputes over religious authority in the seventeenth century. Simon Patrick tells us that the Latitudinarians 'had their rise at Cambridge' 'before his Majesty's most happy Return.'[73] At the time of the Restoration of Charles II in 1660, the Anglican Church found itself under pressure. Those Anglican divines who had been committed to the Church of the Interregnum during England's brief period of republicanism and who then later declared their fidelity to the post-Restoration Church justified their loyalty to both regimes by identifying basic principles of Christianity which held more theological importance than the various less essential aspects of ritual and doctrine. This earned the disdain of those who had refused to conform to the Interregnum church and the label 'latitude-men' was coined as a pejorative term levelled directly at their inclusiveness.[74] Drawn from within the Anglican Church, the Latitudinarians developed a reputation for the breadth of their views, and they were known as gentlemen 'of a wide swallow.' They stressed the unity of English Protestants rather than their divisions, and they took a political stance against both divine right and hereditary succession, thus making them precursors of the form of Anglicanism that would later be called Low.[75]

The Interregnum of 1649–1660 had seen Parliament and the religious mood of the country dominated by Puritanism. The term 'Puritan,' also originally a term of abuse, has its origins under the rule of Elizabeth I. It tended to refer to those Protestants for whom the Church of England was not reformed enough. They longed to purify it by making it more akin to the reformed Continental churches. Theologically, they disputed salvation through the sacraments of the church, preferring instead a soteriology of grace. Those who were Calvinist denied human freedom in accepting grace and were particularly opposed to Arminianism, a Protestant movement that followed the Dutch Reformed theologian Jacobus Arminius. Arminianism promoted the free acceptance or rejection of God's grace, had a much higher view of reason than Calvinism and stressed the importance of good works in gaining salvation. The contrast with the Calvinist insistence on the depravity of reason and salvation by grace through faith alone was blunt. Tensions between Calvinist Puritans and those of Arminian leanings simmered before the Interregnum and then came to a boil when William Laud, Bishop of London and then Archbishop of Canterbury, republished the Thirty-Nine Articles in 1629 with a new preface that was unashamedly Arminian in tone.[76] Arminianism in England thus came to be known as Laudianism, and it resulted in many Puritans fleeing England for the New World in the decades that followed. Laud himself promoted a form of authority that sought to combine the religious and the secular, the earthly and the spiritual powers in a unity of church and state governed by the king. He did not embrace Arminianism in its entirety, however. He agreed with Arminius that God's grace can in principle be freely accepted, but disputed the means by which this acceptance takes place. For Laud, it is only through the Anglican sacraments that grace is imparted and salvation attained. Benjamin Carter affirms that 'this emphasis on the sacramental was peculiar to the English anti-Calvinism of Laudianism.'[77]

Cambridge before the Restoration contained a hub for Puritanism in the form of Emmanuel College. Founded in the sixteenth century as a centre for educating young minds in the Puritan faith, it managed to resist the pressure to succumb to Laud's reforms.[78] A forceful reaction against Calvinistic Puritanism, however, was to emerge from within the very establishment set up to propagate Puritan ideas. This reaction took the shape of several thinkers who drew on the philosophy of the ancients, particularly Plato and Plotinus, to promote a theology that endeavoured to bring together Athens and Jerusalem in a vision of unified reason and revelation. As a result of these thinkers, as Powicke puts it, the 'citadel of Puritanism and Calvinism became . . . the cradle of a movement animated by the spirit of Plato and devoted to the golden mean in every sphere of thought and life.'[79]

The originator of the movement should be recognised as Benjamin Whichcote who entered Emmanuel as a student in 1626 and remained there as a fellow until 1643. He gives a good insight as to why he refused Calvinism and embraced a much higher view of reason. Everyone has to depend on his teacher at first, he says, but

> let him not depend upon his teacher more than needs must . . . for you ought not to think that you must be in the state of a learner all the days of your life. A child must believe what is told him at first . . . but after a while he comes to see the reason thereof as well as his teacher; and will not be content always to be in the state of a child . . . He is a very unhappy man that. . . [has never used] reason, understanding and judgment . . . nor put forth any of those acts which do most properly belong unto him, as a rational being.[80]

This affirmation of reason is characteristic of Whichcote's thought. Resisting Calvinism and the religion of the enthusiasts, who claimed the authority of inspiration, he embraced instead the compatibility of philosophy and faith together with freedom of the will, all the while placing an emphasis on divine love rather than power. His rationalism and his belief that reason and religion could be harmonised led him to a positive assessment of pagan philosophy– an attitude picked up by his immediate spiritual successors within the university.[81]

In the nineteenth century, the term 'Cambridge Platonist' was coined to refer to those thinkers who were associated with the University of Cambridge and who followed Whichcote's lead in rejecting Calvinism for a rational religion of latitude, all the while refusing so much as 'to mention "original sin." '[82] They were noted for their affirmation of human reason, positive assessment of ancient Greek pagan philosophy and proposed harmony of philosophy and theology. Furthermore, they rejected the ethical voluntarism associated with Calvinism. They could not countenance the suggestion that God's will might determine truth or value. For a Calvinist such as William Perkins (1558–1602), 'God's justice is that which he in all things willeth that which is just'[83] – an ethic entirely rejected by the

Cambridge Platonists who gave eternal unchanging justice primacy over will. That reason is 'the candle of the Lord,' a phrase adapted from Proverbs 20:27, which became the motto of those Cambridge Platonists. It was used as a metaphor for the power of reason to apprehend a truth and goodness that are not dependent on will,[84] and through this aphorism, they wove the language of the scriptures together with a commitment to a Platonic account of the intellect.

The expression 'Cambridge Platonists' should be used with some caution. Those who have retrospectively been identified as belonging to the group did not call themselves Platonists, and there is no evidence they saw themselves as an organised school of philosophy.[85] In fact, they followed the philosophy of Plotinus as much as Plato, borrowing heavily along the way from Stoicism and Aristotle.[86] Nevertheless, as Sarah Hutton suggests, Cambridge Platonism can find a place as a 'label of convenience' for the philosophical thinkers who were educated at the University of Cambridge and who held a more positive view of reason than many of their more Calvinist contemporaries.[87] Ralph Cudworth (1617–1688) and Henry More (1614–1687) should be identified as primary figures in the group with John Smith (1618–1652), Nathaniel Culverwel (1619–1651), Peter Sterry (1613–1672) and other significant members together with Benjamin Whichcote, their spiritual and intellectual mentor.

Although they did not follow the historic Plato on some key issues (for example, the pre-existence of matter and the conception of God as a demiurge), they can be called Platonic in a general sense: they read with approval the writings of Clement of Alexandria, Origen, Augustine and Florentine Renaissance Platonists, particularly Marsilio Ficino.[88] Their Platonism has thus been called an 'eclectic Neoplatonism' reminiscent of Florentine Neoplatonism and receptive to the aspects of seventeenth-century philosophy and science that appeared compatible with their beliefs.[89] They were all deeply committed to a Platonic account of goodness and saw this, rather than will, as the primary attribute of God. They combated Calvinism with a rationality informed by the Platonic tradition, extolled reason as a divine gift – the turn to which would, they believed, reap rich epistemological rewards – and they resisted key elements of Laudianism. Their belief that reason can accept or reject God's grace freely meant that reason took precedence for them over sacramental theology, conformity to doctrine or hereditary succession.

The Cambridge Platonists adopted an Arminian-informed emphasis on reason and spun it into a Platonically informed theology. After the Restoration, their younger followers, including Simon Patrick (1626–1707) and Edward Fowler (1632–1714), embraced the concern for the primacy of reason and broad-minded attitude, and came to be known as Latitudinarians.[90] As Fowler stated,

> We do not suffer any man to reject the Thirty-Nine Articles of the Church of England at his pleasure; yet neither do we look upon them as

essentials of Saving Faith, or Legacies of Christ and his Apostles. . . . we [do not] oblige any man to believe them, but only not contradict them.[91]

Fowler's statement points to a sharp tension with more Laudian divines within the Anglican Church. The Restoration in 1660 meant a restoration of the monarchy but also the House of Lords and the Church of England, and the restored Church inherited many of its previous Laudian characteristics. Collins describes the Restoration Church as exhibiting a 'Churchmanship more elevated than even that of Laud.' This 'High' Church attitude was often characterised by hatred towards the Puritans and devotion to sacramentalism and ceremonialism, aspects of the church that became particularly notable after the Restoration. The result was a defence of episcopacy on the grounds of divine right, resulting in a hegemony that went beyond what Laud himself had hoped for.[92] In contrast to the Laudians, who itched to enforce conformity, the Latitudinarians preached a broader church and disputed the necessity of uniformity of liturgy because salvation required, they thought, commitment only to a small number of beliefs.

The Cambridge Platonists thus gave rise to Latitudinarianism and they shaped a rationalist strand of theology within Anglicanism that deliberately positioned itself against the enthusiastic religion of the radical Puritans and Calvinists but also against Laudian ideals. One characteristic of the Latitudinarians was their openness to the partiality of human viewpoints. They lacked, as Shapiro puts it, the confidence the enthusiasts had that their views were correct and insisted instead that hostility arising from different opinions was 'intellectually indefensible and socially destructive.'[93] With this, they were suspicious of any allegiance grounded in a claim to unchallengeable authority – a position that grounded their commitment to moderation and latitude in the established church. This is an important aspect of their thought, and it underpins a stress on epistemic humility, which colours their philosophical theology.

In addition to shaping the tradition of Latitudinarianism, the Cambridge Platonists also inspired the more liberal wing of English Dissent, the English Presbyterians, first led by Richard Baxter. Baxter promoted a more moderate Calvinism by appealing to reason in matters of controversy, and his belief in the right of private judgement played a pivotal role in shaping the education at Dissenting Academies in the eighteenth century.[94] By the mid-eighteenth century, the figureheads of Dissent were Isaac Watts (1674–1748) and the Puritan Phillip Doddridge (1702–1751) who was principal of the Dissenting Academy in Northampton from 1729 until he died. Doddridge's academy moved on his death to Daventry whereupon its first student was Joseph Priestley. As part of the late seventeenth-century tradition of moderate Puritan Churchmen, Doddridge was wary of the enthusiasts and equally wary of deism. He was firmly planted in the tradition of Baxter's thought. Schofield notes that the Cambridge Platonists and the later Latitudinarians numbered among some of the authorities he cited most in his lectures together with the Dutch Arminians, English Presbyterians and Newtonian physico-theologians.[95] Doddridge combined his Calvinism with tolerance and his piety with a Cambridge Platonist inspired rationalism – the reconciliation of faith and reason was central to his theology and education – and he formed an approach that was instrumental in shaping the theology of subsequent generations of Rational Dissenters although many of them went on to develop positions he himself would not have embraced.[96]

The early Dissenting Academies were dominated by Cartesianism initially. Originally founded to train Dissenting ministers, the academies mostly taught in English, whereas Doddridge eventually stopped teaching in Latin altogether. One consequence of this was that much newer texts came to take precedence over more traditional Latin works. There is evidence that John Ker's academy in Bethnal Green recommended Henry More's *Enchiridion* alongside Cartesian texts, and it is the *Enchiridion* that consolidates the move made by the Cambridge Platonists away from the scholastic method of providing distinctions, against a concern with sacrament and dogma and in favour of a renewed interest in moral attitude.[97]

The theological distinction between Latitudinarianism and Rational Dissent was therefore decidedly blurred for much of the eighteenth century. Priestley studied Henry More at Daventry, although he was in fact far more entranced by the Latitudinarian David Hartley. Priestley even went as far as to claim – to the disdain of Hartley's daughter, Mary – that Hartley was not Latitudinarian at all but rather Unitarian.[98] The Rational Dissenter John Disney declared the Latitudinarian William Paley's *The Principles of Moral and Political Philosophy* (1785) 'most excellent,' and it was cited approvingly in Samuel Heywood's *The Dissenters Right to a Compleat Toleration Asserted* (1787).[99] As will be proposed later in this volume, Richard Price was familiar with the works of Henry More and Ralph Cudworth, and it was Cudworth in particular who had an essential role in shaping Price's conceptions of reason and freedom.

It must be recognised that the contexts of the Cambridge Platonists, the wider seventeenth-century Latitudinarians and the eighteenth-century Rational Dissenters were very different. For one thing, as Spellman reminds us, the latitude-men of the seventeenth century adopted the Thirty-Nine Articles, approved the Anglican liturgy and obeyed the Church's government. Acceptance of the Thirty-Nine Articles was a given, and they strived to reunite the Nonconformists with the established Church. They also made the doctrine of the fall, together with their Christology, central to their theology.[100] Nevertheless, as Martin Fitzpatrick states, there are many intellectual links between the eighteenth-century Latitudinarians and Rational Dissenters, and they result in commonalities of theological, philosophical and political outlook.[101] The traffic between them was fluid, and the boundaries were loose.

This close relationship between Rational Dissent and Latitudinarianism and its commitment to a scriptural theology unsettles the accounts of

Enlightenment rationalism discussed in the first half of this chapter because it makes it difficult to propose that theology gave way to an antithetical Enlightenment philosophy in any straightforward way. The complexity of English thought at this time and the commonalities between Latitudinarianism and Rational Dissent render the suggestion of a relentless war on theological ways of viewing the world increasingly difficult to sustain. The Rational Dissenters are Enlightenment thinkers, but their links with Latitudinarianism and their scriptural theology means that they do not belong to an enlightenment that dichotomises the philosophical and the theological.

In addition to this, the context of the eighteenth century shows that the issue at stake was ultimately one of power and authority: who claims the power to determine legitimate Biblical authority and how can claims to truth be distinguished from claims based only on arbitrary will? The enthusiasts appealed to individual inspiration as their authority, whereas those who were later called High Church appealed to tradition and the authority of the bishops. In response to this, the Rational Dissenting prioritising of reason had much in common with Anglican Latitudinarianism. Their search was not necessarily for a religion of reason but for a harmony of faith and reason, which had deep roots in the Christian-Platonic tradition.

Re-reading the heterodox enlightenment

In conclusion, this chapter has made the case for a closer look at the history of eighteenth-century philosophy and theology in considering the future of the philosophy of religion. Analytic philosophers of religion have tended to view their discipline in terms of the methods of the sciences, seeking objective justification for belief. They see themselves as continuing a tradition of natural theology that long predates the rise of the method of analysis in the 1970s. Many of them, particularly those who embrace arguments for God's existence and those who focus on the attributes of God, see precursors to their approach in the eighteenth-century natural theologians, albeit in an imperfect form. This ancestry helps to legitimise the use of scientific epistemology in the search for a scientific objectivity. In the process, it drives a wedge between what is deemed a 'pure' philosophy and faith-based theology. The same reading of history is present in the thought of many recent theologians who refuse the philosophy of religion. Ideals such as abstraction, objectivity and coherence have been branded secular and anti-Christian – foreign imports from modernity. This shows that the eighteenth century matters for the philosophy of religion. The dominant narrative that helps to fuel both the despisers and defenders of analytic philosophy of religion is one that puts theology at odds with secular reason and distinguishes sharply between pre-modernity and Enlightenment.

This chapter has given reason to doubt the legitimacy of distinguishing so clearly between a *philosophe*-driven radical Enlightenment and a counter-tradition of (more moderate and conservative) theological thinking. The Rational Dissenters certainly did, as Israel suggests, challenge ecclesiastical authority relentlessly, together with the forms of institutional religion that they saw as socially and politically oppressive, but their rational position cannot be understood without its close links to Anglican Latitudinarianism. The suggestion that the theologians of Rational Dissent had 'become philosophers' in the sense of adopting a foreign imported secular reason should be resisted. Rather than an invasion of Christian theology by scientific rationalism, what develops instead is a conception of reason shaped substantially by a theological reaction to an established church that was experienced as a form of oppressive hegemony and a profoundly Biblical form of faith.

These ideas are taken up further in Chapter 3, which investigates in greater detail the connections between Rational Dissent and Latitudinarianism and the origins of modern philosophy of religion in England, both forged against the backdrop of various claims to power. Before that, the next chapter examines in more detail Rational Dissenting conceptions of reason. Although Price and Priestley share a Presbyterian and Latitudinarian inheritance, they offer very different understandings of rationality and the self. This highlights the multifaceted nature of Rational Dissent and hints at two very distinct traditions of English Rational Dissenting reason. Price's more Platonic account of reason uncovers the development of a strand of Platonic physico-theology in the mid-late eighteenth century, which prioritises ethical concerns and epistemic humility over the justification of propositional metaphysical belief.

Notes

1 Richard Swinburne, "Philosophical Theism," in *Philosophy of Religion in the 21st Century*, ed. D. Z. Phillips and Timothy Tessin (Basingstoke: Palgrave Macmillan, 2001), 40; Richard Swinburne, "The Value and Christian Roots of Analytical Philosophy of Religion," in *Faith and Philosophical Analysis: The Impact of Analytical Philosophy on the Philosophy of Religion*, ed. Harriet A. Harris and Christopher J. Insole (Aldershot: Ashgate, 2005), 40.

2 William J. Wainwright, "Philosophical Theology at the End of the Century," in *Philosophy of Religion in the 21st Century*, ed. D. Z. Phillips and Timothy Tessin (Basingstoke: Palgrave Macmillan, 2001), 21–2; Jonathan Edwards shows a notable influence from the Cambridge Platonists, particularly Henry More and John Smith (I am grateful to the anonymous reviewer for bringing this to my attention). See, e.g., John J. Bombaro, *Jonathan Edwards's Vision of Reality: The Relationship of God to the World, Redemption, History and the Reprobate* (Oregon: Wipf and Stock, 2011), 31.

3 Victoria S. Harrison, "What's the Use of Philosophy of Religion?" in *God, Goodness and Philosophy*, ed. Harriet A. Harris (Farnham: Ashgate, 2011), 31.

4 John Milbank, Graham Ward, and Catherine Pickstock, "Introduction: Suspending the Material: The Turn of Radical Orthodoxy," in *Radical Orthodoxy: A New Theology*, ed. John Milbank, Catherine Pickstock, and Graham Ward (London: Routledge, 1999), 1.

5 John Milbank, *Theology and Social Theory: Beyond Secular Reason* (Oxford: Blackwell, 1993), 280.

6 Martin Fitzpatrick, "Enlightenment, Dissent and Toleration," *Enlightenment and Dissent* 28 (2012): 42.

7   Colin Gunton, *Enlightenment and Alienation: An Essay toward Trinitarian Theology* (Basingstoke: Marshall Morgan and Scott, 1985), 64.
8   Alister McGrath, *The Renewal of Anglicanism* (London: SPCK, 1993), 15; Linell E. Cady, "Foundation vs. Scaffolding," *Union Seminary Quarterly* 41 (1987): 46.
9   Anthony Pagden, *The Enlightenment and Why It Still Matters* (Oxford: Oxford University Press, 2013), 26.
10 See, e.g., J.G.A. Pocock, *The Varieties of British Political Thought 1500–1800* (Cambridge: Cambridge University Press, 1993); J.C.D. Clark, *English Society 1660–1832: Religion, Ideology and Politics during the Ancien Regime* (Cambridge: Cambridge University Press, 2000).
11 Jonathan I. Israel, *Enlightenment Contested: Philosophy, Modernity, and the Emancipation of Man, 1670–1752* (Oxford: Oxford University Press, 2006), 669.
12 Michael J. Buckley, *At the Origins of Modern Atheism* (Yale: Yale University Press, 1987), 37–8.
13 Kelvin Knight, ed., *The MacIntyre Reader* (Cambridge: Polity Press, 1998), 70.
14 Terry Eagleton, *Culture and the Death of God* (London: Yale University Press, 2014), 4, 12, 19, 191, 198; See also Max Horkheimer and Theodor W. Adorno, *Dialectic of Enlightenment: Philosophical Fragments*, trans. Edmund Jephcott (Stanford: Stanford University Press, 2002), 6, 63.
15 William Cantwell Smith, *The Meaning and End of Religion: A Revolutionary Approach to the Great Religious Traditions* (London: SPCK, 1962), 42; Beverley Clack, "Radical Orthodoxy and Feminist Philosophy of Religion," in *Interpreting the Postmodern: Responses to Radical Orthodoxy*, ed. Rosemary Radford Ruether and Marion Grau (London: T&T Clark, 2006), 216; Talal Asad, *Genealogies of Religion: Discipline and Reasons of Power in Christianity and Islam* (London: John Hopkins University Press, 1993), 45–8.
16 Peter J. Stanlis, *Edmund Burke: The Enlightenment and Revolution* (London: Transaction Publishers, 1991), 116.
17 Richard A. Muller, "Philip Doddridge and the Formulation of Calvinistic Theology in an Era of Rationalism and Deconfessionalization," in *Religion, Politics and Dissent 1660–1832: Essays in Honour of James E. Bradley*, ed. Robert D. Cornwall and William Gibson (Farnham: Ashgate, 2010), 65; Isaiah Berlin, *The Age of Enlightenment: The Eighteenth-Century Philosophers* (Oxford: Oxford University Press, 1979), 19, 27.
18 Israel, *Enlightenment Contested*, 669, 685, 696.
19 Clack, "Radical Orthodoxy," 216.
20 John Milbank, *Being Reconciled: Ontology and Pardon* (London: Routledge, 2003), 163.
21 James K.A. Smith, *Introducing Radical Orthodoxy: Mapping a Post-Secular Theology* (Grand Rapids, MI: Baker Academic, 2004), 31, 32–3.
22 Jonathan I. Israel, "Enlightenment! Which Enlightenment?" *Journal of the History of Ideas* 67, no. 3 (2006): 528–9.
23 Jonathan I. Israel, *A Revolution of the Mind: Radical Enlightenment and the Intellectual Origins of Modern Democracy* (Princeton: Princeton University Press, 2010), 35, see also 18–19.
24 Israel, "Enlightenment!" 528; Israel, *Revolution*, 12.
25 J.G.A. Pocock, "Post-Puritan England and the Problem of the Enlightenment," in *Culture and Politics from Puritanism to the Enlightenment*, ed. Perez Zagorin (London: University of California Press, 1980), 91–111; See esp. Roy Porter, *The Enlightenment* (Basingstoke: Macmillan, 1990), 5–11; Clark, *English Society*; for a clear introduction to Clark and Bradley's criticism of his reading see Robert D. Cornwall and William Gibson, "Introduction," in *Religion, Politics*

and Dissent 1660–1832: Essays in Honour of James E. Bradley, ed. Robert D. Cornwall and William Gibson (Farnham: Ashgate, 2010), 1–14.

26 Buckley, *Origins*, 33.

27 Buckley, *Origins*, 40. See also 354.

28 Buckley, *Origins*, 345, 356.

29 Charles Taylor, *A Secular Age* (Cambridge, MA: Belknap Press of Harvard University Press, 2007), 221, 291–4.

30 Ruth Watts, "Introduction: Rational Dissenting Women and the Travel of Ideas'," *Enlightenment and Dissent* 26 (2010): 14 makes this case; Roy Porter is dismissive of the significance of Rational Dissent, calling its members "a hot-head minority." but John Seed challenges this view: John Seed, "'A Set of Men Powerful Enough in Many Things': Rational Dissent and Political Opposition in England, 1770–1790," in *Enlightenment and Religion: Rational Dissent in Eighteenth-Century Britain*, ed. Knud Haakonssen (Cambridge: Cambridge University Press, 1996), 140–68. Although J. C. D. Clark calls them a "small radical intelligentsia," he still sees them as important for challenging the establishment: Clark, *English Society*, 345.

31 Israel, *Enlightenment Contested*, 102.

32 Knud Haakonssen, "Enlightened Dissent: An Introduction," in *Enlightenment and Religion: Rational Dissent in Eighteenth-Century Britain*, ed. Knud Haaksonssen (Cambridge: Cambridge University Press, 1996), 4; J. G. A. Pocock, "Conservative Enlightenment and Democratic Revolutions: The American and French Cases in British Perspective'," *Government and Opposition* 24 (1989): 97–8.

33 J. A. I. Champion, *The Pillars of Priestcraft Shaken: The Church of England and Its Enemies* (Cambridge: Cambridge University Press, 1992), 23.

34 Champion, *Pillars of Priestcraft*, 19.

35 Samuel Clarke, "A Discourse Concerning the Unchangeable Obligations of Natural Religion, and the Truth and Certainty of the Christian Revelation," in *The Works of Samuel Clarke*, vol. ii (London: Printed for John and Paul Knapton, 1738), 605.

36 Quoted in Simon Mills, "Scripture and Heresy in the Biblical Studies of Nathaniel Lardner, Joseph Priestley, and Thomas Belsham," in *Dissent and the Bible in Britain, c.1650–1950*, ed. Scott Mandelbrote and Michael Ledger-Lomas (Oxford: Oxford University Press, 2013), 101; Soame Jenyns, "A Free Inquiry into the Nature and Origin of Evil: In Six Letters to –, " in *Miscellaneous Pieces in Verse and Prose* (London: Printed for J. Dodsley, 1770), 232.

37 Mills, "Scripture and Heresy," 86.

38 A. M. C. Waterman, "The Nexus between Theology and Political Doctrine in Church and Dissent," in *Enlightenment and Religion: Rational Dissent in Eighteenth-Century Britain*, ed. Knud Haakonssen (Cambridge: Cambridge University Press, 1996), 197.

39 Thomas C. Pfizenmaier, "Why the Third Fell Out: Trinitarian Dissent," in *Religion, Politics and Dissent 1660–1832: Essays in Honour of James E. Bradley*, ed. Robert D. Cornwall and William Gibson (Farnham: Ashgate, 2010), 17; Cornwall and Gibson, "Introduction," 2.

40 Cornwall and Gibson, "Introduction," 2.

41 William Gibson, "Dissenters, Anglicans and Elections after the Toleration Act, 1689–1710," in *Religion, Politics and Dissent 1660–1832: Essays in Honour of James E. Bradley*, ed. Robert D. Cornwall and William Gibson (Farnham: Ashgate, 2010), 130.

42 Isabel Rivers and David L. Wykes, "Introduction," in *Joseph Priestley, Scientist, Philosopher and Theologian*, ed. Isabel Rivers and David L. Wykes (Oxford: Oxford University Press, 2008), 5.

43 Gibson, "Dissenters," 130.
44 David L Wykes, "Religious Dissent, the Church, and the Repeal of the Occasional Conformity and Schism Acts, 1714–19," in *Religion, Politics and Dissent 1660–1832: Essays in Honour of James E. Bradley*, ed. Robert D Cornwall and William Gibson (Farnham: Ashgate, 2010), 181.
45 James E. Bradley, *Religion, Revolution, and English Radicalism: Nonconformity in Eighteenth-Century Politics and Society* (Cambridge: Cambridge University Press, 1990), 89.
46 Wykes, "Religious Dissent," 182.
47 Rivers and Wykes, "Introduction," 11.
48 Mark Philp, "Rational Religion and Political Radicalism in the 1790s," *Enlightenment and Dissent* 4 (1985): 36.
49 Knud Haakonssen, *Enlightenment and Religion: Rational Dissent in Eighteenth-Century Britain* (Cambridge: Cambridge University Press, 1996), 4.
50 Two comprehensive biographies of Priestley are F. W. Gibbs, *Joseph Priestley: Adventurer in Science and Champion of Truth* (London: Thomas Nelson & Sons, 1965); John Ruskin Clark, *Joseph Priestley, a Comet in the System* (San Diego: Torch Publications, 1990); The best biographical study of Price remains D. O. Thomas, *The Honest Mind: The Thought and Work of Richard Price* (Oxford: Clarendon, 1977).
51 Joseph Priestley, "Memoirs," in *Works*, ed. John Towill Rutt, vol. i (London: Printed by George Smallfield, 1817), 35.
52 Joseph Priestley, "Letters to Dr Horsley in Answer to His Animadversions of the History of the Corruptions of Christianity," in *Works*, ed. John Towill Rutt, vol. xviii (London: Printed by George Smallfield, 1831), 40.
53 Mills, "Scripture and Heresy."
54 R. K. Webb, "The Emergence of Rational Dissent," in *Enlightenment and Religion: Rational Dissent in Eighteenth-Century Britain*, ed. Knud Haakonssen (Cambridge: Cambridge University Press, 1996), 36.
55 Priestley, "Memoirs," 1817, 36, 39; Mills, "Scripture and Heresy," 101.
56 Priestley, "Letters to Dr Horsley," 1817, 40; Mills, "Scripture and Heresy," 99.
57 J. G. McEvoy and J. E. McGuire, "God and Nature: Priestley's Way of Rational Dissent," *Historical Studies in the Physical Sciences* 6 (1975): 329.
58 Thomas, *Honest Mind*, 16.
59 More in depth biographical details of Price's life can be found in Carl B. Cone, *Torchbearer of Freedom: The Influence of Richard Price on Eighteenth Century Thought* (Lexington: University of Kentucky Press, 1952) and Thomas, *Honest Mind*.
60 Thomas, *Honest Mind*, 8.
61 Richard Price, *Sermons on the Christian Doctrine* (London: Printed for T. Cadell, 1787), 85; Richard Price, *Thoughts on the Progress of Socinianism; with an Enquiry into the Cause and the Cure. In a Letter Humbly Addressed to Learned, Orthodox, and Candid Ministers of All Denominations: With a Particular View to the Writing of Dr. Priestley. To Which Is Added, a Letter to Dr. Price, on His Late Sermons on the Christian Doctrine* (London: J. Buckland and J. Johnson, 1787), 3, 19.
62 Price, *Thoughts on Socinianism*, 2, 35, 18n.
63 Price, *Thoughts on Socinianism*, 18n.
64 Price, *Christian Doctrine*, 87. See also 25, 48–9.
65 Mills, "Scripture and Heresy," 88.
66 Jamie C. Kassler, *Seeking Truth: Roger North's Notes on Newton and Correspondence with Samuel Clarke c.1704–1713* (Farnham: Ashgate, 2014), 210–11.
67 Joseph Priestley, "Letters to Dr Horne, Dean of Canterbury," in *Works*, vol. xviii, 1817, 338.

68 Buckley, *Origins*, 33–4, 357.
69 B. W. Young, *Religion and Enlightenment in Eighteenth-Century England: Theological Debate from Locke to Burke* (Oxford: Clarendon, 1997), 44.
70 David Hartley, "Of the Rule of Faith," in *Observations on Man, His Frame, His Duty, and His Expectations* (London: Printed for T. Tegg and Son, 1834), 540 This book was originally published in 1749.
71 Anthony Page, *John Jebb and the Enlightenment Origins of British Radicalism* (London: Praeger, 2003), 11.
72 Philp, "Rational Religion," 36.
73 S. P. [Simon Patrick], *A Brief Account of the New Sect of Latitude-Men Together with Some Reflections upon the New Philosophy* (London, 1662), 3; Robert Grove, *A Vindication of the Conforming Clergy from the Unjust Aspersions of Heresie* (London: Printed for Walter Kettilby, 1676), 24.
74 John Gascoigne, *Cambridge in the Age of Enlightenment: Science, Religion and Politics from the Restoration to the French Revolution* (Cambridge: Cambridge University Press, 1989), 40.
75 Edward Fowler, *The Principles and Practices of Certain Moderate Divines of the Church of England* (London: Printed for Lodowick Lloyd, 1670), 10; John Gascoigne, "Anglican Latitudinarianism, Rational Dissent and Political Radicalism in the Late Eighteenth Century," in *Enlightenment and Religion: Rational Dissent in Eighteenth-Century Britain*, ed. Knud Haakonssen (Cambridge: Cambridge University Press, 1996), 224.
76 Charles Taliaferro and Alison Teply, "Introduction to Cambridge Platonism," in *Cambridge Platonist Spirituality*, ed. Charles Taliaferro and Alison Teply (Mahwah, NJ: Paulist Press, 2004), 45.
77 Benjamin Carter, *'The Little Commonwealth of Man': The Trinitarian Origins of the Ethical and Political Philosophy of Ralph Cudworth* (Leuven: Peeters, 2011), 7.
78 James Deotis Roberts, *From Puritanism to Platonism in Seventeenth Century England* (The Hague: Martinus Nijhoff, 1968), 44.
79 Frederick J. Powicke, *The Cambridge Platonists: A Study* (London: J. M. Dent, 1926), 3.
80 Benjamin Whichcote, *The Works of the Learned Benjamin Whichcote* (Aberdeen: Printed for A. Thomson, 1751), 155–6.
81 Sarah Hutton, "A Radical Review of the Cambridge Platonists," in *Varieties of Seventeenth- and Early Eighteenth Century English Radicalism in Context*, ed. Ariel Hessayon and David Finnegan (Farnham: Ashgate, 2011), 161–82.
82 Mark Goldie, "Cambridge Platonists (act. 1630s-1680s)," in *Oxford Dictionary of National Biography Online*, ed. Lawrence Goldman (Oxford: Oxford University Press, 2015), http://www.oxforddnb.com/view/theme/94274. Last accessed 01/05/16; C. A. Patrides, " 'The High and Aiery Hills of Platonisme': An Introduction to the Cambridge Platonists," in *The Cambridge Platonists*, ed. C. A. Patrides (Cambridge: Cambridge University Press, 1969), 38.
83 Quoted in Carter, *Commonwealth*, 3.
84 Benjamin Whichcote, *Moral and Religious Aphorisms* (London: Printed for J. Payne, 1930), §916; John Smith, *Select Discourses* (London: Printed by J. Flesher, for W. Morden, bookseller in Cambridge, 1660), 448; David Pailin, "Reconciling Theory and Fact: The Problem of 'Other Faiths' in Lord Herbert and the Cambridge Platonists," in *Platonism at the Origins of Modernity: Studies on Platonism and Early Modern Philosophy*, ed. Douglas Hedley and Sarah Hutton (Dordrecht: Springer, 2008), 93–112 discusses the varied interpretations of the scope of reason but acknowledges that all the Cambridge Platonists had a substantial belief in the power of reason as a religious and ethical guide.
85 Hutton, "Radical Review," 165.

86   Lloyd P. Gerson argues that Plato's philosophy is itself one version of Platonism: *From Plato to Platonism* (London: Cornell University Press, 2013), 9.

87   Sarah Hutton, "Lord Herbert of Cherbury and the Cambridge Platonists," in *British Philosophy and the Age of Enlightenment*, ed. Stuart Brown (London: Routledge, 1996), 23.

88   Charles Taliaferro, *Evidence and Faith: Philosophy and Religion since the Seventeenth Century* (Cambridge: Cambridge University Press, 2005), 16; In terms of their interpretation of Plato, the Cambridge Platonists were certainly influenced by Marsilio Ficino's reading of Plato, see, e.g., Patrides, "Introduction," 1; Sarah Hutton, however, argues for the fact that Cudworth both read and interpreted Plato for himself. Hutton reports that Ficino and Jean de Serres were the two most important translators of Plato in the Renaissance, but Cudworth was alert to the differences between his interpretation of Plato and theirs: Sarah Hutton, "Introduction," in *A Treatise Concerning Eternal and Immutable Morality with a Treatise of Freewill*, ed. Sarah Hutton (Cambridge: Cambridge University Press, 1996), xix. Cudworth was therefore clearly aware of other editions and translations of Plato's works but was not dependent on them.

89   Hutton and Brown, "Herbert of Cherbury," 23.

90   Hutton and Brown, "Herbert of Cherbury," 23.

91   Quoted in Roger D. Lund, "Introduction," in *The Margins of Orthodoxy: Heterodox Writing and Cultural Response, 1660–1750*, ed. Roger D. Lund (Cambridge: Cambridge University Press, 1995), 4.

92   Jeffrey R. Collins, "The Restoration Bishops and the Royal Supremacy," *Church History* 68, no. 3 (1999): 558.

93   B.J. Shapiro, "Latitudinarianism and Science and Seventeenth-Century England," *Past and Present* 40 (1968): 30.

94   Robert E. Schofield, *The Enlightenment of Joseph Priestley: A Study of His Life and Work from 1733 to 1773* (University Park, PA: Pennsylvania State University Press, 1997), 50; David L. Wykes, "The Contribution of the Dissenting Academy to the Emergence of Rational Dissent," in *Enlightenment and Religion: Rational Dissent in Eighteenth-Century Britain*, ed. Knud Haakonssen (Cambridge: Cambridge University Press, 1996), 121, 126.

95   Webb, "Emergence," 29; Schofield, *Enlightenment of Joseph Priestley*, 51.

96   Webb, "Emergence," 34, 36.

97   Wykes, "Dissenting Academy," 112; Ernst Cassirer, *The Platonic Renaissance in England*, trans. James P. Pettegrove (New York: Nelson, 1953), 27–8.

98   Joseph Priestley, *Memoirs of the Rev. Dr. Joseph Priestley to the Year 1795 / Written by Himself with a Continuation to the Time of His Decease by His Son Joseph Priestley* (London: Unitarian Societies in England, 1809), 16–17; Jack Fruchtman Jr, "Late Latitudinarianism; The Case of David Hartley," *Enlightenment and Dissent* 11 (1992): 6.

99   Martin Fitzpatrick, "Latitudinarianism at the Parting of the Ways: A Suggestion," in *The Church of England c.1689-c.1833: From Toleration to Tractarianism*, ed. John Walsh, Colin Haydon, and Stephen Taylor (Cambridge: Cambridge University Press, 1993), 210.

100 W.M. Spellman, *The Latitudinarians and the Church of England, 1660–1700* (Athens, GA: University of Georgia Press, 1993), 158–9.

101 Fitzpatrick, "Latitudinarianism," 209.

2 Godliness and Godlikeness
Deiform reason and the honest mind

It is no surprise that Richard Price has been thought of as epitomising the trend towards an 'enlightened' and modernistic world view, especially given the ethics of rationalist intuitionism he advances. His philosophy has been described as the 'culmination of eighteenth-century rationalism,' and he is most usually depicted – particularly influentially by Alasdair MacIntyre – as a prime example of an Enlightenment moralist who was forced to search for an alternative justification for ethics following the eighteenth-century rejection of Aristotelianism and Christian teleology.[1] According to Jonathan Israel, Price, along with the other Rational Dissenters, should be placed in the tradition of 'Christian-Unitarianism,' part of what he calls the radical Enlightenment, which by the time of the French Revolution had 'come to form a powerful rival "package logic" – equality, democracy, freedom of the individual, freedom of thought and expression, and a comprehensive religious toleration.' Israel associates Christian-Unitarianism closely with Socinianism, and he posits an alliance between Socinianism and Spinozism. These two thought systems are aligned, he argues, through their commitment to materialism with both promoting a one-substance metaphysic that operates by 'conflating body and mind into one, reducing God and nature to the same thing, excluding all miracles and spirits separate from bodies, and invoking reason as the sole guide in human life.'[2]

This assumption underpins the perception, noted in the previous chapter, of the radical Enlightenment as anti-theological at its heart. As stated in the last chapter, Israel sees these two Enlightenments as entirely separate by the second half of the eighteenth century. The linking of the tradition of Christian-Unitarianism with the atheist radical Enlightenment does much to reinforce the view that theology took a philosophical turn in the eighteenth-century, rendering it anti-theological, in a move that replaced revelation with reason as part of a war against theological ways of understanding the world. This complements the account of a link between heterodox and radical Enlightenment and nurtures the view that concepts of equality, democracy and the like are part of a liberal anti-Christian secular tradition.

The 'moderate' Enlightenment, which is thought to culminate in Edmund Burke, is characterised by a two-substance dualism for which reason is immaterial and divine, as well as a gift to humankind, and which raises us above other non-human life. This Enlightenment, according to Israel, clips the wings of reason in favour of faithfulness to tradition and ecclesiastical authority. Furthermore, he insists that these two Enlightenments are diametrically opposed: between them, 'no compromise or half-way position was ever possible, either theoretically or practically.'[3] The dichotomy between an atheist-leaning rationality and a more conservative traditional theology is thus entrenched, and the fracture between Enlightenment philosophy and religious faith looks inevitable.

This chapter, however, challenges the suggestion that the moderate and radical Enlightenments can be distinguished so easily. This is important for uncovering a Platonic-Rational-Dissenting strand of theological reason in the eighteenth century and its associative natural theology. A closer look at Price and Priestley shows they present significantly different understandings of reason, coloured by the different intellectual sources they draw upon: Price from Platonist epistemology and metaphysics, and Priestley from Hartley's understanding of the self, coloured by his conversion to Socinianism. Appreciating the Platonism and theology of Price's account of reason and contrasting it with Priestley's alternative not only affirms the difficulty with distinguishing between a radical Enlightenment and a theologically informed more moderate Enlightenment but also challenges those narratives of the eighteenth century that propose it was dominated by a turn to a new form of secular philosophy that was by definition anti-theological. Price's Rational Dissenting understanding of reason was not part of a Socinian-Spinozian tradition but was instead part of a religiously inspired model of reason as the divinity within. This leads to a very different – and limited – conception of the nature and scope of reason.

Innate ideas and the human soul: disputes within Rational Dissent

The question of the relationship between mind and matter formed the most contentious point of disagreement between Price and Priestley – a dispute played out through a series of letters published in 1778 under the title *A Free Discussion of the Doctrines of Materialism and Philosophical Necessity in a Correspondence between Dr. Price and Dr. Priestley*. Although a good-tempered disagreement, it signalled a deep disparity of epistemology and metaphysics. As Fitzpatrick points out, there were enormous differences in the way the Rational Dissenters perceived of reason and of how they thought human beings could best understand themselves.[4] Although Price and Priestley had a shared commitment to reason, they developed it in two notably divergent directions.

Wholly material not wholly spiritual: Priestley's Hartlean monism

Priestley saw himself as at least in part a Lockean. There are important connections between Locke and the Cambridge Platonists, not least the fact that Locke greatly admired Whichcote and heard him preach many times in London and the friendship between Locke and Damaris Masham, Ralph Cudworth's daughter. John Rogers suggests that the most important link between them was their commitment to reason as the primary intellectual virtue. Reason is a powerful source of religious knowledge – an epistemology defined in opposition to the target of enthusiasm.[5] What attracted Priestley to the philosophy of Locke, however, was his attack on the doctrine of innate ideas. He praised Locke's recognition that all our ideas come from the senses, including all rational knowledge of our own nature.[6] With this stance against innate ideas, Priestley positioned himself resolutely against the epistemology of Platonism. In fact, he regarded Platonists with nothing but complete disdain because he considered the Platonist doctrine of the immateriality of the soul as the root of every corruption of Christianity. The philosophy led, he thought, to the idea of the Logos as the second God and ultimately to the doctrine of the Trinity.[7]

Disparaging the immateriality of the soul, Priestley developed a monistic conception of nature and the human person. 'Mr Hobbes' he proclaimed 'was the first who understood and maintained the proper doctrine of philosophical necessity,'[8] and he took from Anthony Collins the view that most people's actions are determined by fear or hope. More prevalent than their influence, however, was that of the Latitudinarian David Hartley. While at Daventry, Priestley read Hartley's *Observations on Man* and quickly became a zealous convert to its materialistic psychology. He reported that reading Hartley increased his 'disposition to piety' and liberated him from his Calvinist background. He adopted from his intellectual idol the doctrine of necessity and then later embraced the association of ideas derived from sensory experience.[9]

In *Observations*, Hartley proposed that actions always follow from motives, which arise in the mind through sensation and association; hence, in this way, they are necessary. Free will in the philosophical sense is therefore impossible, although he maintained (whereas his critics remained unimpressed) that there is still such a thing as practical liberty in that we have at least the impression of freedom. *Observations* offered a materialistic explanation of how the brain receives sense data, and it proposed that simple ideas have their origin in the physical structure of the brain, produced in response to the senses by vibrations in the nervous system and spinal marrow. These simple ideas produce complex ideas through a process termed 'association.' He drew directly from Locke's account of knowledge as forged from the association of ideas in the mind, arising from the data of sense experience.

Priestley adopted Hartley's psychology and proposed what could be called a one-substance metaphysic, moving away from dualism towards a materialistic account of the human person. He saw human beings as '*wholly material*,' rather than '*wholly spiritual*,' and by 1775, he had moved towards the view that 'the whole man is of some *uniform composition*' rather than made up of the different substances of matter and spirit and that the 'property of *perception*, as well as the other powers that are termed *mental*, is the result . . . of such an organical structure as that of the brain.'[10] There is a clear development, galvanised by his reading of Hartley, towards an emergence theory of the mind.

Although Priestley proposed human beings to be 'wholly material,' he cannot be classified as a straightforward materialist especially not in the Epicurean sense. It had been Newton's view that there is a 'subtle spirit which pervades and lies hid in all gross bodies.'[11] Building on Hobbes's theory of the association of ideas, Hartley interpreted this 'subtle spirit' to be the force that animates living things rather than an incorporeal substance.[12] Priestley then developed this philosophy to insist that the infinite solidity of atoms is not absolute. There is no real difference he argued between matter and force: 'Matter has, in fact, no properties but those of *attraction and repulsion*.'[13] What he denied was the existence of two distinct substances of matter and spirit by seeing matter as possessing extension, and the powers of attraction and repulsion. This means that electricity, light and gravitation became more fundamental than complex bodies. For Priestley, therefore, matter ultimately resolves into force. This was something that Price, who adopted an atomistic idea of matter, could not agree with. Despite their contention about this, one important point to note is that Priestley proposed a materialism that is irreducibly theological. All forces are essentially passive and could not exist without an active cause, which is God. If matter can be called active for Priestley, it is only in the sense that divine causality becomes immanent in nature. There is 'no active force in nature but that of God.'[14] God becomes the infinite force which unites all matter and which is continual action. This explains how he could claim that although human nature is material rather than wholly spiritual, he still had the option of calling it wholly spiritual. He could just as much, he insisted, call his account spiritualism as materialism and thus was definitely no atheist.

It is for this reason that Henri Laboucheix argues that if 'matter' is defined as atoms made up of forces that hold them together and if by forces we mean the powers of attraction and repulsion that make up the atom as well as those external to it, then Priestley should not really be thought of as materialist so much as someone who proposes a dynamic theory of the universe. The dynamism of the universe should not be equated with God, he thought, proposing instead a monism in which the divine being has the nature of 'filling all in all.'[15] Even for Priestley, nature cannot be understood without God organising it. He might best be seen, as Laboucheix suggests, as reaching back beyond Socrates to revive a form of Democritus's philosophy.[16]

Nevertheless, he marks an important shift in the way the relationship between God and nature was conceived. His account was truly Unitarian because it refused a distinction between matter and spirit, temporal and eternal, God and human beings, comprehensible and incomprehensible.[17]

In contrast, Price insisted that the experience of reflecting on ourselves teaches us that the exercise of our mental powers depends on the brain and the nerves, but not that the mind *is* the brain and the nerves. He explicitly rejected any emergent theory of the human soul because he embraced the theory of soul as a different *substance* to matter, one that could not have arisen from matter. At the heart of Price's disagreement with Priestley about the substantial difference between the brain and the mind lies Price's conviction in the unbridgeable distinction between the activity of mind and passivity of matter. He simply could not countenance that a number of particles disposed and moved in one particular way are what he calls torpid matter but moved in another way are perception, judgement and reason: '*Matter* is something that is solid, and extended, and figured and moveable. *Spirit* is something that thinks, and wills, and judges.'[18] The principles of thought and reason are not only distinct from the body, he believed, but also independent of it with respect to existence rather than operation. By this he meant that the *principles* of thought and reason are independent of the body, but he believed that the mind is dependent on the body for the exertion of the soul's powers. Matter must, according to Price's psychology be innately inactive, which means it cannot begin motion in itself, and it has no *agency*. The mind, however, he sees as active because it can begin motion in the body. Our minds are active in that we have command over our thoughts and determinations: 'Mind is prior to body, and the cause of all its motions and properties.'[19]

The impasse between Price and Priestly on the nature of the soul and the activity or inactivity of matter was to a significant degree the result of their varying reactions to a Platonic metaphysic. Whereas Priestley abandoned Platonism in favour of a Hartlean monism, it was a commitment to Platonic epistemology that grounded Price's dualistic metaphysics. This had as its main concern the defence of the reality of ethical value.

Active intellect and the eternal mind: Price's Platonic epistemology

In contrast to Priestley, Richard Price was enthusiastic about the Platonic tradition. In a letter to Lord Monboddo dated 1780, he declared, 'I was always a warm admirer of Plato among the antients and of Cudworth and Clarke among the moderns.'[20] He even went as far as to agree avidly with Lord Monboddo's estimation of Plato as a 'Philosopher truly Divine,' and he gives us evidence that he had read, among others, Alcinous, Plotinus, Cudworth and Henry More. Like so many of the Renaissance Neoplatonists, he never attempted to distinguish between the different philosophies of the Platonic tradition and exhibited instead a reading of Plato coloured by both the Cambridge Platonists and Middle Platonism (the term given, since the nineteenth century, to the Platonism that developed between the first century BCE and Plotinus in the third century, which includes the thought of Alcinous).[21]

When it comes to reason, Price's account of it is thoroughly Platonic. He grounds it in the Platonic doctrine of participation in which the ultimate aim of the soul is deiformity, to become like God.[22] Most notably, it is this philosophy that underpins Price's commitment to a dualistic understanding of the human person. In fact, the defence of what might be termed a substance dualism is most fundamentally about ethics. There was a danger apparent to Price in Hartley's model, also evident in any moral epistemology that tried to ground morality in moral sense. The doctrine of the association of ideas, as acknowledged by Hartley himself, perceived the moral sense to be generated by 'piety, benevolence, and rational self-interest,' carrying 'its own authority with it.'[23] Anthony Page argues that unlike the Scottish philosophers who saw the moral sense as an innate human quality, Hartley saw it as 'mechanically produced by experience on the "white paper" of the mind.'[24] Hartley's morality becomes in effect a form of hedonism, which for Price could be nothing more than relativism by another name.

The activity of the soul became vital for Price in the cause of safeguarding knowledge and morality. He drew on a basic Platonic principle that knowledge is not to be sought in sense, or matter, but in a superior part of the soul. In this his greatest influence was Cudworth, for whom 'the soul is not a mere naked and passive thing, a *rasa tabula*,' with no innate active principle of its own, because 'if it were so then there could not possibly be any such thing as moral good and evil, just and unjust.'[25] The argument goes right back to Plato and his insistence that perception, or sense experience, cannot act as a foundation to knowledge: 'perception and knowledge cannot ever be identical' because truth and justice cannot arise from, or be caused by, matter.[26] In Cudworth and then in Price's hands, this is developed into an argument that if all knowledge and being is derived from the body and from sensation, it will have less 'reality' than if it was derived from the mind and we will be led into both epistemological and moral relativism. Knowledge and truth will become 'airy' and insubstantial.[27] Cudworth believed this was a danger of Hobbes's position, and Price saw it as a danger of Hutcheson's idea of the moral sense. In the *Review*, Price refers to Socrates' argument in the *Theaetetus* that reason is the soul acting by itself separately from matter. Knowledge is not to be sought for in sense but in the superior part of the soul, reason: for if knowledge claims to rest on sensation, it is reduced to individual perception and one is led straight to Protagoras's suggestion that 'man is the measure of all things.'[28]

The epistemological argument of the *Review* has its roots in the Platonic concern to promote the immutable nature of ethical value. It takes the following form. First, Price argues that knowledge consists of simple ideas, discerned by what he calls 'the understanding.' Second, he argues that this same faculty of the understanding discerns *moral* ideas. This leads Price to his conclusion that moral concepts are simple ideas. This means for him that morality is eternal and immutable, and discerns the real characters of actions. Morality is grounded in the nature of things and, because of this, we do not require further justification for our moral principles.

In unpacking the concept of simple ideas, three different sources of belief are identified. Two of these, sensation and reflection, he adopts from Locke. 'Sensation' refers to the effects arising in us from the impressions made on our minds by external objects and is the experience of sense perception.[29] Locke's understanding of reflection sees it as the mind's observation of its internal operations. Price sometimes calls it deduction as it involves the mind reflecting on ideas that it has already received through sensation. In this way, it is an internal sense – the power by which the mind distinguishes and compares ideas to make more complex ideas. As Price puts it, it involves 'the compounding, dividing, abstracting, or enlarging ideas *previously in the mind*.'[30] Whereas for Locke 'simple ideas' are the product of sensation, uncompounded and incapable of being divided, complex ideas are ideas made by the mind by combining, relating or abstracting simple ideas.[31] The presence of complex ideas in Locke's epistemology does not mean he is suggesting all our ideas come immediately from sensation and reflection, but they are all *ultimately derived* from sensation and reflection. 'Whence has [the mind] all the materials of reason and knowledge? To this I answer, in one word, from *experience*. In that all our knowledge is founded, and from that it ultimately derives itself.'[32] There are, for Locke, no new ideas involved in the process of reflection or deduction.

Price was no Lockean when it came to epistemology, however. Contradicting Locke's empiricism, he envisaged a third source of belief, which he called 'the understanding,' reason or intuition. His conception of this faculty was Platonic. It alone, the *Review* argues, can perceive simple ideas, making it the only source of knowledge. In this argument, Price's meets Locke head-on. Locke had earlier insisted that the mind cannot make simple ideas: 'It is not in the power of the most exalted wit, or enlarged understanding, by any quickness or variety of thought, to *invent* or *frame* one new simple idea in the mind.'[33] For Price, it is crucial that 'the power that *understands*; or the faculty within us that discerns *truth,* and that compares all the objects of thought, and *judges* them, is a spring of new ideas.' Sensory perception as he sees it cannot account for all the ideas that the human mind contains: 'Sense consists in the obtruding of certain impressions upon us, independently of our wills; but it cannot perceive what they are, or whence they are derived.'[34]

This is a direct contradiction with the Hartley-Priestley model of simple ideas arising solely through the physical structure of the brain. The simple ideas Price identified as being of most importance include ideas of right and wrong; the moral values by which we live our lives. These cannot, as he saw it, be accounted for solely in terms of our sense perception. We do not perceive moral value through our five senses, nor is it an invention of the mind composed by deduction. There must, therefore, be another source of these ideas. If there isn't, we are in a vicious circle containing nothing but sensation: 'One sense cannot judge of the objects of another . . . The faculty therefore which views and compares the objects of *all* the senses, cannot be sense.'[35]

This is territory well trodden by Cudworth in his *Treatise Concerning Eternal and Immutable Morality*, particularly in his argument that 'no sense judges either of its own passion, or of the passion of any other sense.'[36] For both thinkers, the understanding is necessary as a power that discerns truth by judging the ideas of the mind and comparing the objects of thought. It is in this way that it becomes, for Price, a source of new ideas. This philosophy rests on a Platonic account of reason as the mind's eye capable of perceiving far more than what can be discovered through sensation alone. For Plato,

> When the mind's eye is fixed on objects illuminated by truth and reality, it understands and knows them, and its possession of intelligence is evident; but when it is fixed on the twilight world of change and decay, it can only form opinions.

Price picks up this argument in its entirety:

> As bodily sight discovers to us *visible* objects; so does the understanding, (the eye of the mind, and infinitely more penetrating) discover to us *intelligible* objects.[37]

The primary dualism here is between sense and knowledge, and it fits with a commitment to the inferiority and passivity of sense experience contrasted with the clarity and superiority of the knowledge of reason. Plato's *Republic* contrasts the knowledge of intelligence with the world of change and decay, and concludes that the intuition of the mind is superior. Plotinus states, 'Sense perception is our messenger, but intellect is our king.'[38] It is this contrast between sense and reason that is picked up by Cudworth. Sense, because of its associations with the body, is seen as confused, indistinct and encumbered. It is contrasted with the clear, satisfactory and awakened knowledge of the intellect. In language used later by Price, Cudworth takes up this passivity of sensory perception: 'Sense, that suffers from external objects, lies as it were prostrate under them, and is overcome by them.'[39]

Price's *Review* directs readers to the Fourth Book of Cudworth's *Treatise of Eternal and Immutable Morality* and takes from it the argument that there are many objects of our mind that we can neither see, hear, feel nor taste and which did not enter the mind by sense. They have sprung instead from the active power and innate fecundity of the mind itself, because of the failure of the corporeal objects of sense to imprint any such things upon it.

Were not *sense* and *knowledge* entirely different, we should rest satisfied with sensible impressions, such as light, colours, and sounds, and
enquire no farther about them . . . Whereas, on the contrary, we necessarily desire some farther acquaintance with them, and can never be
satisfied till we have subjected them to the survey of reason.[40]

The vantage point of an elevated reason enables it to abstract general ideas
from particular instances. This epistemology of simple ideas perceived by
active reason serves to ground Price's aesthetics. It is only the 'universal'
vantage point of intellect in action that can appreciate order and proportion, design, connection and art – all properties of the unity of any given
thing. What is presented is a Platonic vision of the realm of the senses akin
to the shadows of the cave, which are mere reflections of the intelligible
realm. Knowledge, on the other hand, is an 'active energy.'[41] It is different in
kind to what Locke conceived of as deduction, which has only the power to
work with ideas already perceived by the senses. Perception or sense experience cannot act as a foundation to knowledge in the Platonic scheme; it is
only reason that can apprehend what is true.

The Platonic theory of innate ideas should be understood in conjunction
with this distinction between reason and sense. It has been assumed that
Price rejected this particular doctrine. In a brief direct reference to Cudworth's adoption of innate ideas, Price reports, 'I should not care to be
obliged to defend it.'[42] This apathy does not give the whole story, however,
as it is likely Price misread Cudworth's notion of innate ideas for a cruder
notion of Platonic recollection. What Price, Plato, Cudworth and other
Cambridge Platonists meant by innate ideas is itself a debatable issue. One
thing that is certain is that innate ideas must be distinguished from the doctrine of recollection and the pre-existence of the soul. Price may well have
been against a crude notion of innate ideas but, as Dominic Scott points
out, so were Cudworth and More. Both these Cambridge Platonists believed
ideas to be innate in the sense that 'human thought is not the product of
material bombardments on our senses but stems from the creative activity
of the mind, that is, from its own intrinsic nature.'[43] Cudworth described
how the intelligible forms by which things are understood, or known, are
not stamps or impressions printed passively on the soul from without but
ideas actively exerted from within the soul itself.[44]

Active reason is the key principle here. The power in the soul that is innate is that which gives it the ability to raise intelligible ideas from within
itself. The Platonic theory of *anamnesis* (reminiscence) is not linked by Cudworth to the pre-existence of the soul; it is not to do with remembering
something we have known in another life, but is instead the mind's inward
comprehending of things – the active power of the mind from which knowledge can be drawn forth.[45] The same account of reason explains More's
rejection of innatism understood as 'a certain number of *Ideas* flaring and
shining to the *Animadversive faculty* like so many *Torches* or *Starres* in the

Firmament to our outward sight' and his preference instead of 'an active and *actual Knowledge* in a man, of which these outward objects are rather the reminders than the first begetters or implanters.'[46]

Understood in this way rather than in terms of the pre-existence of the soul, Price would have been all too happy to accept the innate quality of what he termed simple ideas. It is with approval that he quoted Cudworth's suggestion that the mind is furnished with certain previous inward anticipations, ideas and instructions.[47] For both Cudworth and Price, the idea of the indivisibility of mind safeguarded the belief that mind was different in kind to matter, and the activity of the mind enabled it to act as a source of knowledge. Knowledge and understanding are thus made superior to matter and cannot be caused by it. They think entirely in unison on this:

> For since the mind and intellect is in itself a more real and substantial thing, and fuller of entity than matter and body, those things which are the pure offspring of the mind, and sprout from the soul itself, must needs be more real and substantial than those things which blossom from the body.[48]
>
> It may at least be said, that thought, knowledge, and understanding, being the original and causes of all particular *sensibles*, and therefore *before* them and *above* them, cannot be derived from them, or dependent upon them.[49]

Dominic Scott is right that the activity of ideas constitutes the common strand of Cambridge Platonist innatism,[50] and in accepting this, Price is entirely at one with them. This marks a considerable divergence between Price and Priestley. Their different attitudes to the possibility of innate ideas give them a very different account of the power of reason. For those, including Price, in the Platonic tradition, active reason is the power of contemplation linked with the divine. For Priestley, the rejection of innate ideas led towards a materialistic epistemology and ultimately to a utilitarian ethic.

Becoming like God: the theology of deiformity

Price's epistemological argument rests ultimately on theology. The understanding is able to perceive truth precisely because truth has a divine nature: 'That infinity of *abstract* truth and of *knowables* which I see to be necessary and eternal, I think to be the *Divine eternal mind*.'[51] God is 'pure and perfect reason,' which makes all other instances of rationality derivatives of the divine. Knowledge is therefore only possible because truth is God and human reason is part of divine reason. This model of God as the intelligence from which all things arise guarantees the possibility of knowledge.

In this, too, Price's position was characteristically Platonic. He referred his readers to Volume One of Cudworth's *True Intellectual System* in which Cudworth depicts the mind of God as the archetypal intellect from which all particular created intellects are derived.[52] The middle Platonist Alcinous, too, to whom Price appeals in defence of his idea of reason, described God as intellect and truth itself. This Platonic conception of ideas as active living powers originating in God contrasts sharply with Lockean epistemology. For Price and the Platonists, it is *because* rationality is from God that the human soul has the faculty to perceive eternal truth and to see and know God: God is 'the divine, uncreated, infinite *reason and power,* from whence all other reason and power are derived.'[53] Price thus followed the Platonists, including Cudworth, in seeing the intellectual part of human nature (the soul) as 'immortal and divine,' 'an emanation from the supreme intelligence.' Human reason is ultimately derived from God because God is 'the divine, uncreated, infinite reason and power, from whence all other reason and power are derived.'[54]

It is not only knowledge of God that was important for Price but also actively becoming like God. The language of deiformity is not present in Price's *Review,* but it is a strong theme in some of his sermons and highlights the theology behind the moral philosophy of the *Review.* True religion consists in 'being like God' and we should aim at resembling him and, 'making ourselves partakers of a divine nature.'[55] Present here are two important Platonic ideas: kinship between reason and the divine, based on resemblance, and the concept of participation, developed in terms of deiformity. For Plato, kinship between the Forms and the soul is necessary because the soul must be like the Forms in order for knowledge to occur.[56] This is a theme taken up by the Cambridge Platonists in their insistence that the knower can attain knowledge because he or she has a kinship with the thing known. For the Cambridge Platonists, it is participation in God that grounds human knowing. Reason allows us the very possibility of knowledge because it is akin to the divine. Central here, for Price, is the influence of Ralph Cudworth's epistemology in which the mind of God is the archetypal intellect and all particular created intellects are derived from God.[57]

If deiformity involves using our reason to 'become like God,' what might this mean in practice? Price suggests in his sermons that acquiring a 'likeness to God' means becoming God's 'genuine offspring,'[58] which is accomplished by fixing our minds on truth and right in order to participate in the moral excellence of God. The ethical weight of Price's thought is clear here: partaking in God's nature means the imitation of God's ethical perfections. This is a theme of considerable importance within certain branches of the Platonic tradition. Although Plato himself was not explicitly theistic, Socratic thought envisaged deiformity in theistic terms, and it lends itself well to the Platonic linking of virtue with holiness. Socrates described his mission of service to God in terms of divine supervision with holiness depicted as a moral virtue.[59] David Sedley draws attention to the fact that although Plato did not share Socrates' theology, it still cohered with his own intention to link justice with holiness and with the philosophy of becoming like God that develops throughout the more 'Platonic' dialogues of the *Republic,*

Phaedrus and *Theaetetus*.[60] In the *Theaetetus*, becoming like God is the escape from earth to heaven, involving a change to becoming 'just and pure, with understanding.'[61] Ethics is clearly central to this doctrine.

Difficulties of interpreting Plato's position and of cohering the dialogues abound: for the middle Platonists, including Alcinous, becoming like God was envisaged in explicitly practical and ethical terms, but Plotinus and the Neoplatonists have often been interpreted as embracing a more mystical flight from the world and a more literal union with the One.[62] Perceived tensions within the Platonic tradition have resulted, compounded by the fact that the theological aspect of this doctrine only becomes explicit with Augustine's Christianizing of Plato. If the Cambridge Platonists or Price were aware of these tensions, however, they did not consider them problematic when reading the ancient Platonic texts.[63] It is likely, therefore, that Price would have seen the Cambridge Platonist notion of deiformity as one that cohered neatly with Plato's own view, in keeping with Alcinous's interpretation of the doctrine. The harmony in the 'Platonic' position can be explained by the influence of Stoicism on Platonism, including the thought of Price, Benjamin Whichcote and Cudworth. Within Stoicism, no great conflict was accepted between the ethical and other-worldly strands of the doctrine, whereas rationality was linked to virtue. This made deiformity a matter of living morally within this life rather than escaping from it. The influence of Stoicism on Price perhaps explains how he could have accepted this ethical interpretation, as it would have fitted neatly with his reading of Plato and the Cambridge Platonists. Rightly or wrongly, then, Price seems to have followed the middle Platonists and interpreted the Cambridge Platonists accordingly by embracing an ethical understanding of Plato's concept of becoming like God, based on a theology of the participation of human reason in divine reason.

In fleshing out his understanding of what 'becoming like God' entails, Price closely followed Benjamin Whichcote's account of the doctrine, which also formed much of the basis for Cudworth's interpretation of the idea.[64] Price endorsed the distinction made by Whichcote between the natural and moral characteristics of God. Some of the classical attributes are listed (Price called them 'natural attributes,' Whichcote 'perfections') including independence, omnipotence, omniscience and eternity. As it was obvious to both that imitation of God could not consist of the acquisition of these aforesaid characteristics, they focused on the imitation of God's moral attributes. To Whichcote's call that 'it is only in the exercise of his power and the direction of [God's] will that we can be like him,' Price echoed, 'We imitate [God] when our wills are likewise directed by truth and reason.'[65] God is truth and right, and God's will is orientated to truth and goodness meaning each human's will ought to be orientated in the same way too. For both Whichcote and Price, becoming like God is based on rectitude of the will, which involves cultivating a charitable temper and being ready to assist others. Although both conceded that it is impossible for us to be virtuous in exactly the same way that God is (because God is the eternal law itself), it is possible for us to aim for our wills to be guided by the same principle as God's: in this sense, we can aim to become like God. Becoming like God, therefore, means imitating God's moral characteristics. We can never imitate God's omnipotence or omniscience, but it is possible, on this distinction, to imitate God's moral perfections by allowing our will to be guided by truth and right. 'Let us think of the order that governs nature. Let us exhibit that order in our own conduct that we may share in the infinite happiness which it has been established to produce.'[66]

Many of these themes are also present in Cudworth. That God is goodness and truth makes holiness the 'conformity of our wills to the will of God.' Ethics is central. The 'great mystery of the Gospel, is to establish a Godlike frame and disposition of spirit . . . in the hearts of men.'[67] His understanding of the doctrine was, however, inseparably linked to his Christology, uncovering a significant difference in emphasis between him and Price. In Cudworth's theology, it is the descent of the Logos into human likeness in the incarnation that enables participation in the divine nature. Any godlike frame and disposition we have is enabled by Christ's death on the cross, and the spark of divinity within all human beings is the 'immortal seed' of the Logos acting immediately upon human nature: 'Christ formed in us': 'God was therefore incarnated and made man,' Cudworth states, paraphrasing Athanasius, 'that he might deify us, that is . . . make us partakers of the Divine nature.'[68]

Whichcote's theology is not without a Christological element – that Christ died for our sins, he believes is just as indispensable to religion as morality – but his understanding of the doctrine of deiformity is more strongly rationalistic, lending itself to Price's prioritising of moral action over religious belief.[69] Adopting Whichcote's interpretation of the doctrine would have enabled Price to take Cudworth at his word when he stated that goodness and holiness are more fundamental than Christological speculation and would have enabled Price to avoid seeing any contradiction between Cudworth's view and his own. An entirely other-worldly interpretation of the union of the individual with the world soul and the flight from the body is largely rejected by Cudworth but also by Whichcote, More and John Smith.[70] The result that the overriding importance of the ethical in Price's account grants him is a distinct harmony with the general spirit of the Cambridge Platonist tradition and their interpretation of the Platonic doctrine.[71]

True religion and the tripartite division of the soul

Price's Platonism is particularly apparent in his view of the human person, a psychology grounding both his epistemology and his theology of deiformity. He adopted the tripartite division of the soul and a concern that reason should govern human action. In the *Review*, Price identifies first certain 'instincts' which human beings share with animals. These include our feelings of hunger, thirst and sexual attraction, and, following the philosophy of the *Phaedrus* and the *Republic*, Price calls them 'appetites' or 'passions.' Second, he makes a distinction between these instincts and what he calls 'affections,' by which he means the desires had by reasonable beings, which are the result of rationality, for example, benevolence, or love of truth. Affections seem to be very much akin to the 'spirit' element of the soul postulated by Plato. Whereas passion (sometimes called instinct) has nothing to do with reason, affections are depicted as dependent on reason; they are something that animals do not experience because only human beings possess reason.[72] The term 'will' is used to cover this second aspect of the soul. Appetites are placed under the direction of reason, the third aspect of human nature, and are intended to be subject to it. Reason is the superior, controlling aspect of the soul; the intellect, the understanding, the eye of the mind, which examines, judges, decides and directs. To defend his claim of the pre-eminence of reason, Price appeals both to Alcinous, and to Plato for whom goodness is the discipline of keeping the passions and affections in subjection to reason.[73]

In a nod towards Plato's *Republic*, Price links morality with proper order in the soul. For Plato, 'each of us will be just . . . only if each part of him is performing its proper function,' and for Price, 'goodness in mankind is the "sound state of our natures" restored and established.'[74] Deiformity is thus not an escape from the body but a proper ordering of the soul. In this, Price has much in common too with John Smith and Henry More for whom Cartesian dualism was rejected ultimately for its cleaving apart of body and soul: 'Wherefore the Passions of the Body are not to be quite extinguished, but regulated, that there may be the greater plenitude of life in the whole man.'[75] Imitation of God can only occur when reason governs the soul and kind affections are cultivated.

A distinctive definition of religion itself results from this. For both Whichcote and Price, it is the imitation of God's moral perfections that form the locus of true religion:

> In these doth religion consist; viz. in a divine nature, in the imitation of God in respect of his moral perfections, of holiness, goodness, righteousness and truth: and in the guidance and superintendency of the divine spirit over our minds.[76]

True religion on this view becomes moral goodness and it is goodness that constitutes the supreme *telos* of human nature. In thinking this, Price was closer to Whichcote than Plato. His epistemological foundation may have come largely from Plato, but he adopted Whichcote's religious understanding of becoming like God, which fitted his insistence that the actual imitation of God, rather than the possession of reason as such, gives human beings their dignity. The imago Dei is not a faculty of the mind, nor is it a separate soul, but rather shows itself in our 'maintaining an invariable regard to truth and right.'[77] The similarity of language and thought between Price and Whichcote is perhaps at least partly explained by the influence of Samuel Clarke upon Price. The idea of conformity of our will to God's is present in Clarke and forms the basis for his account of obligation. Whether Clarke borrowed directly from Whichcote's theology is not clear, but in 1707, he anonymously published a fourth volume of Whichcote's sermons, which suggests at the very least that Whichcote's ideas cohered with his own.[78]

Despite the general coherence between Price and a broadly Cambridge Platonist account of becoming like God, however, any similarity must be tempered by the lack of any strong theology of grace in Price's work. The Cambridge Platonists were concerned to harmonise their Platonism with a Christology of the incarnate *Logos*. John Smith perhaps has the strongest theology of grace, going as far as to see becoming like God in terms of the union between Christ and God and a result of grace, but he died before he could complete his exposition of God's 'communication' to humankind.[79] Although More, Whichcote and Cudworth understood deiformity in highly ethical terms, they still speak of its possibility in terms of the 'seed' of God. Price certainly had a higher Christology than Joseph Priestley or the Socinians would allow, but he had little theology of grace or incarnation in relation to deiformity. The shadow of Pelagius lurks in the background here. If reason renders divine assistance superfluous, what use is grace?

This tension, inherent in the Cambridge Platonists' commitment to rationalism and grace, is resolved by Price through his increased ethical conception of religion and is consolidated by the Latitudinarian emphasis on simplicity of doctrine.[80] This sits with his reading of scripture, but it is not without difficulties. Foreshadowing the problems of the later Rational Dissenters who followed him, he wished to maintain a role for Christ as saviour but struggled to say what it is that human beings are to be saved from.[81] This is worked out primarily in ethical terms: human beings are rescued from an unethical existence. Price's anti-Trinitarianism therefore marks a break with Logos theology. Despite this divergence, Price's theology was not entirely at odds with an Arminian concept of grace that emphasised free human acceptance or rejection and the importance of good works. The Cambridge Platonists were at odds with the Laudian model in which grace is dependent on Anglican sacraments. The Platonic philosophy of deiformity would have offered fertile soil for a Dissenter who rejected the Anglican liturgy and forms of worship, and an Athanasian or Calvinist theology of grace, in favour of what he saw as a more Biblical faith.

Most crucially, what Price shares with the Cambridge Platonists is a conviction that ethical conduct is only possible because of the divinity of reason. This is a far cry from the secular conception of reason most often associated with the Enlightenment period. Whereas Priestley laid the blame for the corruption of Christianity at the door of the Platonists, Price believed the key to preserving Christianity from the dangers of Calvinism and relativism could be found in a Platonic epistemology and metaphysics of the soul. This results in two remarkably different accounts of the self, rooted in diametrically opposed metaphysics, but both are nonetheless irreducibly theological in their own way. This confirms that Rational Dissent was by no means homogenous. Furthermore, Israel's two Enlightenments must be rethought in the light of this strand of Platonically informed thought that refuses the strict dichotomy between radical materialism and conservative dualism. Price represents the continuation of a tradition of Platonic thought in the eighteenth century that is centred on a deiform conception of reason and resistance to a more materialistic monism.

The honest mind: candour, epistemic humility and the limits of knowledge

The implications of these divergent strands of thought within Rational Dissent are substantial. Both Price and Priestley held reason in high esteem, but Price's Platonic account of deiform reason should be appreciated primarily for its emphasis on epistemic humility and the limits of human knowledge. Reason is not extolled without a recognition of its limits.

A community of discussants: knowledge and candour

The Rational Dissenters shared many assumptions with other Enlightenment thinkers, particularly about the value of reason and the search for knowledge, and there is a good argument to be made that Priestley shared many features of what Israel calls the radical Enlightenment. Their commitment to the principle of *sola scriptura* and their connections to Latitudinarianism, however, mean that both Price and Priestley interpreted the broad themes of the Enlightenment in their own particular way. Even Priestley who came closer to embracing what might be considered key Enlightenment values, including reason and empiricism as sources of knowledge, human beings as part of the material world and nature as self-regulating, cannot be considered 'enlightened' without some caveat.[82] His materialism is in key respects doubtful and his understanding of the world thoroughly theological.

In fact, although Priestley rejected a Platonic concept of the soul, his appeal to reason was in many ways a development of Nonconformist appeals to a supposed divine element of human reason, which justified the following of conscience and rejection of conformity.[83] This explains D. O. Thomas's comment:

> It is a remarkable characteristic of many of the English Dissenters that they did not believe that the pursuit of knowledge is detrimental to religion; on the contrary they thought that the exercise of reason is a duty owed to the Deity, and that only false forms of religion are vulnerable to the search for truth.[84]

An essential part of this rational pursuit of knowledge was the practice of candour, and it had important social and political implications.

Candour required debate with others, conducted with respect to differing opinions, but also with genuine engagement and openness. It was fostered in the Dissenting Academies when students were presented with a diverse range of argument and encouraged to think carefully for themselves, and it came to fruition in the many gatherings attended by Dissenters and others sympathetic to them for the purposes of discussion and debate. In 1758, Price moved to Newington Green with his wife, Sarah, and became a preacher in the Presbyterian chapel there. The place was somewhat of a magnet for Dissenters. The chapel treasurer, Daniel Radford, was the nephew of Matthew Henry who penned the noteworthy *Commentary on the Bible* (1708–10). The Rational Dissenter and political radical James Burgh, author of *Political Disquisitions* (1774), was a neighbour, and Price, together with Burgh and the rector of Stoke Newington, formed a weekly supper club. Burgh, who counted Benjamin Franklin as a friend, was a member of the 'Honest Whigs,' and Price quickly became a member of that circle of mostly Dissenting ministers who met at St. Paul's Coffee House fortnightly on Thursdays during the season to discuss the 'topics of the day.'

Priestley was a member of the circle for many years, and other attendees included Andrew Kippis, Theophilus Lindsey, William Rose (co-editor of the *Monthly Review*), John Jebb and John Cartwright (who with Jebb founded the republican Society for Constitutional Information), Richard Oliver (founder of the Bill of Rights Society), Abraham Rees (editor of *Chamber's Dictionary*), Sir George Savile (a member of Parliament) and James Boswell. Some of them, including Franklin, Kippis, Rees, Priestley and Price were fellows of the Royal Society and many were tutors at Dissenting Academies. By March 1772, the club had moved to the London Coffee house on Ludgate Hill and attracted sizeable numbers of those with an 'open mind.'[85] Political matters were more often than not discussed in a spirit of the mutual search for truth, embodying the practice of candour. Candour involved more than just regular meetings, however, and was not simply a method of debating different sides of an argument. It was, in the words of Mark Philp, a virtue nurtured through close family and friendship, strengthening intellectual and emotional ties. Rational Dissent should, therefore, be characterised by its becoming a 'community of discussants' who, through candid engagement with one another, sought to uncover religious and moral truth.[86] This truth did not emerge merely through abstract rational analysis but through genuine conversation, which meant actively engaging with others' points of view.

For Price, a Platonic and ethical interpretation of 'becoming like God' together with the embrace of candour led to a prioritizing of the ethical in place of doctrinal uniformity. In matters of religion, he called merely for an honest mind: one that has sought knowledge with integrity and sought the good. In the face of divergent doctrines of God, 'there is but one thing fundamental, and that is, an honest mind.'[87] Conformity to specific theological doctrines thus becomes unnecessary for him. This represents not a replacement of theology with the ethical life, however, but recognition of the complexity of theological hermeneutics and a respect for caution with regard to imposing one's own theology on others. Price offers a direct echo of Cudworth's own sentiment of latitude. Cudworth had insisted,

> Surely, the way to heaven that Christ hath taught us, is plain and easie, if we have but honest hearts . . . no man shall ever be kept out of heaven, for not comprehending mysteries that were beyond the reach of his shallow understanding; if he had but an honest and good heart.[88]

There is little of significance here in the change of vocabulary from heart to mind, despite what Rational Dissent's critics might have claimed. Later on in the eighteenth century, Burke fostered carefully the myth that the rationalist is cold, pitiless and without heart,[89] and his criticisms of Price led to it becoming widely accepted that Price was indeed a cold-hearted rationalist. This slight is undeserved, however, both on the personal front and from the perspective of his philosophy. In terms of ethical philosophy, what was of crucial importance for both Cudworth and Price is inner attitude: an openness to strive for the attainment of knowledge and the pursuit of goodness. Elsewhere Price states, 'nothing is essential but an honest heart, and that right practice which must prepare us for eternity.'[90]

Candour was vital for the Rational Dissenters and scrutinised the demands of the honest mind. It checked any tendency towards enthusiasm and pre-empted any call to the authority of mystery. It ensured that freedom of conscience is not the freedom to do whatever one feels. The obligation to act according to conscience, therefore, gave rise to the obligation to debate with others to fulfil the requirements of candour: 'According to Price, honesty of mind requires nothing less than an unremitting search for truth and an unrelenting criticism of the claims of conscience.'[91] There is a need, he says, for the constant criticism of the claims of conscience and a need for us to discipline ourselves to perceive and accept the duties of our vocation to conduct the service of God.

Candour denies that truth is something mysterious or private to any given person or group of people. This means opinions should not be accepted uncritically, and everyone should think for themselves. Part of its obligation therefore involved fostering an appreciation for 'the importance of fair discussion and the sufficiency of a sincere desire to know and do the will of God.'[92] The commitment to rationality is thus born of a desire to search for truth and value. One of Price's favourite principles he says in a letter to Hume is that 'nothing is fundamental besides a faithful desire to find out and to practice truth and right.' In this way, the practice of candour shapes the apprehension of religion in terms of ethical action: 'In religion there is nothing so essential as charity, candour, and benevolence.'[93]

The Rational Dissenting concern for candour placed considerable emphasis on the importance of rational debate but the ability of reason to attain truth was very much embedded in the society of dissent. Candour meant that knowledge could not be attained through Cartesian-style meditations or individual rational reflection, but it involved instead a lived community. This fact is usually overlooked when considering the thought of the Rational Dissenters but it is an important part of their understanding of rationality. Martin Fitzpatrick describes their concern to create 'a polity in which truth could naturally progress' starting with their immediate community. This resulted in the cultivation of an open and supportive community and, furthermore, one in which Rational Dissenters strived to promote societal change by living in practice what their philosophical ideals preached.[94] A sense of solidarity and social activity was essential. So too was honesty and openness. They embodied a spirit of listening and engaging with the other. They were definitely selective in who the 'other' was – there was little evident attempt, for example, to engage with those from less privileged backgrounds or to challenge social exclusion – but the general principle was that of fostering consideration of others' experiences and knowledge claims in the mutual search for a better more truthful understanding.

Epistemic humility and the honest mind

When it comes to what certainty rational knowledge can yield, Price and Priestley have very different opinions. Their differences illustrate the division between Socinianism and Arianism, the most prominent schism within Rational Dissent in the eighteenth century. Priestley had a much 'higher' view of reason in that he bought into the possibility of certainty, whereas Price's rationalism had much greater emphasis on the limits of reason. The distinction is important not only because it points to a much more complex Enlightenment than is typically envisaged but also because epistemic humility is important for Price's natural theology, discussed further in Chapter 4.

In his assessment of the scope of reason, Priestley was much more akin to Hartley, who thought that the critical study of scriptures would end disagreements about doctrine, seeing them replaced by a rational Christianity revealed to all who would look. Whereas Locke refused to speculate about the nature of the mind or matter and made a sharp distinction between what can be demonstrated and what is only speculative, Priestley held nothing opaque to human rationality.[95] Once he had converted to Socinianism, he denied anything not in accordance with the dictates of human reason. The Socinian Racovian Catechism, for example, denied Christ's divinity because it is against reason to claim that two persons possessing opposite qualities (mortal and immortal, or having a beginning and eternal) could make up one substance, and the Socinian creed subjected all knowledge to rationality making reason the determiner of truth.[96] Embracing these ideas meant for Priestley, any 'mystery' at all is always evidence of 'corruption.'

Ritual, symbol, artistic or poetic imagery is always 'superstitious' and must be eliminated completely by the 'rational.' Mystery is associated with secret parts of heathen worship admitting only select people to its number. So it was, he thought, with the mystery of the Eucharist. Those who did not partake of the ordinance and who were not in communion were excluded. The light of reason sits in judgement of everything to the extent that whatever is untenable should be abandoned by genuine and rational Christianity, 'whatever is not rational ought to be abandoned on principles that are even not Christian.'[97]

Weeding out the corruptions of Christianity became an obsession for Priestley, and it was reason together with a scripturally based materialism that served as the benchmark for what should be retained. 'By the help of the system of materialism . . . the Christian removes the very foundation of many doctrines, which have exceedingly debased and corrupted Christianity.'[98] Priestley's Socinianism fitted with his Nonconformist theology of conscience and the principle of *sola scriptura,* resulting in an account of reason as the sole interpreter of the Bible. The 'most obvious sense of the Scriptures,' he says, is 'in favour of those doctrines which are most agreeable to reason.'[99]

Fitzpatrick charts a difference in emphasis between Latitudinarianism and Rational Dissent when it comes to reason: whereas so many of the Latitudinarians were keen to stress the failings of reason, the Rational Dissenters began to place more weight on its clarity and its similarity in kind to the truths of science.[100] Priestley certainly saw his own extremely high view of reason as a common feature in Dissenting thought: the more '*rational* part of the Dissenters' hold that religion ought to be 'put upon the same footing with other branches of knowledge.' Priestley thus encouraged his readers to judge theological knowledge by the same standards of scientific and philosophical knowledge. Christianity, he thought, really ought to be capable of being 'properly *understood.*' Believers in the purified core of Christianity, excised of all corruptions, will perceive a manifest argument for its truth.[101] John Jebb, one of the most radical of the Rational Dissenters, is another example in this line of thought. He proposed that religion is a 'science,' inspired by the 'Newtonian and Maclaurin method of proving a deity,' which he saw as providing such an obvious conclusion that frankly he was baffled by anyone who did not accept it. The truths of religion he insisted are 'few in number, easy of comprehension, propounded with the utmost perspicuity and plainness.'[102]

This was not the view shared by all the Rational Dissenters, however. In complete contrast to Priestley, Price tells us he is not confident on theological matters. He does not feel assured of the truth of Christianity and feels 'difficulties and wonder' at the confidence of those who think no honest person can doubt. He claims instead only that his beliefs are a result of preponderance, something he sees as more in keeping with candour. Socinian rationality irks him so much that he even verges on sarcasm – a striking diversion from his usual mild manner – in criticising its tendency (particularly apparent he thinks in Theophilus Lindsey's musings) to argue that the evidence for theological belief is so obvious that '*all* the rational are seeing it every day more and more and so vast that every eye *must* see it that is not wholly blinded by prejudice.'[103] Unlike Priestley and Lindsey, Price is far from convinced that reason can attain a view from nowhere or absolute certainty when it comes to theological truth claims.

In addition to this, he thinks there is an ethical imperative *not* to aim for certainty because therein lies a dangerous autocracy, ironically not that far removed from enthusiasm. In the face of Socinianism or those who force conformity, even the most able thinkers who dare to disagree are in danger of being unfairly dismissed for seeing 'things thro' a mist.' Such an attitude, Price thought, stood to contravene the very requirements of candour itself. In practical terms, candour meant not only giving respect to those with whom one disagrees but also a spirit of openness and a willingness to accept throughout the possibility that one is mistaken.[104] The place of reason in religion was to encourage the pursuit of knowledge in a spirit of humility: humility in the face of conflicting truth claims and humility in the face of a truth much more expansive than could ever be grasped.

It is for these reasons that, as far as Price saw it, Socinianism is made 'ignorant and gloomy' by its over-reaching rationality and its abandonment of the belief in any truth beyond reason. Ironically, just like the enthusiasts, those who follow such a rationalising religion have 'narrow minds bound down to a system.'[105] Reason overreaches itself when it is not first and foremost mindful of its limits. What gives the honest mind its honesty is its avoidance of the dangers of superstition and enthusiasm. Even something that seemed as obvious to Price as providence is treated with caution. Enthusiasm, he worried, imagines that the direction of God's providence can be duly observed, which means that if something favourable happens, it is assumed God willed it that way.[106] The same argument of the enthusiasts was used by some of those within the established church who wished to defend aspects of the *ancien régime*, including Edmund Burke in his *Reflections on the Revolution in France* (1790). Burke's unwavering belief in providence underpinned his conservatism. God has established the 'nature of things' in which the state embodies God's power and goodness. Prescription and tradition are to be respected. This was a typical argument by those with more conservative sympathies, and Price was not unaware of the political implications of the epistemological confidence embedded in Socinian: enthusiastic and more conservative positions.

Price and Priestley also exhibit very different views on the issue of whether the truth will make itself apparent eventually. Priestley encouraged debate and the criticism of religion, but he had a sincere belief that the time would come when everyone would agree on basic religious truths. He spoke of 'a permanent and rational uniformity'[107] that although not in evidence at present, would certainly manifest itself in the course of time. For Priestley, the basic doctrines of Christianity are so plain that the learned and unlearned are on a level with respect to it. Lindsey agreed that debate would most definitely lead to truth, embracing an assumption that the truths of religion will become apparent under the interrogation of reason.[108] This confidence resulted in a spirit of evangelism. Priestley's belief in the uniformity of truth encouraged him to proselytise to the corruptors of Christianity and the unbelievers in favour of the most rationally credible version of Christianity.[109] He quite clearly saw himself as presenting rational arguments for the purpose of converting all those who would only make the effort to examine them properly. In a letter to Price, it becomes clear that this is the only reason he put pen to paper, exclaiming he is 'professed to write with no other view than to make proselytes' and could not even see 'any other rational object in writing at all.'[110] If conversion comes, thinks Priestley, it will be through the power of reason alone and its demonstration of the most rational, sound theological system.

Such optimism for rational argument was not uniform among the Rational Dissenters, however. Price did not want to assume that rational inquiry would lead to uniformity, his religion being 'a tolerant and catholic religion, not a rage for proselytism.'[111] As Fitzpatrick states, this makes Price and Priestley essentially figureheads for the widely divergent viewpoints about rational persuasion found within Rational Dissent.[112] Price writes,

> I feel no disposition to be very anxious about bringing you over to my opinion. The rage for proselytism is one of the curses of the world. I wish to make no proselytes except to candour, and charity, and honest enquiry.

Price was not an anomaly among the Rational Dissenters on this issue. Robert Robinson complained even more loudly that 'the idea of uniformity is neither the idea of a philosopher nor of a christian . . . Make religion what you will.'[113] Dissenters of Price's stripe did not seek rational argument purely for the purposes of persuading others to their point of view; rather, they adopted it as a means to further the imperative of becoming divine and truth seeking. Toleration of other positions for Rational Dissenters such as Price and Robinson was seen as valuable for its promotion of individual conscience and candour for its promotion of epistemic humility. The contrast with Priestley, for whom toleration and candour are primarily important for their hastening of the day when universal truth will be accepted by everyone, is notable.

Priestley is conscious of this difference, quite openly stating that he would rather not be like Price; 'For I would not lose the satisfaction that arise from a persuasion of having found any valuable truth, nor willingly continue any longer than is necessary in a state of 'doubt' than which nothing is more painful and distressing.'[114] For Priestley, candour involves presenting all the evidence on both sides of a debate and allowing the reader to decide, whereas doubt is painful for him, something to be eliminated through rational inquiry, which when done properly would present truth. Such unwavering confidence in rationality explains why he was clearly often irked when others would not concede to his position.[115] From where he was standing, religious truths are in principle comparable to scientific truth and are capable of the same clarity. Price, however, refuses to commit to the principle that truth will necessarily be clear to all, or that there will ever necessarily be uniformity. Doubt is not distressing for him, quite the opposite. He is acutely conscious of human epistemic limits and the ongoing nature of the mutual search for inexhaustible truth and goodness.

Rational intuition and participation in the divine life

The doctrine of becoming like God underlies Price's concept of intuition and the self-evidence of simple ideas, another important aspect of his epistemology. That he called these ideas 'self-evident' does not conflict with his denial of the uniformity of belief or extolling of doubt. 'Intuition' is the term Price used for the intellect's discernment of the self-evident ideas of moral right and wrong, and it is an active power of reason described as apprehending immediate truth that cannot be discerned through sensation. The concept has deep Platonic resonances. We may observe individual actions through our senses, Price argued, but what we intuit is right in itself, or rectitude, which is a law.[116] D.D. Raphael, in his introduction to the third edition of the *Review*, suggests Price was the first to apply the word 'intuition' to moral judgement, and it has been generally accepted that Price was the first philosopher to speak of the intuition of moral truth. This innovation is thought to have been a conscious and novel extension of Descartes's concept of intuition to moral epistemology.[117] Price's application of intuition to moral knowledge was not entirely original, however, and it should be thought of as Platonic rather than Cartesian.

Reason, for Price, can intuit truth because it participates in God, which enables us to perceive truth, and so for him, like the Cambridge Platonists, reason is the 'candle of the Lord.' For Price, we are capable of perceiving truth by intuition, because the intellect is derived ultimately from God who is the source of all knowledge. Henry More, for example, made this point clear when he describes the immediate apprehension of certain moral principles, which arise out of the intellect, or *nous*.[118] More did not use the term 'intuition,' but his account of how we know these basic axioms is very similar to Price's account of intuition. The intellect is described as an image of the divine Logos, and in it is found the wisdom of God. The connection of intuition with ethical knowledge makes Price much closer here to the Cambridge Platonists than to Descartes. Although his simple ideas do show a close similarity with Descartes's clear and distinct ideas, and although he adopts the criterion of clarity and distinction for truth, the way in which intuition is described and discussed shows a deep influence from the Platonic, and particularly Cambridge Platonist, tradition.

It is upon a largely Cambridge Platonist view of reason that Price's distinction, made throughout the *Review*, between reason and reasoning is based. Reasoning is mere deduction and is passive and self-contained. Reason, or intuition, however, involves partaking in the divine nature and seeing by divine light:

> Truth is the proper object of mind, as light is of the eye. . . . Truth and science are of infinite extent; and it is not conceivable that the understanding can be indifferent to them . . . or that, with the prospect before it of unbounded scope for improvement and endless acquisitions, it should be capable of being equally contented with error, darkness, and ignorance.[119]

Price was not, therefore, introducing an entirely new concept when he spoke of the intuition of moral truth. Given the use of the notion of intuition in the eighteenth century, and given the influence upon him of the Platonic tradition, it is not surprising that he appealed to the idea of the intuition of moral knowledge, as it was in many ways a development of the Christian idea that there is an intelligible natural law that we can perceive through reason.

Leaving aside any debate as to the worth of contemporary deontological intuitionism, it is certainly inaccurate to suggest, as MacIntyre does, that for Price the meaning of duty and obligation is immediately obvious to any rational being in the sense of 'self-evident' to all as it might have been for twentieth-century intuitionism.[120] Self-evidence in Price's thought was connected to a deiform account of reason and the divine life understood in ethical terms. Price saw the mind as able to intuit simple ideas that are self-evident because these ideas cannot be inferred or deduced from other beliefs. The same is true of our basic moral ideas. Our perceptions of right and wrong must be immediate, he thought, because they cannot be analysed and cannot be deduced or inferred from a prior principle. This, he believed, is shown by the fact one can always ask whether that ethical principle is right:

> There are, undoubtedly, some actions that are ultimately approved, and for justifying which no reason can be assigned; as there are some ends, which are ultimately desired, and for choosing which no reason can be given.[121]

This is the notion of right and wrong as 'simple' or prior, and it grounds the notion of self-evidence and immediacy. Price was attempting to show here that the meaning of 'good' is not derived from any other concept, and in this way, he thought it was basic or simple. Immediacy does not mean obviousness, but ensures that immediate truths are not derived from other ideas in the mind. We cannot explain virtue by saying that it is 'conformity to the relations of persons and things,' because one can always ask whether it is right to conform oneself to the relations of persons and things. If this question is asked, 'we shall find ourselves obliged to terminate our views in a simple perception, and something ultimately approved for which no justifying reason can be assigned.'[122] The existence of objective rightness is something that we have to postulate in order to make sense of our experiences, and in this way, right and wrong are ideas that force themselves upon us because they 'in some form or other, always remain, even when we think we have annihilated them.'[123] The good, therefore, remains behind all our experiences of particular goods, and moral ideas are self-evident, not because they are discerned through reasoning but because such simple ideas make reasoning possible. Self-evidence does not call to mind the acknowledgment of obvious statements but points to the active power of the mind.[124]

The value of Price's intuitionism is that it points towards a morality that is a quality of insight and an account of perception that is grounded very much in a commitment to the idea of the good and to a religious world view. This becomes particularly important when considering the tradition of natural theology of which Price is a part, which is taken up in Chapter 4. Intuition is not a strange ghostly function of the mind, nor is it used as a last-ditch Enlightenment attempt to ground morality following an eighteenth-century rejection of Aristotelianism and Christian teleology. Instead, all knowledge, including that of the sciences, religion or morality, is therefore a form of revelation.

Price's account of reason is best seen as a middle way between Calvinism and Socinianism. This, for him, was the true Unitarianism. He had, he claimed, a better right to the title 'Unitarian' than the Socinians.[125] Chapter 1 noted that Price accepted the doctrines of atonement and the pre-existence of Christ as orthodox because such doctrines are laid down in the scriptures. Both Price and Priestley held to a scriptural theology, and as the next chapter argues, they both rejected the rationalism of deism and could not have countenanced John Toland's insistence that there is nothing in Christianity 'above' reason.[126] Price, however, could not embrace the harder more Socinian rationality adopted by Priestley. By adopting Platonic epistemological and theological arguments and by using them to consolidate his position against Priestley, Socinianism and ratiocination, Price forged a rationalist philosophy that tried to resist the rationalism of both the Socinians and the deists. Although Price never explores the more mystical Platonic inward path to knowledge of God explicitly, which distinguishes him from the Plotinian elements of the Cambridge school, his account of reason, the soul and the *telos* of the human person in becoming deiform were essentially Platonic.

This chapter has highlighted distinct strands of Rational Dissent, and they exhibit remarkably different conceptions of reason. Israel's division of moderate and radical Enlightenments is therefore rendered too neat. Price and Priestley's metaphysics are diametrically opposed. The two Enlightenments of moderate two-substance dualism and radical one-substance monism cannot therefore be so easily identified. Priestley's conversion to Socinianism is a shift to a harder model of rationality grounded on a monistic epistemology, but not all of his fellow Dissenters shared his approach. Price's dualism and rationalism represents a development of a Cambridge Platonist tradition of thought woven into the phenomenon known as Rational Dissent. For Price, as for the Platonic tradition from which he borrows, there was no strict dichotomy between the rational and spiritual because the spiritual is the highest form of the rational. All this does much to shed doubt on the existence of any one form of Enlightenment secular rationality that rejected transcendent values and abandoned theology.

The next chapter goes on to show that despite differences within the tradition, the Rational Dissenting conception of reason was united by being at once both deeply theological and ethico-political. In their rational response to deism and enthusiasm, the Rational Dissenters refused an appeal to mystery in a move that had deep political implications.

Notes

1 W. B. Peach, "The Ethics of Richard Price" (PhD, Cambridge, MA, 1951), 100; Alasdair MacIntyre, *After Virtue: A Study in Moral Theory*, 2nd ed. (London: Duckworth, 1985), 236.

2 Jonathan I. Israel, *Democratic Enlightenment: Philosophy, Revolution, and Human Rights 1750–1790* (Oxford: Oxford University Press, 2011), 12; Jonathan I. Israel, *A Revolution of the Mind: Radical Enlightenment and the Intellectual Origins of Modern Democracy* (Princeton: Princeton University Press, 2010), 19.

3 Israel, *Democratic Enlightenment*, 11; Israel, *Revolution*, 15, 17–18, 35, 221.

4 Martin Fitzpatrick, "Rational Dissent and the Enlightenment," *Faith and Freedom* 38, no. 2 (1985): 87.

5 G. A. J. Rogers, "Locke, Plato and Platonism," in *Platonism at the Origins of Modernity: Studies on Platonism and Early Modern Philosophy*, ed. Douglas Hedley and Sarah Hutton (Dordrecht: Springer, 2008), 202.

6 James A. Harris, "Joseph Priestley and 'The Proper Doctrine of Philosophical Necessity'," *Enlightenment and Dissent* 20 (2001): 23.

7 Joseph Priestley, "Letters to Dr. Price," in *Works*, vol. xviii, 1817, 455; Joseph Priestley, "An History of Early Opinions Concerning Jesus Christ," in *Works*, vol. vi, 1817, 152.

8 Joseph Priestley, "The Doctrine of Philosophical Necessity Illustrated," in *Works*, vol. iii, 1817, 455.

9 R. K. Webb, "Perspectives on David Hartley," *Enlightenment and Dissent* 17 (1998): 33; James Dybikowski, "Joseph Priestley, Metaphysician and Philosopher of Religion," in *Joseph Priestley, Scientist, Philosopher and Theologian*, ed. Isabel Rivers and David L. Wykes (Oxford: Oxford University Press, 2008), 83.

10 Joseph Priestley, "Letter to Dr. Kenrick," in *Works*, vol. iv, 1817, 142; Joseph Priestley, "Introductory Essays to Hartley's Theory of the Human Mind," in *Works*, vol. iii, 1817, 182.

11 Isaac Newton, "General Scholium," in *Mathematical Principles of Natural Philosophy*, vol. 2 (London: Benjamin Motte, 1729), 393.

12 Henri Laboucheix, "Chemistry, Materialism and Theology in the Work of Joseph Priestley," *Price Priestley Newsletter* 1 (1977): 37.

13 Joseph Priestley, "Disquisitions Relating to Matter and Spirit," in *Works*, vol. iii, 1817, 230.

14 Priestley, "Disquisitions," 218–19, 226; Laboucheix, "Chemistry," 38.

15 Priestley, "Disquisitions," 301.

16 Laboucheix, "Chemistry," 45.

17 Anthony Page, "The Enlightenment and a 'Second Reformation': The Religion and Philosophy of John Jebb (1736–86)," *Enlightenment and Dissent* 17 (1998): 72.

18 Joseph Priestley, *A Free Discussion of the Doctrines of Materialism and Philosophical Necessity. In a Correspondence between Dr. Price and Dr. Priestley. To Which Are Added, by Dr. Priestley, An Introduction, Explaining the Nature of the Controversy, and Letters to Several Writers Who Have Animadverted on His Disquisitions Relating to Matter and Spirit or His Treatise on Necessity* (London: T. Cadell, 1778), 332; C.f. Richard Price, *The Nature and Dignity of the Human Soul: A Sermon Preached at St. Thomas', January the Fifth, 1766* (London: A. Millar, 1766), 7.

19 Richard Price, *Sermons on Various Subjects*, ed. W. Morgan (London: Longman, 1816), 307; c.f. Richard Price, *A Review of the Principal Questions in Morals*, 3rd ed. (Oxford: Clarendon, 1948), 22, 26.

20 Richard Price, *The Correspondence of Richard Price*, ed. W.B. Peach and D.O. Thomas, vol. II (Cardiff: University of Wales Press, 1991), 65. Price to Monboddo, 2 August 1780.

21 Price, *Correspondence*, 1991, II: 70 and 87. Monboddo to Price, 15 September 1780 and Price to Monboddo, 11 December 1780; Price, *Review*, 217n; Richard Price, *Four Dissertations* (Bristol: Thoemmes, 1990), 49; The difficulties of interpreting Plato's philosophy were not unappreciated in the eighteenth century: See, for example, Martha K. Zebrowski, "John William Thomson's 1728 Edition of Plato's 'Parmenides': A Calvinist Humanist from Königsberg Reads Platonic Theology in Oxford," *British Journal for Eighteenth Century Studies* 30, no. 1 (2007): 113–31.

22 On becoming like God as a central feature of Plato's thought see David Sedley, "The Ideal of Godlikeness," in *Plato*, ed. Gail Fine (Oxford: Oxford University Press, 2000), 791–810; Julia Annas, *Platonic Ethics, Old and New* (London: Cornell University Press, 1999); L.P. Gerson, "What Is Platonism?" *Journal of the History of Philosophy* 43 (2005): 253–76.

23 David Hartley, *Observations on Man, His Frame, His Duty, and His Expectations* (London: T. Tegg and son, 1834), 312, 532.

24 Page, "Enlightenment," 65.

25 Ralph Cudworth, *A Treatise Concerning Eternal and Immutable Morality with a Treatise of Freewill*, ed. Sarah Hutton (Cambridge: Cambridge University Press, 1996), 144–5.

26 Plato, *Theaetetus*, trans. Robin A.H. Waterfield (London: Penguin, 1987), 186e, 210a; Alcinous, *The Handbook of Platonism*, trans. John Dillon (Oxford: Oxford University Press, 1993), §4.3–4, 6.

27 Price, *Review*, 32n, 37n; Cudworth, *Treatise*, 145–9.

28 Price, *Review*, 37n.

29 Price, *Review*, 19.

30 Price, *Review*, 18, my emphasis.

31 John Locke, *An Essay Concerning Human Understanding*, vol. 1 (Dublin: Printed for H. Saunders, W. Sleater, D. Chamerlaine and J. Potts, 1777), 2.II.i p. 80–1; 2.XII.i, p. 124, c.f. 2.I.ii, p. 81; 2.I.iv, p. 68; 2.II.i, p. 116.

32 Locke, *Essay*, 1:2.I.ii p. 67.

33 Locke, *Essay*, 1:2.II.ii p. 82.

34 Price, *Review*, 18–19.

35 Price, *Review*, 19.

36 Cudworth, *Treatise*, 54.

37 Plato, *The Republic*, trans. Desmond Lee, 2nd ed. (London: Penguin, 1987), 508d; Price, *Review*, 38.

38 Plotinus, *Enneads*, trans. A.H. Armstrong, Loeb Classical Library (London: Heinemann, 1966) V.3.3 and also III.6.6.

39 Cudworth, *Treatise*, 54.

40 Price, *Review*, 19–20 c.f. Cudworth, *Treatise*, 80.

41 Cudworth, *Treatise*, 57, c.f. 96–7; Price, *Review*, 20.

42 D. Daiches Raphael, "Introduction," in Richard Price, *A Review of the Principal Questions in Morals* (Oxford: Clarendon, 1948), xiv; Price, *Review*, 31n.

43 D. Scott, "Platonic Recollection and Cambridge Platonism," *Hermathena* 149 (1990): 77.

44 Cudworth, *Treatise*, 73–4, 83.

45 Cudworth, *Treatise*, 78. This idea is expressed by Plotinus in Enneads V.5.1.

46 Henry More, *An Antidote against Atheism: Or, an Appeal to the Naturall Faculties of the Minde of Man*, ed. G.A.J. Rogers (Bristol: Thoemmes Press, 1655), 223.

47 Price, *Review*, 20n.

48 Cudworth, *Treatise*, 149.

49 Price, *Review*, 31n.

50 Scott, "Platonic Recollection," 85.

51 Price, *Correspondence*, 1991, II: 67. Price, *Correspondence*, 1991, II: 67. Price to Lord Monboddo, 12 August 1780.

52 Cudworth, *Treatise*, 77, 128; Price, *Review*, 88n.

53 Price, *Review*, 88; Price, *Various Subjects*, 307–8.

54 Price, *Various Subjects*, 148; Price, *Nature and Dignity*, 11. See also Plato, *Timaeus*, trans. Desmond Lee (London: Penguin, 1977), 41d, 61c, 65a; Price, *Review*, 88.

55 Price, *Various Subjects*, 379, 376.

56 See Plato, *Phaedo*, trans. David Gallop (Oxford: Oxford University Press, 1999), 78b–84b. Gerson discusses Platonic kinship in considerable depth in Gerson, "Platonism."

57 Cudworth, *Treatise*, 77, 128; Benjamin Whichcote, *The Works of the Learned Benjamin Whichcote*, 4 vols. (Aberdeen, 1751) I, 32, 53; II, 189, 201; IV, 299; Benjamin Whichcote, *Moral and Religious Aphorisms* (London: Printed for J. Payne, 1753), §460; John Smith, *Select Discourses* (Cambridge: Cambridge University Press, 1660), 2–3.

58 Price, *Various Subjects*, 382.

59 Plato, "The Apology," in *The Last Days of Socrates*, trans. Hugh Tredennick (London: Penguin, 1959), 29d – –30a.

60 The Phaedrus has a very different interpretation of the idea, but Sedley gives a persuasive argument for reading the doctrine as coherent in the light of the Timaeus in Sedley, "Godlikeness," 796.

61 Theaetetus, 176b, Republic, 613a-b. See, however, Julia Annas, "What Are Plato's 'Middle' Dialogues in the Middle Of?" in *New Perspectives on Plato, Modern and Ancient*, ed. Julia Annas and Christopher J. Rowe (Harvard: Harvard University Press, 2003), 1–23 for a challenge to the developmental understanding of Plato's dialogues.

62 See, however, Kevin Corrigan, " 'Solitary' Mysticism in Plotinus, Proclus, Gregory of Nyssa, and Pseudo-Dionysius," *The Journal of Religion* 76, no. 1 (1996): 28–42 for an argument that the two interpretations can be unified.

63 John H. Muirhead, *The Platonic Tradition in Anglo-Saxon Philosophy* (London: Macmillan, 1931), 53.

64 Michael B. Gill, "The Religious Rationalism of Benjamin Whichcote," *Journal of the History of Philosophy* 37 (1999): 288.

65 Price, *Various Subjects*, 366; Whichcote, *Works*, II, 385.

66 Price, *Various Subjects*, 382.

67 Ralph Cudworth, "A Sermon Preached before the House of Commons," in *The Cambridge Platonists*, ed. C. A. Patrides (Cambridge: Cambridge University Press, 1969), 98, 102.
68 Cudworth, "Sermon," 101, 104–6.
69 Whichcote, *Works*, II, 293.
70 I am grateful to one of the reviewers of this manuscript for pointing out that Smith's Plotinian account of becoming divine is moral, not metaphysical.
71 C. A. Patrides, "'The High and Aiery Hills of Platonisme': An Introduction to the Cambridge Platonists," in *The Cambridge Platonists*, ed. C. A. Patrides (Cambridge: Cambridge University Press, 1969), 18 points out that the Cambridge Platonists resisted Plotinus's call for isolation from the world. C.f. More, *Antidote*, A5.
72 Plato, *Republic*, 439d; Price, *Review*, 74, 79.
73 Price, *Review*, 17, 38, 217n; Plato, *Timaeus*, 29b; Plato, *Phaedrus*, trans. Walter Hamilton (Harmondsworth: Penguin, 1973), 246; Alcinous follows Plato's Republic Book 4, 441d-e by distinguishing between reason and the affections, suggesting that the soul has three elements. Alcinous, *Handbook*, §24.35–45, 31–2.
74 *Republic*, 441d-e; Price, *Review*, 217.
75 Henry More, "Conjectura Cabbalistica," in *A Collection of Several Philosophical Writings of Dr. Henry More* (London: Printed by Joseph Downing, 1712), 214; For a discussion of the different accounts of becoming like God in Smith and More, see J. E. Saveson, "Differing Reactions to Descartes among the Cambridge Platonists," *Journal of the History of Ideas* 21 (1960): 560–7.
76 Whichcote, *Works*, II, 385; see also 386; John Smith, *Select Discourses* (London: Printed by J. Flesher, for W. Morden, bookseller in Cambridge, 1660), 390–1.
77 David Pailin, "Reconciling Theory and Fact: The Problem of 'Other Faiths' in Lord Herbert and the Cambridge Platonists," in *Platonism at the Origins of Modernity: Studies on Platonism and Early Modern Philosophy*, ed. Douglas Hedley and Sarah Hutton (Dordrecht: Springer, 2008), 93–112 points out that for Whichcote, man is not deified as a rational animal (inferior creatures are rational too) but as a religious creature; Price, *Various Subjects*, 367–8; 371 c.f. Whichcote, *Works*, I, 53–4.
78 This point is made by James Deotis Roberts, *From Puritanism to Platonism in Seventeenth Century England* (The Hague: Martinus Nijhoff, 1968), 240.
79 Smith, *Select Discourses*, 340. I am grateful to the anonymous reader of the manuscript for this point. See also John Worthington's "An Advertisement" in the 1660 edition of the *Select Discourses*, p. 280.
80 See Gill, "Religious Rationalism," 271 for an argument that there is an inherent tension between Whichcote's rationalism and his Christology.
81 A. M. C. Waterman, "The Nexus between Theology and Political Doctrine in Church and Dissent," in *Enlightenment and Religion: Rational Dissent in Eighteenth-Century Britain*, ed. Knud Haakonssen (Cambridge: Cambridge University Press, 1996), 216 makes this point in relation to Price and Priestley's theories of church and state.
82 Fitzpatrick, "Rational Dissent," 90.
83 Richard Ashcraft, "Latitudinarianism and Toleration: Historical Myth versus Political History," in *Philosophy, Science and Religion in England, 1640–1700*, ed. Richard Kroll, Richard Ashcraft, and Perez Zagorin (Cambridge: Cambridge University Press, 1992), 151–77.
84 D. O. Thomas, *The Honest Mind: The Thought and Work of Richard Price* (Oxford: Clarendon, 1977), 12–13.
85 Richard Price, *The Correspondence of Richard Price*, ed. W. B. Peach and D. O. Thomas, vol. III (Cardiff: University of Wales Press, 1994), 42n; See Thomas, *Honest Mind*, 143 for more information about the Honest Whigs.

86   Mark Philp, "Rational Religion and Political Radicalism in the 1790s," *Enlightenment and Dissent* 4 (1985): 37, 41.
87   Richard Price, *Sermons on the Christian Doctrine* (London: Printed for T. Cadell, 1787), 25.
88   Cudworth, "Sermon," 11.
89   Thomas, *Honest Mind*, 316.
90   Price, *Correspondence*, 1994, III: 190. To William Adams, 16 December 1788.
91   Thomas, *Honest Mind*, 110–11.
92   Price, *Correspondence*, 1994, III: 190. To William Adams, 16 December 1788.
93   Price, *Correspondence*, 1991. Letter to Joseph Priestley 14 May 1778, 22.
94   Martin Fitzpatrick, "Heretical Religion and Radical Political Ideas in Late Eighteenth-Century England," in *The Transformation of Political Culture: England and Germany in the Late Eighteenth Century*, ed. Eckhart Hellmuth (Oxford: Oxford University Press, 1990), 352. See also 352.
95   Page, "Enlightenment," 53; Rogers, "Locke," 204.
96   Faustus Socinus, *The Racovian Catechisme* (Amsterdam: Printed for Brooer Janz, 1652), 28.
97   Joseph Priestley, "Letters to a Philosophical Unbeliever," in *Works*, vol. iv, 1817, 446.
98   Priestley, "Disquisitions," 257.
99   Joseph Priestley, "An Appeal to the Serious and Candid Professors of Christianity," in *Works*, vol. ii, 1817, 385.
100 Martin Fitzpatrick, "Toleration and Truth," *Enlightenment and Dissent* 1 (1982): 12.
101 Joseph Priestley, "An History of the Corruptions of Christianity," in *Works*, vol. v, 1817, 10, 493.
102 Fitzpatrick, "Toleration," 12; John Jebb, *The Works, Theological, Medical, Political, and Miscellaneous of John Jebb with Memoirs of the Life of the Author by John Disney*, vol. II (London: Printed for T. Cadell, 1787), 5, 8, 178.
103 Price, *Correspondence*, 1994, III: 175. To Theophilus Lindsey, 26 May 1788.
104 Fitzpatrick, "Toleration," 17.
105 Price, *Correspondence*, 1994, III: 175. To Theophilus Lindsey, 26 May 1788.
106 Price, *Four Dissertations*, 92–3.
107 Quoted in Fitzpatrick, "Toleration," 18; Priestley, "Corruptions," 480–1.
108 Fitzpatrick, "Toleration," 19.
109 Fitzpatrick, "Toleration," 25.
110 Priestley, "Letters to Price," 373.
111 Richard Price, "Observations on the Importance of the American Revolution and the Means of Making It a Benefit to the World," in *Richard Price: Political Writings*, ed. D. O. Thomas (Cambridge: Cambridge University Press, 1991), 136.
112 Fitzpatrick, "Toleration."
113 Quoted in Fitzpatrick, "Toleration," 20.
114 Priestley, "Letters to Price," 370.
115 Fitzpatrick, "Toleration," 27.
116 Price, *Review*, 110.
117 Raphael, "Introduction," xix; A. S. Cua, *Reason and Virtue: A Study in the Ethics of Richard Price* (New York: H. Wolff, 1966), 78.
118 Henry More, *An Account of Virtue: Or, Dr. Henry More's Abridgement of Morals* (London: Printed for Benjamin Tooke, 1690), 1.4.2.
119 Price, *Review*, 73.
120 Alasdair MacIntyre, *A Short History of Ethics: A History of Moral Philosophy from the Homeric Age to the Twentieth Century* (London: Routledge, 1967), 176.

121 Price, *Review*, 41.
122 Price, *Review*, 112, 127.
123 Price, *Review*, 112.
124 Price, *Review*, 98; More, *Antidote*, 20; Cudworth, *Treatise*, 78. This idea is also expressed by Plotinus in Enneads, V.5. See also Scott, "Platonic Recollection."
125 Price, *Christian Doctrine*, 143.
126 John Toland, *Christianity Not Mysterious or, a Treatise Shewing, That There Is Nothing in the Gospel Contrate to Reason, nor above It: And That No Christian Doctrine Can Be Properly Call'd a Mystery* (London, 1702), 6.

3 State cozenage and political fictions
Reason, revelation and the politics of conformity

In 1675, John Standish, a fellow of Peterhouse College Cambridge and royal chaplain to Charles II, lamented a trend he identified in the established church to

> supplant *Christian* Religion with Natural Theologie; and turn the Grace of God into a *wanton* Notion of *Morality* . . . making *Reason, Reason, Reason,* their only Trinity, and sole Standard, whereby to measure both the Principles and Conclusions of *Faith*.[1]

This dangerous craze, he thought, came not from the atheists or those who dissented from Anglican Communion but from those who were already part of the established church. Standish's culprits were the latitude-men: those Anglican divines who embraced what would later be called a Low Church ecclesiology and who went on to welcome the Revolution settlement of 1688. They were renowned, as Standish illustrates, for embracing a rationalistic natural theology.

Standish was not the only one to express alarm. His contemporary Miles Barne (also a Peterhouse man and royal chaplain) delivered his own sermon in the same year in which he blasted Latitudinarianism for being essentially 'Libertinism.'[2] When boiled down, the problem was that anyone who holds to the clearness of scriptures has a tendency to 'despise their Ecclesiastical Superiors' and 'throw off all obedience to Christ's Ministers.'[3] This exposes the deep-seated worry behind their attitude: the threat to the authority of the established church. Reverence for authority was paramount for both divines, forming the basis of the state and the heart of God's revelation: in fact, it was part of what revelation *meant*, as revelation could not be conceived of aside from the establishment church's role as custodian and sole interpreter of God's word. Calvinism, according to Barne, had threatened passive obedience to the Lord's Anointed, but the latitude-men posed a particular worry lurking right inside the belly of Anglicanism.[4] It did not escape him that reason, and rationalist natural theology, was a direct threat to the establishment.

Standish and Barne took an exceptionally hostile view of reason. Although not universally shared by their contemporaries, their opinions still make for a good illustration of the inherently political character of seventeenth- and eighteenth-century English debates about reason, revelation and natural theology. This is important for considering the relationship between reason and revelation. That the two are opposed, or that they at least operate separately in different spheres, has become a widespread assumption from which the definition of natural theology often takes its cue, as demonstrated by James Barr:

> Traditionally, 'natural theology' has commonly meant something like this: that 'by nature,' that is, just by being human beings, men and women have a certain degree of knowledge of God and awareness of him, or at least a capacity for such awareness; and this knowledge or awareness exists anterior to the special revelation of God.[5]

Barr goes on to state that natural theology is thought of most usually as received prior to being revealed and is possible – or even preferable – without any appeal at all to revealed theology. It is common (particularly by its critics) for natural theology to be coupled with reason and defined in opposition to revelation.

That natural theology and revelation should be defined as antithetical to one another, or at least as entirely independent; however, it is an assumption that buys into the dichotomy set up and exploited by Anglican divines such as Standish and Barne. This dichotomy is implicit in the dominant narratives of Enlightenment discussed in Chapter 1. On this assumption, the eighteenth-century natural theologians are seen to embrace secular reason – to become 'philosophers' – in order to engage in debate with the atheists, all the while hewing out the theological ground beneath their feet. Contextualising the rationalism of some of these key seventeenth- and eighteenth-century thinkers, however, suggests instead the prevalence of a deeply theological account of reason that underpins a conception of reason and a natural theology that was at once both ethical and political. This makes theological reflection on the social-political consequences of theologies of reason and revelation unavoidable and highlights how depoliticised more recent natural theology and philosophy of religion has become.

This chapter will make two main points. First, although the English natural theologians of the seventeenth and eighteenth centuries were responding to a perceived threat from atheism, their main concerns were ethical rather than purely about the justification of belief. Their worries about atheism cohered with worries about Calvinist voluntarism, and the concerns were not new to the era: they have deep roots in the Platonic tradition. Their conception of reason, and the resulting natural theology, is therefore inherently ethical. Second, this chapter will highlight that the shape of English rationalist natural theology was forged by political disputes within the Anglican Church. Concerns about atheism and enthusiasm were a strong unifying bond between Anglicans of all persuasions in the late seventeenth and eighteenth centuries.[6] Responses, however, tended to vary enormously according to political allegiance. The critique of reason which was heard commonly on the lips of those who might later be called High Anglican and Tory contrasted sharply with those who had a much higher view of reason and who proposed varying forms of natural theology: they tended to be Latitudinarian (and in the mid-late eighteenth century also Rational Dissenting) and politically Whig.

This is not to claim that every natural theologian would have proposed his or her argument primarily as a political exercise, or that, as the late seventeenth and eighteenth century wore on, the critics of reason would necessarily have been High Church Anglicans, but lines of political allegiance can be drawn. For Standish and Barne, the Latitudinarian menace was at once both theological and political. The appeal to reason and natural theology represented a political hazard that could be countered only by abandoning rationality and re-asserting revelation in its stead. For the Latitudinarians and Rational Dissenters who appealed to reason, an overbearing ecclesiastical authority was seen to have much in common with the dangers of atheism, Calvinism and voluntarism.

What this shows is that debates about reason and revelation, and about the nature and worth of natural theology, cannot be captured in terms of the justification of belief or in terms of debates about whether God's existence can be demonstrated rationally, but were to a significant degree politically charged disputes concerning religious and civil authority and the relationship between church and state. Understanding the political nature of the rationality of this era brings to centre stage the power structures of High Church ecclesiology and the establishment theology that the natural theologians were making it their business to challenge. Behind arguments against atheism, and debates about the reach of the established church, lay disputes about the nature of power and the reality of ethical value. Engaging in natural theology or rejecting it was an inherently political activity.

The philosophy of religion in England: power, will and the immutability of goodness

The first use in English of the term 'philosophy of religion' is attributed to Ralph Cudworth, who described himself as putting forward such a philosophy in his *True Intellectual System of the Universe Wherein All the Reason and Philosophy of Atheism Is Confuted and Its Impossibility Demonstrated* (hereafter *TIS*): 'The main thing, which the book pretends, to . . . being the philosophy of religion.'[7] This multi-volume work, of which the first part was published in 1678, was nothing short of an attempt, colossal in its proportions, to bring together all the arguments for atheism under one roof in order to dismiss them en masse. The final product looked suspicious to some. Cudworth was accused of promoting the cause of unbelief, having produced effectively what looked to his detractors as something strikingly like an atheists' handbook. It is doubtful he was any kind of subversive atheist, however. His work was an endeavour to confirm and establish 'the belief of a God, by philosophic reasons,' thereby establishing that theology is not full of 'inconsistent and contridictious notions' and that the idea and existence of God is not 'the confounded nonsense of astonished minds.'[8]

Cudworth's target, however, was not in a straightforward sense what we have come to understand by atheism today: the denial of the propositional belief in God. The seventeenth and eighteenth century use of the term atheism is difficult to define, not least because it was used primarily as a term of abuse. Cudworth at times seems to equate it with materialism, but the word was often associated with a lack of any sense of divine justice and was used to include deists, materialists, freethinkers and, later on, Unitarians.[9] It is evident that the term sometimes encompassed more than just a materialistic world view. Henry More proposed that it is a position that is wont to confuse the nature of good and evil, and its origins lie in 'those dreadful decrees by virtue of which God can damn man, apparently through sheer willfulness.'[10] Atheism, for the Cambridge Platonists, is an ethical issue. It is not a straightforward proposition of fact about the non-existence of God but involves a stance taken towards the reality of ethical values. What tends to unify those deemed atheist is voluntarism; the belief that ethical value is created by the will as opposed to having independent objective existence. Atheism for Cudworth has at its heart the rejection of eternal and immutable reality, in other words the real distinction between right and wrong. Cudworth's tome and its philosophy of religion was a response to the ethical dangers perceived in an adherence to the supremacy of will. Atheism and its consequent materialism turn out to be but one symptom of this voluntaristic malaise.

Descartes and Hobbes were the prime voluntarist targets of the *TIS*. The arguments of Descartes's *Meditations* rest on a commitment to the goodness of a God who would not deceive. Cudworth, however, remained unconvinced by the circularity of the reasoning. Descartes proposed a good God as guarantor of the accuracies of our rationality but at the same time asserted that our rationality establishes the goodness of God, producing an argument that, as Cudworth pointed out, proves absolutely nothing and leaves the objective nature of goodness in a precarious position.[11] No power, not even omnipotence, can make a true thing false, or a false thing true. This is the core of Cudworth's entire philosophy. The primary attribute of God, he argues, as many of the later eighteenth-century natural theologians went on to insist, is benevolence, not power. Power – envisaged as divine will – cannot compromise the nature of truth. When the *TIS* embarks on a rational investigation of God's attributes, therefore, it is first and foremost an effort to curb the arbitrariness of power through a regard to the absolute nature of ethical truth.

This forms the context of Cudworth's promotion of abstract ideas as a guide to truth capable of comprehension clearly and distinctly. As explained in the previous chapter, this line of reasoning is what lies behind Price's conception of simple ideas. Their clarity was promoted by Cudworth to oppose the reduction of truth to power. The essence of the truth of abstract things is their clear perceptibility and most certainly *not* the omnipotence of God. Thus he insists, contra Descartes, that God could not create beings that have clear and distinct ideas of falsehoods, 'no power, how great soever . . . can make any thing to be indifferently either true or false.'[12] The assertion that even God cannot do contradictory things, that truth might be perceived clearly and distinctly, and that the divine nature itself might conform to the laws of logic, are presented as a much-needed alternative to the consequences of the Cartesian argument that reduces truth to a matter of power. If the laws of logic have any validity to discern the nature of the Deity, it is because they prevent the divine will from indiscriminately determining truth.

Cudworth's method of using reason in religion – what he termed the philosophy of religion – is not, therefore, for the primary purpose of epistemic justification in the face of non-belief but for the wider purpose of the defence of the reality of absolute ethical value. The difference is subtle but important. If God is said to do only non-contradictory things, this is not to gain merely a propositional statement of fact about the divine but to open up a debate about the relationship between knowledge and power. For Cudworth, it is imperative that knowledge should be the measure of all power, which is a position upheld in direct objection to the ancient Protagorean assertion that 'man is the measure of all things – of the things that are, that they are; of the things that are not, that they are not.'[13] That truth is, contra-Protagoras, 'public, catholic and universal. . . [obtaining] every where' presents the ideal of a view from nowhere, but it is a claim born from Cudworth's concern to restrict the whims of arbitrary power against anyone who in Protagoras's terms would think all truths are 'private and relative' and that 'no one man's opinion was righter than another's.'[14] His stance is both firmly anti-relativist and anti-voluntarist.

The voluntaristic threat from Hobbes was the most immediate menace in Cudworth's eyes, and he was the main perpetrator of the 'atheism' referred to throughout the *True Intellectual System*. His antithetical attitude to the philosophy of religion is clear. As Hobbes saw it, the entire enterprise should be brought to an abrupt halt:

> We ought not to dispute of God's nature; He is no fit subject of our philosophy. True religion consisteth in obedience to Christ's lieutenants, and in giving God such honour, both in attributes and actions, as they in their several lieutenancies shall ordain.[15]

Hobbes's reason for disdaining the rational investigation of divinity is not because its arguments fail logically, but because the essential rights of sovereignty preclude the rational analysis of religious belief. For 'Christ's lieutenants,' we should read 'civil magistrate,' and it was he (exclusively 'he') who should judge in all matters of religious controversy. The will of the magistrate reigns supreme in the Hobbesian ideal state, with the result that any attempt to undertake the philosophy of religion is a direct threat not only to the power of the magistrate but also to the entire edifice of the leviathan. These words cannot have been lost on Cudworth. Hobbes's assertion that religious belief is made convincing not with regard to how reasonable it is but on account of the power and authority of those who enforce it was countered by Cudworth's rational investigation into the attributes of God and the coherence of belief. In Cudworth's hands, the philosophical contemplation of religion is a political act – a deliberate obstruction to the ever-looming peril of Hobbes's authoritarian idyllic government.

The issue with Hobbes's voluntarism is an ethical one, as it is with Descartes. If all power is passed over to the magistrate, then who is to be obeyed if Christ's lieutenant should command contrary to the laws of God or nature?[16] This is the question of Plato's *Euthyphro* – is the holy loved by the gods because it is holy or is it holy because it is loved by the gods?[17] – and it dominates the nature and shape of the philosophy of religion advocated in the *TIS*. From where do truth and goodness come? Do they come from the will of the gods or those in power? Or do they transcend the power of will? How this dilemma is answered has deep political connotations.

Political concerns had been at the forefront of Cudworth's mind for some time. In 1647, 30 years before the publication of the first part of the *TIS*, Cudworth delivered a sermon to the House of Commons. The English Civil War had started five years earlier and Cudworth's homily was delivered as a plea to limit political power with justice and humility.[18] The majority of his audience for this particular sermon would have been Presbyterian Reformers, notable for their earnest acceptance of Calvinist predestination and its particular view of providence. Their Calvinistic enthusiasm subjected everything to the will of God. Cudworth's main theme takes up the sovereignty of goodness as opposed to the primacy of self-love, appetites or desires. Two concepts of God are contrasted: the God of goodness and the God of power. Worshipping a God of sheer power can celebrate only vanity – a trait 'symptomatic of a community incapable of conceiving of a good that transcends self-will.'[19] Cudworth was working from the recognition that our conceptions of the divine have unavoidable societal and political consequences, meaning that it can only be a mistake to shape God 'according to the model of ourselves' by making the Deity 'nothing but a blind, dark, impetuous Self-will, running through the world.'[20] His argument is therefore essentially anti-Machiavellian.[21] Reason is not merely instrumental, and power not what is supreme. Both should bow instead to the immutable nature of goodness.

Frederick Beiser notes that the early writings of the Cambridge Platonists do not even mention Hobbes, which means their refutation of ethical voluntarism predates Hobbes's *On Human Nature* (1640) and *De Corpore*

Politico (1642). The conclusion he draws is that their theology positions itself against the voluntarist God of Calvinism (which as they saw it had atheistic implications) rather than against propositional atheism itself.[22] Douglas Hedley is right, however, that the Cambridge Platonists were doing more than just responding to Calvinism.[23] Cudworth, together with John Smith, was later concerned to argue against what Hedley calls 'speculative' atheism – the materialistic assertion that there is no God (what we would call atheism today) – just as much as he tried to rebut Calvinism. This means the Cambridge Platonists represent the development of a form of radical Protestantism with deep historical roots in Alexandrian Christian Platonism and the mystical medieval tradition, and they often, as Cudworth does in the *TIS*, associate atheism with the materialistic empiricism of Epicureanism.[24]

The important point for the concerns of this book is that the argument against atheism, in its different Calvinist and Epicurean incarnations, was at its heart an ethical one. Atheism was regarded as a threat to the immutability of goodness. This concern for the voluntarist implications of materialistic atheism goes back to Plato and grounds the worries the Cambridge Platonists had for the voluntarism implied by both atheism in its Epicurean form and by the atheist implications of Calvinism. The connection made by Cudworth between religion, reason and morality is part of an anti-naturalism that can be traced to Plato's *Laws*: for Plato, 'atheism is a "disease" of the soul because it subverts the respect for Good.'[25] As Hedley points out, the very motto of Cudworth's *TIS* is taken from the *Laws*.[26] The arguments of the *Laws*, proposed against the errors of the atheists when they argue the gods do not exist, do not care for us or can be corrupted, show that 'for Plato the essential point of theism is its relation to morality, God must be conceived of as good, and concerned about virtue.'[27] The *Laws* argue not only that the gods exist but also they care for human beings and do not use us merely for their sport. It is a theme of so many other Platonic dialogues too that a commitment to the transcendence of the good is contrasted with the relativism of those, such as Thrasymachus, who would see justice as nothing but the interests of the stronger, or the aforementioned Protagoras who would make human will the measure of all things. This is precisely why atheism, for Plato, is linked with immorality and the corruption of the state.[28]

It seems fair to accept then that Cudworth was aware of the difference between Calvinism and Epicurean atheism. Calvinism is atheist in its implications rather than in the theoretical sense of Epicurean materialism. Both, however, are united through their voluntarist implications, and these have strongly ethically relativist consequences. Cudworth's concern to defend the immutability and objectivity of goodness against both materialism and Calvinism is rooted in these ethical considerations. It is a concern for goodness that characterises the beginning of the *TIS*, and it draws together the theoretical and practical, the metaphysical and ethical, into a Platonic theism that refuses to see nature as a random collection of matter, or truth as a matter of will. In such a universe, there can be no goodness.[29]

It presents no problem for this argument that the Cambridge Platonist Peter Sterry was a Calvinist, as he in fact shared deep concerns about voluntarism with the rest of the Cambridge school. He prioritised the love and goodness of God and saw it as the only means through which God's justice is dispensed. For this reason, unusual for his time, he rejected the doctrine of eternal punishment. God's goodness, he insisted, takes precedence over God's will, and God's will is not capricious. In this, he was entirely in harmony with the other Cambridge Platonists: will alone, he maintained – even the will of God – cannot determine the nature of goodness.

Grounding religion 'upon the instincts of nature, and upon solid reason' is for Cudworth, therefore, essential for showing that religious truth cannot be determined by arbitrary power and the 'fiction or imposture of politicians.'[30] The gods, as Plato put it in the *Laws*, cannot be bribed and their power is not arbitrary. While Cudworth was writing the *TIS*, speculation about the political nature of religious belief was rife. Isaac Le Peyrère, Claude Saumaise and Baruch de Spinoza had suggested that religion was the result of human superstitions ignited and utilised for the purpose of wielding political power, and Hobbes had played with that idea in the *Leviathan's* proposal that this is true of all religions, apart from Judaism and Christianity.[31] Despite Hobbes's sop to the Judeo-Christian tradition, it would hardly have been a giant leap to tar these religions with the same explanatory brush. The implications would have been clear for all to see, and they were not lost on Cudworth. Furthermore, there was another anti-religious plot afoot. Henry Oldenburg from Oxford claimed in 1656 that a theory, ominously dubbed the *Trois Imposteurs*, was doing the rounds. It stated that Moses, Jesus and Mohammed were political schemers who had propagated religious views for the purposes of political power. There was a rumour of an accompanying book, but the work proved elusive even to Queen Christina, who failed to flush it out with a one-million-dollar reward. Despite the lack of a tangible adversary, a response was penned for good measure by Adam Boreel in the form of his *Jesus Christ, Legislator of the Human Race*. Although his ruminations never reached the press, Robert Boyle and Henry More had copies of the work, and it is most likely that Cudworth was familiar with it too.[32] Although Cudworth may not have been privy to the arguments in their original form, Boreel's response would have made him all too aware of the suggestion that religion is just another name for the wielding of political power.

The taxonomy of the various religious beliefs compiled in the *TIS* constitute Cudworth's attempt to argue instead that different religions demonstrate something of God's revelation, even if they have very much corrupted it. If religious belief is a mere phantasm peddled by those aspiring to cling on to power, there can be no defence against the leviathan's all-encompassing authority. Cudworth's philosophy of religion in the *TIS* was motivated, therefore, by the endeavour to fulfil the mutually reinforcing goals of denying the reduction of Christianity to sociological and political explanation on the one hand and the defence of the reality of truth and ethical value on the other. The atheists, he tells us, have tried to show that religious belief is a means of social-political control, but it cannot be that which serves only political interest. Belief in God is therefore not mere 'state cozenage,' the 'arbitratious fiction of law-makers and politicians.'[33] Atheists both ancient and modern (the most notable of whom is clearly identified as Hobbes) have produced 'a mormo, bugbear, or terriculum, a frightful, hurtful and most undesirable thing' in their suggestion that religion is a mere tool of government, utilised to make the citizenry tamer and more obedient.[34]

Cudworth's account of the scope of human rationality must be placed within the context of this political consideration of religion. The attributes of God, in Cudworth's eyes, should be considered philosophically not for the primary purpose of justifying theistic belief against propositional atheism, but because if they are not considered in this way, God's attributes will come to signify nothing true or false in nature but only what is in the interests of civil law. Voluntarism is wrong that 'all things whatsoever, even the natures of good and evil, and all truth and falsehood, do so depend upon the arbitrary will and power of God' and likewise political authority comes from the moral law not from fear: 'no Lawgiver has just right to inforce his laws beyond equality and justice.'[35] Words like 'infinite' and 'eternal' signify something real, not just the political machinations of the powerful. Cudworth's answer to the Euthyphro dilemma denies not only that divine will is paramount but also that religion might be a political invention, derived from the will of commanding civil sovereigns.

God and religious belief are therefore posited as subjects of philosophy precisely because religion is not a matter of law and arbitrary constitution. Voluntaristic power is opposed to the commitment to the objectivity of truth without which religion can too easily become a figment of fear and fancy, 'a mere political scare-crow.'[36] Hobbes's atheism and Calvinism's enthusiasm make for two sides of the same voluntaristic coin. They dissolve goodness into power and have worrying despotic political implications. The Calvinist's jealous and suspicious fear of God conceived of as an 'arbitrary and tyrannical Being' lies at the heart of superstition and makes atheists of those who 'grossly mistake the notion of God' by thinking of God differently and regarding the divine 'as a thing which is only to be feared, and must consequently be hated.'[37] Calvinism insisted on a theocratic social order, and Hobbes was adapting rather than challenging this by making the state a 'mortal God' – the only legitimate source of religion and the dictator of the law. In these systems, faith and the individual is subject to, and subordinated by, absolute will. Calvinism and Hobbes's empiricism demand obedience to will: 'Both recognise an absolute Being, which, as absolute power, not only limits the capacities of the understanding and will, but finally absorbs them altogether.'[38]

The anti-enthusiasm of Cudworth's earlier sermon before the House of Commons and its prioritising of goodness over will is married to his anti-Hobbesian stance in the *TIS*. The result is a model of philosophy of religion that utilises reason to curb the power of those who would bend the nature of truth and value to their will. The affinities with Plato's campaign against the Sophists are clear. Participation in reason reveals the poverty of the claim that human beings, especially those in power, are the measure of all. It is rather the nature of the good that grounds the legitimacy of power. The central message of Plato's *Laws* that the gods care for human beings makes Cudworth's philosophical apprehension of the goodness of God a continuation of the Platonic endeavour to reassure us of the absolute nature of moral value. The result is a philosophy that proposes immutable goodness as the locus for political power rather than arbitrary will. Whereas Hobbes's scheme posits political communities grounded in fear rather than in eternal morality perceived by reason,[39] Cudworth's rational alternative has distinctly radical undertones. This comes across more clearly in his unpublished works, where he insists that it is not laws and conventions that make something just and unjust but rather that the laws of the land are themselves 'accountable to a greater power.' This means that authority can be 'refused if the dictates of natural justice were circumvented by the commander.'[40]

The mid- to late seventeenth century recognised that no philosopher of religion could be free of political concerns. The political implications of Cudworth's anti-atheism and with it his anti-voluntarism were far-reaching and potentially subversive. If the nature of goodness cannot be determined by God's will or human will, no monarch or parliament has the power to dictate moral goodness. Beliefs about divine power inevitably ran parallel to beliefs about political power, including the power of the Church, Parliament and the crown. Cudworth's attempt to consider beliefs about the divine in the light of reason necessarily implied strict limits to political power.[41]

Toleration and the reasonableness of religion

The anti-voluntarism of Cudworth's *TIS* was in practice more than a challenge to Hobbes's atheism and Calvinism. The immediate political context was a debate about the relationship of church and state. Hobbes's atheism promoted the state as the arbiter of religious matters. What was after 1688 called 'High Church' Anglicanism linked church establishment with political power insisting on conformity prescribed by one recognised communion. The Cambridge Platonists, however, had no wish to reintroduce any one Anglican liturgy within the University of Cambridge. They called for toleration, reflecting their concerns to resist the Laudian (and later High Church ideal) of a national church that had coercive state power at its fingertips to help it personify holiness through uniform liturgy and ordered theology.[42] Cambridge Platonist anti-voluntarism thus resulted in a call for toleration and the rejection of enforced subscription. That Cudworth called for the examination of religious beliefs by philosophical reason would have made for a rebuke of non-tolerant ecclesiastical hierarchy in an era when the issue of conformity was becoming increasingly politically charged.

It is evident that the word Latitudinarian became much more widespread after the Restoration in 1660. It was a term used to criticise those who, as some Laudians saw it, pledged allegiance to the restored church and monarchy out of expediency, not conviction.[43] The more 'elevated' Laudian clerics favoured strict ritualistic and doctrinal conformity in order to protect the church from what they perceived to be the chaos of the Interregnum. Standish's disdain for natural theology came from the same position of fear for the safety of the establishment, which in turn cloaked his dichotomising of reason and revelation and his outright rejection of the former as anti-church.

Cudworth's commending of reason was in effect nothing short of a direct critique of the principles behind what was to become High Church Anglican theology. Affirming the use of reason in religion and the immutable nature of goodness constituted an argument against the reverence of arbitrary authority and passive obedience to power. True religion and conscience are encapsulated in the demand that God should be obeyed, not human will. This was how the more 'highly minded' Anglicans saw it too. Joseph Beaumont griped against Henry More that 'the drift of his desperate and blasphemous opinion is chiefly, if not solely, to usher in this Liberty of Conscience.'[44] The appeal for toleration by the Cambridge Platonists and the call for the superiority of conscience in place of the subjection to the will of others included not only the critique of arbitrary divine power and the power of the state but also the enforcing of conformity on those of a different theological persuasion. The account of reason developed in Cudworth's *TIS* defends the Latitudinarian drive towards the refusal of subjection to civil magistrates, its apathy towards tradition and its denial of the mystical theology of monarchy: all of which countered what would go on to be the defining characteristics of High Anglicanism.[45]

This forms the context for the Cambridge Platonists' openness towards the 'new philosophy' of the physical sciences on which their natural theology is based. Attention to nature was promoted as part of a move away from the authority of scripture as mediated through the teaching and tradition of the Anglican Church.[46] Apparent debates between the Cambridge school and their adversaries about the nature and limits of natural and revealed theology should more accurately be interpreted as disputes about the authority of history and tradition. Conformity to traditional liturgies, observances and sacramental theology was, according to their clerical opponents, the defining feature of what constitutes a true Anglican. In response, the emphasis on the fundamental principles of Christianity, on the new philosophy and on natural theology comprised an argument that enabled Anglicans who rejected these ideals to go on to claim their place within the Restoration Church.[47]

The spirit of Cambridge Platonism was evidently clear in the younger generation of Restoration Latitudinarians who emphasised, as John Moore put it, 'the reasonableness of our religion' as opposed to any one ecclesiastical model.[48] This advocacy for rationality earned John Tillotson and Simon Patrick an attack by the House of Lords for a pamphlet in which Tillotson had defended private judgement in religious matters. The Cambridge Platonists heavily influenced another broad-minded divine, Edward Stillingfleet, graduate of St. John's College Cambridge and later vicar of Sutton in Sussex. Although he elected to become part of the Anglican establishment, his Latitudinarianism denied the 'necessity of any one form of [Church] government' because he could find no prescribed model of church government in the scriptures.[49] As a result, he faced the wrath of the High Church Simon Lowth who defended the doctrine of Episcopal succession fiercely.[50] The Latitudinarians' denial of the necessity of conformity arose from a theology of individual conscience that challenged the automatic authority of ecclesiastical hierarchy. Stillingfleet's argument was grounded in a refusal to claim supremacy for a particular form of ecclesiastical organisation. It was epistemic humility that he thought curbed the will to theological power – a humility that went on to characterise the thought of many later Latitudinarians and, as the previous chapter argued, the Rational Dissenting thought of Richard Price.

The rationalism of the Cambridge Platonists and later seventeenth-century Latitudinarianism must be distinguished from both Cartesianism and deism. Their critics unfortunately often conflated them. Simon Patrick reports that the latitude-men were associated with Cartesianism, which was reputed to have 'poisoned' the fountain of Cambridge[51] despite the fact that it is quite clear that the Latitudinarians had serious reservations about the philosophy of Descartes. Cudworth was concerned to avoid both the extremes of Spinozian pantheism (a theology that regards God as the same substance as the cosmos, in which God and nature are synonymous) and Descartes's voluntaristic theism of transcendence. Cartesian metaphysics was too closely related to Epicurean materialism because it makes God's interaction with the world problematic: it cannot give a satisfying answer as to how the material and the spiritual interact.[52] Cambridge Platonist philosophy of religion represents instead an attempt to combine a commitment to revelation with a rationalism that recognises reason's limits and which pays close attention to the study of the natural world. The imagery of the candle of the Lord in the hands of the Cambridge Platonists did not take away from the importance of supernatural light, however.[53] For them, it was still God's grace which bestowed salvation. The proper use of reason cannot be attained without careful guidance, which means ethical conduct can only be a result of a life of faith and a restoring of a pre-Fall nature. This puts them at considerable distance from the deist's virtual elimination of revelation by means of rational theology.

They were at one with the deists, however, in acknowledging that the mystery of Christianity could be used all too easily as a means of suppression by the powerful, and they shared a concern to challenge conformity with a much higher view of reason and an emphasis on moral behaviour. The deists' figurehead, John Toland, complained that the clerical divines demand that 'we must adore what we cannot comprehend,' and they enforce their incomprehensible views on the rest of the population, 'making the most noise out of what can be least understood.'[54] Although it might seem that the deists were not that far removed ideologically from the Cambridge Platonists and the Latitudinarians when it comes to the role of reason in religion, the small step the deists took to eliminate the scriptures with natural theology was in fact a giant leap that gave rise to a view of reason neither the Cambridge Platonists nor their Latitudinarian successors could countenance.[55] Gone was the Thomist insistence that 'certain things that are true about God wholly surpass the capability of human reason,'[56] and gone was the recognition reason is limited with the all-too-real possibility of corruption.

The divine rational candle of the Cambridge Platonists should, therefore, be located a long way from the reason of the deists. Their Anglican opponents may have tried to promote the opposite opinion, but the two models of reason were very different. The latitude of Cambridge Platonist rationality was an anti-voluntarism that resisted the ethical relativism of atheism, enthusiasm and authoritarian tradition. They saw the Calvinists as advancing an irrational '*sola fidianism*': a 'naked, unoperative faith' grounded in the will of the enthusiast,[57] the atheists as advancing a Epicurean universe in which goodness can have no real existence beyond what is willed and those who refused tolerance as asserting the reverence of authority – and human will – above and beyond what is truly good.

The rise of reason, the establishment church and the long shadow of 1688

After 1688, Latitudinarianism became a much better defined movement moulded by Newton's scientific advances and by the Whig ethos of the University of Cambridge.[58] The defence of the Revolutionary Settlement and the affirmation of the monarchy of William and Mary necessarily entailed a rejection of the mystery of the divine right of kings and hereditary succession. Many of those of a High Church persuasion were reluctant to coalesce with a church and government that had William as its head because, it was regarded as compromising the principles of those mysteries.[59] Their response was to stress the transcendental aspects of Christianity and the monarchy, placing divinised Episcopal authority and an ecclesiology of mystery at the heart of their theology. The appeal to a revelation that is fundamentally mysterious and anti-rational became a political theology inseparable from the desire to preserve what the High Anglicans regarded as the true monarchy and divine ecclesiology. The Latitudinarians, on the other hand, embraced the new Revolutionary state of affairs and utilised a much higher view of reason to challenge the mystery of authority. Their interest in the new natural philosophy and its resultant natural theology reflected whole-sale this less exalted view of monarchy.[60]

In the previous decade, 1679 had seen the passing of the Exclusion Bill formulated to exclude the Duke of York from the line of succession. Those who opposed the bill were named Tories and those in favour of it, Whigs – a political distinction that was to dominate the shape of English theology and philosophy of religion throughout the rest of the seventeenth century until the end of the eighteenth. High Church Anglicanism came to be dominated by Toryism, which resisted the bill on the grounds of monarchic dynasty. The result of these political disputes towards the end of the seventeenth century was a split between a High Church theology that enshrined the importance of the sacraments, the liturgy and the Thirty-Nine Articles (and opposed reason and revelation to one another), and a Latitudinarian theology (often called 'Low' Anglicanism) that opposed the mystery of divine and kingly power with a belief in the accord between reason and the events of 1688.[61] If Christianity was deemed to be a rational religion by the Latitudinarians, it was at least in part because they refused its necessary collusion with enforced subscription. Consequently, by the early eighteenth century, the Latitudinarians were distinguished by an emphasis on simplicity of doctrine, resolute anti-sacerdotalism and stress on the need to demonstrate the congruity between Christianity and human reason.[62] All these features united the Latitudinarians of the end of the seventeenth century with their pre-Revolution Cambridge Platonist forebears.

Tensions simmered between High and Low Church for half a century following the Revolution, and they were largely centred on the issues of monarchic dynasty, pastoral strategy – should the Church advocate coercive power and kerb toleration of dissent? – and ecclesiology (was the Church a voluntary society – as Locke had claimed – whose members had the right to judge the truth of its doctrines, or was it an apostolic universal body which was owed conformity and obedience?).[63] The eighteenth century brought the monarchy of Queen Anne (r.1702–1714), during which the High Churchmen remained fearful of the dangers they saw facing the established church in the form of the rise of the Low Church Whigs. The Nonjurors were particularly paranoid. They were composed of divines and laymen who had originally rejected outright William's government and his Church for transgressing the principle of divine hereditary kingship. Along with others of a High Church persuasion, they continued to oppose toleration and the lifting of penalties for those who would not conform.

The result was an even greater entrenchment of the dichotomy between natural and revealed religion. The worry that reason was a threat to revelation was, as Stewart tells us, the predictable High Church mentality.[64] Roger North, a lay Nonjuror and a particularly vocal opponent of the new regime, insisted that the battle of reason and revelation must be fought to the death. The enemies of mystery, he says, will reduce revelation 'to Nothing' such that 'all Revealed Religion must Tumble.' There could be no halfway house for him, no marriage of the two: this was war and it must be fought to the bitter end. It is, he states, 'all or None.'[65] The term 'deist' is defined by him in terms of those who are 'apostates' and those who refuse to submit the theological pronouncements of reason to authority.[66] A succinct example of how this was developed into a politics of establishment is provided by the High Church divine Robert South who wistfully reminisced that if only the clergy were given their due respect once again, 'men would be less confident of their own understandings, and more apt to pay reverence and submission to the understandings of those, who are both more conversant in these matters than they can pretend to be, and whom the same wisdom of God has thought fit to appoint over them as their guides.'[67] The appeal to reason thus constituted a defiant act against the hierarchical account of divine providence, and it resulted in a disconnection of the authority of church and king from the authority of God.

Natural theology played a vital role in the Latitudinarian challenge to this High Church ideal of ecclesiastical power, animating the claim that clerics cannot be the sole performers of religious rituals or interpreters of the word of God. This was, as Gascoigne highlights, what unified the Latitudinarians in their front against the doctrine of apostolic succession and its consequent strict theological hierarchy.[68] At the end of the seventeenth century and the beginning of the eighteenth, debates about reason and revelation were inseparable from debates about tradition and the role of Church and clergy as mediators of Christian doctrine.

One major difference is commonly identified between the theology of the Cambridge Platonists and their Latitudinarian intellectual offspring. The Cambridge Platonists' work is often seen to have a distinctly mystical flavour, whereas the later Latitudinarians are deemed much less overtly mystical in their defence of reason. Whether there is such a shift in emphasis is debatable, but even if assumed, it would still be very much in keeping with the spirit of Cambridge Platonism, however. Spellman tells us that mystical concerns became a luxury that the later Latitudinarians could not afford: they were too busy with the practical concerns of their urban parishes, inspiring a new generation in the Christian faith, and he argues that in fact there is more that unites the Cambridge Platonists with later Latitudinarians than divides them.[69] Both embraced reason in opposition both to enthusiasm and to High Church ideals. The later Latitudinarians moved away from mystery, not on account of any desire to diminish revelation, but because of their rejection of the mystery of Episcopal authority and the claim to the supremacy of 'enthusiastic' will.

This is evident in the thought of Benjamin Hoadly. Hoadly was Samuel Clarke's friend and editor, and he argued for the self-evidence of the truths of Christianity. Any hardening of the rational line in favour of self-evidence was politically charged: it undermined the power of ecclesiastical authority to define doctrine and normative worship.[70] Self-evidence left the established church with no authority to arbitrate about doctrine or liturgy. It was not Hoadly's goal to reduce revelation to reason. He allowed that certain truths of revelation go beyond human rationality and saw this as perfectly in keeping with the mutual compatibility of Christianity and reason. The reaction he received was blunt, however. The implicit threat to church authority made him what Leslie Stephen calls 'the best-hated clergyman of the century amongst his own order' and inspired Bolingbroke's snipe that he leaves a bishop as 'nothing but a layman with a crook in his hand.'[71] Hoadly himself did not pursue the natural conclusions of his theology. These were picked up by John Jackson in his *Grounds of Civil and Ecclesiastical Government* (1718) in which the claim is made that the Church has no special powers other than those which are derived from 'the Principles of Natural Reason improv'd by Revelation.'[72] The political application of this is, according to Jackson, that the Church has no power or right to impose any doctrine on anyone if it is not declared necessary in the Gospel. Once again, the principles of reason form the bulwark against any attempt at coercion by the state church.

Samuel Clarke takes up this language of self-evidence, arguing that the principal truths of Christianity are clear to those willing to examine the evidence. He parallels Christian truth and natural philosophy, putting both on the same footing as truths available to rational inspection. Clear political overtones can be detected in his desire to assert the rational character of Christianity. His sermon *The Character of Oppressive Power in Religion* opposes reason to unintelligible doctrine and the 'traditions of men' enforced by means of power – the same objective that underpins the challenge his natural theology makes to the insistence of any independent revealed knowledge that depends on interpretation through clerical hierarchy.[73] Clarke's *Scripture Doctrine of the Trinity* aided the Latitudinarian cause for a broad church: the Articles of the established church allowed, he thought, for varied interpretation because an individual could subscribe to them whenever they could be reconciled with scripture. His rational investigation of scripture and the divine nature rested on a point of significant theological importance: scriptures and doctrinal pronouncements cannot avoid the necessity of interpretation. If reason does not aid the interpretation, it is in danger of resting on the forceful will of establishment.

Clarke's stance did not go down well, and accusations flew in from all over the place. John Ball of Honiton (c.1665–1745) encapsulated the disgruntled reaction of Calvinism to what was seen as the new religion of reason. Newton and Clarke, he complained, 'Think it not just that God should punish Sin committed in this world with eternal Misery. These are the Men that are for rational Enquiries, and free Thought; and shall Dissenters lackey after 'em? God forbid!'[74] From the established church, reactions were every bit as deleterious. North accused Clarke of setting up 'reason against Revelation' and, along with other High Churchmen, categorised Clarke together with Isaac Newton as dangerous Whig ideologues. The Nonjuror response to Newton's philosophy was that it was likely to become 'waste-paper.'[75] The close affinity between Clarke and Newton's natural theology and their strong Whig leanings made them both the target of High Church ire. North's friend George Horne (1730–1792) of Magdalen College, Oxford (a University that had strong Tory inclinations), typified the response to both in his ceaseless championing of the supremacy of revealed over natural theology. Natural religion, he complained, is 'a religion without the *knowledge of God,* or the *hope of salvation;* which is deism.'[76] The result of this position is the assertion that true knowledge can only be sought within the confines of establishment. Not all conservative Anglicans were entirely hostile to Newtonianism. Horsley, for example, gave it a mixed reaction, looking at it as a means of defending the Anglican establishment, but he still stopped short of examining the mysteries of Christianity through the insights of science because of the threat this would present to religious and political stability.[77] Any challenge to the established church was strictly off the table.

It was thus the long shadow of the events of 1688 that dominated English disputes about natural theology at this time, together with debates about the relationship between reason and revelation. Tensions that had been simmering in the decades before concerning toleration and conformity, as well as the divine right of kings and divinised ecclesiology, were sharpened by the political divisions between Tory and Whig that ensued. The concepts of reason and revelation that developed were inseparable from these rifts: High Churchmen who rejected reason tended to prefer a Tory politics and an emphasis on mystery, whereas the nature and shape of natural theology was shaped by the desire to formulate a theological objection to establishment hierarchy. The Low Church Whigs appreciated how mystery and conformity had the tendency to be all too oppressive.

Those sympathetic to Whig politics were careful to resist the High Church portrayal of conflicting reason and revelation. Samuel Clarke himself expressed frustration that any attempt to think carefully about theological matters was immediately dismissed as prioritising individual reason over scripture – an accusation that he saw as utterly unjust. He was adamant that he had all along insisted on scripture rather than natural reason.[78] Advocates of reason evidently felt that they did not get a fair hearing and were unhappy that all appeals to rationality were treated as all of a kind, whether Latitudinarian, deistic or Socinian. Richard Baxter complained of the shortsightedness of Latitudinarian's accusers in making it seem that all those who have rational faith must be Socinian.[79] Entrenching a gulf between reason and the divine, however, became essential work for the Nonjurors in particular, and, consequently, they helped to cement the assumption that natural and revealed theologies were at odds. Distraught by the Glorious Revolution, they found providence unfathomable for a start. How on earth could a martyred king be thrown out of his kingdom and his followers abandoned? Gascoigne explains that this was proof for them that the ways of God are beyond human understanding and that the pride of reason had to be cast down low – a sentiment that led to frequent High Church vitriol against the new natural theology of Newton and Clarke. The High Church clerics thus charted an unholy alliance between Newtonian natural philosophy and Latitudinarianism, and treated the idea of religion without mystery with a considerable degree of suspicion.[80] For the Latitudinarians then, a Cambridge Platonist-informed account of reason was opposed to High Church ideals. Their anti-voluntarism and emphasis on the reality of ethical values consolidated a rejection of any one form of ecclesiastical government or worship. The High Church appeal to mystery was envisaged as a form of arbitrary power, which made it an inadequate and potentially dangerous response both to atheism and enthusiasm.

The frustrations of the Latitudinarians that their conception of reason was much misunderstood had plenty justification. The flourishing of natural theology in the seventeenth and eighteenth centuries did not necessarily signal the abandonment of caution about reason's abilities. Edward Fowler warns against too high an opinion of reason, but the honest soul, he says, has no such conceit about his reason. Such a person will submit reason to divine revelation and *not* the other way around, and there will be no disharmony, because there is nothing contradictory to reason in the scriptures.[81] Reason is only trusted because it is divine, and the scriptures are the ultimate revelation. The Latitudinarians could never, therefore, have accepted the deist claim that reason provides all the necessary grounds of religion, or that it is in principle unlimited. John Toland might have mined Locke's theory of ideas, but Locke himself demanded that one turn to revelation wherever reason fails because reason is only ever subsidiary.[82] The Latitudinarians were not throwing their lot in with a deistic model of rationality but were endeavouring to maintain a nuanced theological position that avoided the pitfalls of the freethinkers and the deists, the atheists, the enthusiasts and the High Church Anglicans.

Despite the tarring of Samuel Clarke with an anti-revelatory brush, he in fact makes very little distinction between Biblical theology and philosophical theology. As far as he is concerned, the relationship between scripture and reason is fluid. Moreover, attaining the light of nature is a struggle, as our reason is often diminished. He draws attention to the fact that even Plato and Cicero, the crème de la crème of pagan thought, failed to discern knowledge of God's ultimate design and ultimately recognised the need for revelation.[83] Scriptural revelation and natural theology are, he affirms, complementary ways to strive towards a single truth, and in promoting this, as Zebrowski argues, he was doing no more than following the method of the Church Fathers who were seeking to respond to pagan assertions that the way of philosophy, the search for wisdom, is superior to the way of Christ, the way of faith.[84] Unlike the High Church Anglicans, the Latitudinarians saw the Church Fathers not as representatives of an authoritative tradition but as theologians whose works could be used to demonstrate the conformity between reason and revelation.[85] Clarke's concern is that everyone should be able to read the scriptures and interpret them without relying on any form of external authority. For these reasons, his ecclesiology reduces the clergy to the role of mere guides and instructors, hence the adverse High Church reaction. Clarke was, as Zebrowski states, a man beset on all sides for good reason.[86] He challenged High Church notions of ecclesiastical authority in *The Scripture Doctrine of the Trinity* (1712), riling the establishment with his anti-Trinitarian Christology, but he also repudiated the more extreme radical politics spawned by Toland's materialism. He was a Whig through and through, but certainly no deist.

This account of reason and revelation means that the Latitudinarians should be positioned, as Spellman suggests, in between the extremes of deism on the one hand, and fideism (both its Catholic and Protestant varieties) on the other.[87] It was not that they opposed reason to a personal relationship with God; rather, they deemed personal relationship with God far more important than conforming to a single form of worship or to specific Articles of faith. Their emphasis on reason and morality was only as prominent as it was because they were responding not only to the threat of atheism but also to a Calvinist emphasis on faith, which neglected works, and to a High Church ecclesiology of conformity. The theology of reason advocated by the Latitudinarians was not, therefore, an attempt to replace theology or revelation by reason. They did not seek to ground religion in secular philosophy but to use a model of reflection on religious belief that has a long history within Christianity. The Latitudinarians were thinking and writing from a position of first-hand awareness of the theological, social and political consequences of a dominant community using divine mystery as a front to enforce conformity through political might.

Rational Dissent and the politics of reason

The Anglican Latitudinarians had an affinity with the Rational Dissenters evident until the end of the eighteenth century. Both embraced a Whig politics, and they were united in their belief in a threat from the High Church of the late seventeenth and early eighteenth centuries. This gave them a natural alliance in their opposition to what they saw as a worrying trend of the divinising of church and state, subjection to civil magistrates in matters of religion, and to subscription for religious or civil office. These made up the basic principles of Rational Dissent.[88] As the eighteenth century wore on, particularly towards the mid-century, the Latitudinarians enjoyed an increased respectability but they shared with their predecessors the conviction in the unity of reason and revelation, a dislike of sacerdotalism and a commitment to the ability of human beings to interpret the scriptures independently, according to their consciences.[89] The Rational Dissenters, as the Latitudinarians, ascribed little importance to tradition and agreed with the repudiation of the divine right of kings. They found natural allies in the Low Church Anglicans for their challenge to High Church mystical ecclesiology and the arguments of the early Latitudinarians against Calvinism were incorporated into arguments against forced subscription.

It was the rejection of what they saw as arbitrary power that grounded for the Rational Dissenters, as much as for the Latitudinarians, the conception of reason. The principles of Rational Dissenting religion were founded equally on reason and revelation and were those that 'bespeak obedience to God, rather than to man.'[90] There was no disharmony detected here between faith and reason: like the Latitudinarians, their concern was to guard against arbitrary civil power.

The Rational Dissenting education system fostered the application of reason to matters of religion and instilled in those who experienced it the value of critically assessing theological claims with the tool of reason. One figure of substantial importance for forming the structure of Dissenting education was Richard Baxter. Baxter offered a qualified Calvinism by stressing the importance of appealing to reason in the event of disagreement. The result was a Dissenting pedagogy that disdained theological schemes and favoured the practice of presenting a defence of both the orthodox and heterodox positions, encouraging students to think for themselves.[91] Doddridge reports that his tutor John Jennings was 'sometimes a Calvinist, sometimes an Arminian, and sometimes a Baxterian, as truth and evidence determine him.'[92] Doddridge was so taken by this method that he used it himself in his Academy at Northampton. He was a Calvinist, but noted for his tolerance and for his fusing of piety with rationality – an approach that inspired several succeeding generations of Dissenters.[93] Doddridge's own students would consider opposing sides of an argument before coming to a judgement – an educational method that became the formal pattern of the Dissenting Academies during the eighteenth century and one that Priestley and Price participated in. This approach necessarily refused the forcing of any particular theology on its pupils and served as a check against any stray tendencies to enthusiasm. It formed an important element of candour and was significantly more 'impartial' than the older educational style it replaced that involved expounding textbooks.[94] The assumption behind it, as Wykes points out, is that rational argument is the means to work towards the attainment of truth, including scriptural and theological truth. The result was the conversion of many orthodox students to heterodoxy particularly Arianism, encouraged in no small part by the encouragement that they should read the Bible for themselves, and by the publication of Clarke's *Scripture Doctrine*.

By and large, the Rational Dissenters prioritised the interpretation of scripture through reason. According to Israel Mauduit, who argued in favour of relaxing subscription for the Dissenters, they 'believe that the holy Scriptures are the only sufficient Rule of faith and can submit to the Authority of no human decisions as a supplemental Amendment to them.' What they rejected was the High Church authority of tradition. They hold, insisted Mauduit, all the while to the scripture containing the whole of revelation.[95] What lies behind their rationalism, and its commitment to a truth that is at least in part accissible and commanding, is a stance against the authority of mystery. The insistence that political and theological truth should be available to all was intended to confound the argument that the members of the Anglican established church necessarily knew better than they how God should be worshipped. Priestley, for example, celebrates the fact that Rational Dissent requires subscription to no Articles of faith and is 'unfettered by authority.' The result gives the faculties of the mind 'free play,' without determining beforehand the results of students' inquiries. Students are thus made wise rather than made the tools of any 'particular party.' The power of the civil magistrate is confronted directly: no civil magistrate should have power to control the press or suppress ideas. A system of uniformity is founded on 'narrow and short-sighted views of polity.'[96] For Price too, the civil magistrate has no authority to impose what he deems to be true, because there is no guarantee this is not fallible human judgement and the assertion of will.[97]

The commitment to reason in religion rested for the Rational Dissenters, therefore, on the right to private judgement. In this, they were at one with the earlier Latitudinarians, tempering the dangers of enthusiasm implicit in *sola scriptura* with an appeal to reason. Fitzpatrick reminds us it was not so much that the Rational Dissenters could not sign up to any particular doctrinal Articles but rather that they rejected subscription to any Articles as a matter of principle. For them, the right to private judgement is a non-negotiable essential part of Christianity.[98] This did not mean that reason *alone* aside from revelation was the guide to divinity but that the Bible, not the Articles of the Anglican Church, was the authority in religion. Truth comes not from scriptures interpreted by the civil magistrate or other such theological authority, but from scriptures interpreted by reason. Their model was not reason set against revelation, but reason *and* revelation set against the scriptures as capriciously interpreted by what they saw as the will of ecclesiastical power.

The previous chapter drew attention to the harder rationalism espoused by Priestley. In his later works, he proposed a synthesis of philosophy and science that judged the doctrines of religion by a Socinian-inspired rationality. In an age of reason, he says, '*Christian knowledge* should keep pace with the *philosophical*.'[99] This is a theologian who seems, as Buckley might suggest, to promote a new form of rational religion grounded on the enlightened values of an empirical way of understanding human beings and the wider world. As Priestley saw it, any theories that went against empirical, historical or logical evidence must be rejected. It should be emphasised, however, that behind Priestley's method is a dispute about power and authority. Reason is pitted first and foremost against mystery: 'If what is called a *mystery of Christianity*, be really a falsehood in philosophy . . . the belief of it must be abandoned altogether.'[100] Mystery was political as much as theological. When Priestley defends Christianity, it is against those who already claim to believe: Calvinists, Trinitarians, Catholics and Platonists.

As he saw it, the Calvinists appealed to mystery through their promotion of enthusiasm. The Trinitarians – especially High Church Anglicans – relied on mystery to prop up the establishment. Catholicism was a religion of mystery for its ecclesiology, and Platonism was to blame for justifying the Trinitarian error in the first place. In all cases, appeals to mystery helped to enforce hegemonic power structures or the subordination of one person under the will of another. 'Distrust, therefore, all those who decry human reason, and who require you to abandon it, wherever religion is concerned. When once they have gained this point with you, they can lead you whither they please.'[101] It was within two church establishments that Priestley found the greatest corruption of Christianity: the Church of England and the Catholic Church. True Christianity, he insisted, would not be allied to the state, and it was 'institutional prejudices' as much as 'Platonic mysteries' that left him distressed over the corruption of Christianity.[102]

Priestley's understanding of natural theology follows on from this. That there can be no mystery means there can be no contradiction between God's word and God's work. Natural religion included in its scope 'all that can be demonstrated, or proved to be true by natural reason,' but Priestley still insisted that what could be demonstrated by natural reason 'was never, in fact, discovered by it; and even though it would be probable that mankind would never have known it without the assistance of revelation.' For Priestley, reason – and with it natural theology – is always, secondary to revelation.[103] He would have complained as loudly as the Latitudinarians about the High Church attempts to divide reason from revelation. It was Priestley's conviction in this harmony between reason and revelation that led him to declare reason the sole interpreter of scripture. It must be remembered that the shared characteristic of all the Rational Dissenters was the conviction that human reason on its own was incapable of understanding the nature and activity of God.[104] John Jebb, as Fitzpatrick argues, came closest to deist theology in his presumption that human reason can independently attain the same truths of revelation but even for him natural religion was only ever a pale imitation of revealed Christianity. Natural religion can only teach us to hope for a hereafter and for forgiveness, but revelation assures us of it.[105] This means that despite Priestley's 'harder' rationalism, he did not abandon revealed for natural theology and, as James Hoecker points out, his appeal to revelation would have actually seemed rather peculiar to those more inclined towards deism.[106] As suggested in Chapter 1, what was essential to debates about reason were disputes about the Bible and who has the power and authority to define and impose orthodox interpretations of it.

What galled the Rational Dissenters was the very fact of subscription. Lindsey reports that Price would have sooner been silenced or imprisoned 'than comply with such a requisition from the civil magistrate, to intitle him to the liberty of worshipping his Maker in his own way.'[107] What he wanted was freedom of worship and he was one of a growing number of voices who decried any authority of the magistrate over conscience. The Rational Dissenters thus interpreted the theology of freedom of conscience, so much a part of Latitudinarian politics, in a very radical way and insisted far more than Locke and their Latitudinarian peers on the separation of church and state.[108] The conception of reason in the period of Enlightenment in England is shaped, therefore, by disputes about power, arbitrary will and theological and political authority in a context of intolerance and the continuous threat of suppression.

The Rational Dissenters shared with the Latitudinarians a theology of divine reason that was opposed to arbitrary human power and the dangers of this implicit in established religion. This led to porous boundaries between moderate Anglicanism and Rational Dissent. In fact, many later eighteenth-century Rational Dissenters were originally part of the Church of England, including Gilbert Wakefield, William Frend, Disney and Lindsey. Webb therefore speaks quite rightly of a continuum of rational religion in which Dissenters are numerically less significant than Churchmen and in which Unitarians do not entirely exhaust Dissent.[109] Jebb, who is perhaps closer to deism, promoted a rational Christianity that has undergone a 'Second Reformation' to purge it of superstition, but his theology was inherently political: orthodox Christianity was in danger of having to rely on political power in an era that saw many conservative Anglicans quarantine orthodox theology from the interrogation of science and philosophy.[110]

What this demonstrates is that apparent disputes about reason and revelation and England in the late seventeenth and eighteenth centuries were often in fact disputes about authority in scriptural interpretation and religious conformity. Epicurean materialism, Hobbesian atheism, Calvinist voluntarism and High Church Toryism shared a common danger for the Latitudinarians and Rational Dissenters: all threatened to subvert the immutability of goodness with the supremacy of will. The result was a philosophy of religion and a conception of reason that was developed in the hands of the Cambridge Platonists, Latitudinarians and, later, Rational Dissenters to curtail the power of will, end the pressure to conform and champion the reality of ethical value. In the eighteenth century, attitudes to reason, including self-evidence, remained political, but reason was not contrasted with revelation. If reason measured faith, as Standish complained, it was not an alternative to revelation but a challenge to arbitrary will determining a normative interpretation of revelation or 'truth,' or demanding conformity. The resultant theological method of both the Latitudinarians and the Rational Dissenters proposed in short that truth could be discovered through rational investigation as opposed to the custodians of the established church.[111] How this works out in some of the specific arguments that comprise natural theology is taken up in the next chapter.

Notes

1 John Standish, *A Sermon Preached before the King at White-Hal, September 26th 1675* (London: Printed by Henry Brome, 1676), 24–5.

2 John Gascoigne, *Cambridge in the Age of Enlightenment: Science, Religion and Politics from the Restoration to the French Revolution* (Cambridge: Cambridge University Press, 1989), 45.
3 Miles Barne, *The Authority of Church-Guides Asserted in a Sermon Prech'd before Our Late Gracious Sovereign King Charles II at Whitehall, Oct 17th 1675* (London: Printed for Richard Green, 1685), 2.
4 Gascoigne, *Age of Enlightenment*, 45.
5 James Barr, *Biblical Faith and Natural Theology* (Oxford: Clarendon, 1993), 1.
6 See, e.g., John Spurr, " 'Latitudinarianism' and the Restoration Church," *The Historical Journal* 31, no. 1 (1988): 67.
7 Ralph Cudworth, *The True Intellectual System of the Universe. . . with a Treatise Concerning Eternal and Immutable Morality*, ed. John Harrison, vol. i (London: Thomas Tegg, 1845), xliv.
8 Cudworth, *TIS*, vol. i, xlviii, 509–10.
9 Ralph Cudworth, "The Digression Concerning the Plastick Life of Nature, or an Artificial, Orderly and Methodical Nature," in *The Cambridge Platonists*, ed. C. A. Patrides (Cambridge: Cambridge University Press, 1969), 323; See Mark Philp, *Godwin's Political Justice* (London: Duckworth, 1986), 323, for more discussion of the term's use.
10 Quoted in C. A. Patrides, " 'The High and Aiery Hills of Platonisme': An Introduction to the Cambridge Platonists," in *The Cambridge Platonists*, ed. C. A. Patrides (Cambridge: Cambridge University Press, 1969), 22.
11 Cudworth, *TIS*, vol. iii, 32.
12 Cudworth, *TIS*, vol. iii, 34–5.
13 Plato, *Theaetetus*, trans. Robin A. H. Waterfield (London: Penguin, 1987), 152a.
14 Cudworth, *TIS*, vol. iii, 35–6.
15 John Bramhall, *The Works of the Most Reverend Father in God, John Bramhall*, ed. A. W. Haddan, vol. 4 (Oxford: John Henry Parker, 1844), 193.
16 This question was posed by Bramhall out of concern for the power Hobbes gave to the civil magistrates. Bramhall, *Works*, 4: 196.
17 Plato, "Euthyphro," in *The Last Days of Socrates*, trans. Hugh Tredennick (London: Penguin, 1959), 10a.
18 Charles Taliaferro, *Evidence and Faith: Philosophy and Religion since the Seventeenth Century* (Cambridge: Cambridge University Press, 2005), 13.
19 Taliaferro, *Evidence and Faith*, 12.
20 Ralph Cudworth, "A Sermon Preached before the House of Commons," in *The Cambridge Platonists*, ed. C. A. Patrides (Cambridge: Cambridge University Press, 1969), 102.
21 Taliaferro makes this point in *Evidence and Faith*, 17.
22 Frederick C. Beiser, *The Sovereignty of Reason: The Defense of Rationality in the Early English Enlightenment* (Princeton: Princeton University Press, 1996), 141.
23 Douglas Hedley, "Real Atheism and Cambridge Platonism: Men of Latitude, Polemics, and the Great Dead Philosophers," in *Platonisms: Ancient, Modern, and Postmodern*, ed. Kevin Corrigan and John D. Turner (Leiden: Brill, 2007), 157; Beiser, *Sovereignty of Reason*, 147.
24 Hedley, "Real Atheism," 156–7, 165.
25 Hedley, "Real Atheism," 160.
26 "Well now, how can one argue for the existence of gods without getting angry?" Hedley, "Real Atheism," 159.
27 Hedley, "Real Atheism," 161.
28 Hedley, "Real Atheism," 159.
29 Hedley, "Real Atheism," 162.

30 Cudworth, *TIS*, vol. ii, 625.
31 Richard H. Popkin, "The Crisis of Polytheism and the Answers of Vollius, Cudworth, and Newton," in *Essays on the Context, Nature, and Influence of Isaac Newton's Theology*, ed. James Force and Richard H. Popkin (London: Kluwer Academic Publishers, 1990), 9 and 22n.
32 Popkin, "Crisis of Polytheism," 16.
33 Cudworth, *TIS*, vol. ii, 626, 630.
34 Cudworth, *TIS*, vol. ii, 569, 564.
35 Cudworth, *TIS*, vol. ii, 533; FM.4983: 22, quoted in Benjamin Carter, 'The Little Commonwealth of Man': The Trinitarian Origins of the Ethical and Political Philosophy of Ralph Cudworth* (Leuven: Peeters, 2011), 235.
36 Cudworth, *TIS*, vol. ii, 557.
37 Cudworth, *TIS*, vol. ii, 576.
38 Ernst Cassirer, *The Platonic Renaissance in England*, trans. James P. Pettegrove (New York: Nelson, 1953), 77–8.
39 Carter, *Commonwealth*, 122.
40 Both quoted in Carter, *Commonwealth*, 127.
41 Taliaferro, *Evidence and Faith*, 13.
42 Gascoigne, *Age of Enlightenment*, 41.
43 Gascoigne, *Age of Enlightenment*, 41.
44 Joseph Beaumont, *Some Observations upon the Apologie of Dr Henry More for His Mystery of Godliness* (Cambridge: Printed by John Field, 1665), 143.
45 G. M. Ditchfield, "Joseph Priestley and the Complexities of Latitudinarianism in the 1770s," in *Joseph Priestley, Scientist, Philosopher and Theologian*, ed. Isabel Rivers and David L. Wykes (Oxford: Oxford University Press, 2008), 150.
46 Gascoigne, *Age of Enlightenment*, 64.
47 Gascoigne, *Age of Enlightenment*, 64.
48 Quoted in Gascoigne, *Age of Enlightenment*, 47.
49 W. M. Spellman, *The Latitudinarians and the Church of England, 1660–1700* (Athens, Georgia: University of Georgia Press, 1993), 29.
50 Gascoigne, *Age of Enlightenment*, 50.
51 Simon Patrick, *A Brief Account of the New Sect of Latitude-Men Together with Some Reflections upon the New Philosophy* (London, 1662), 5.
52 Hedley, "Real Atheism," 171.
53 Spellman, *Latitudinarians*, 26.
54 John Toland, *Christianity Not Mysterious or, a Treatise Shewing, That There Is Nothing in the Gospel Contrate to Reason, nor above It: And That No Christian Doctrine Can Be Properly Call'd a Mystery* (London, 1702), 1.
55 Spellman, *Latitudinarians*, 148.
56 Spellman, *Latitudinarians*, 148; Thomas Aquinas, *Summa Contra Gentiles*, trans. English Dominican Fathers, vol. 1 (London: Burns, Oates & Washbourne, 1923), I.iii.
57 Anon., *A Free and Impartial Inquiry* (London: Printed by J. M., for Richard Royston, 1673) quoted in Spurr, "Latitudinarianism," 80.
58 Ditchfield, "Joseph Priestley," 147.
59 Larry Stewart, "Samuel Clarke, Newtonianism, and the Factions of Post-Revolutionary England," *Journal of the History of Ideas* 42, no. 1 (1981): 62.
60 Gascoigne, *Age of Enlightenment*, 77.
61 Gascoigne, *Age of Enlightenment*, 237.
62 Ditchfield, "Joseph Priestley," 147; Martin Fitzpatrick, "Latitudinarianism at the Parting of the Ways: A Suggestion," in *The Church of England c.1689-c.1833: From Toleration to Tractarianism*, ed. John Walsh, Colin Haydon, and Stephen Taylor (Cambridge: Cambridge University Press, 1993), 211.

63 John Walsh and Stephen Taylor, "Introduction: The Church and Anglicanism in the 'Long' Eighteenth Century," in *The Church of England c.1689-c.1833: From Toleration to Tractarianism*, ed. John Walsh, Colin Haydon, and Stephen Taylor (Cambridge: Cambridge University Press, 1993), 46 discuss this tension in more depth.

64 Stewart, "Samuel Clarke," 64.

65 Quoted in Stewart, "Samuel Clarke," 64.

66 Jamie C. Kassler, *Seeking Truth: Roger North's Notes on Newton and Correspondence with Samuel Clarke c.1704–1713* (Farnham: Ashgate, 2014), 240.

67 Quoted in Robert E. Sullivan, *John Toland and the Deist Controversy: A Study in Adaptations* (Cambridge, MA: Harvard University Press, 1982), 81.

68 Gascoigne, *Age of Enlightenment*, 77.

69 Spellman, *Latitudinarians*, 116–17, 29.

70 Benjamin Hoadly, *A Preservative against the Principles and Practices of the Non-Jurors Both in Church and State* (Dublin: Printed by A. Rhames, for E. Dobson, 1716).

71 Leslie Stephen, *History of English Thought in the Eighteenth Century*, vol. II (London: Smith, Elder & Co., 1876), 152; Bolingbroke quoted in Gascoigne, *Age of Enlightenment*, 116.

72 Gascoigne, *Age of Enlightenment*, 131; John Jackson, *The Grounds of Civil and Ecclesiastical Government Briefly Considered* (London: Printed for James Knapton, 1718), 5.

73 Samuel Clarke, *The Works of Samuel Clarke*, vol. i (London: Printed for John and Paul Knapton, 1738), 631–2.

74 Quoted in Alan P. F. Sell, "Henry Grove: A Dissenter at the Parting of the Ways," *Enlightenment and Dissent* 4 (1985): 53.

75 Gascoigne, *Age of Enlightenment*, 247.

76 Quoted in Gascoigne, *Age of Enlightenment*, 247.

77 Anthony Page, "The Enlightenment and a 'Second Reformation': The Religion and Philosophy of John Jebb (1736–86)," *Enlightenment and Dissent* 17 (1998): 60.

78 John Jackson, *Three Letters to Dr Clarke, from a Clergyman of the Church of England; Concerning His Scripture-Doctrine of the Trinity: With the Doctor's Replies* (London: Printed for John Baker, 1714), 31. Clarke to Jackson, 23 October 1714.

79 Sell, "Henry Grove," 57.

80 Gascoigne, *Age of Enlightenment*, 165, 171.

81 Edward Fowler, *The Design of Christianity; or, a Plain Demonstration and Improvement of This Proposition, Viz. That the Enduing Men with Inward Real Righteousness or True Holiness, Was the Ultimate End of Our Saviour's Coming into the World and Is the Great Intendment of His Blessed Gospel* (London: Printed by E. Tyler and R. Holt, 1670), 274–5.

82 Spellman, *Latitudinarians*, 87.

83 Samuel Clarke, "A Discourse Concerning the Being and Attributes of God," in *The Works of Samuel Clarke*, vol. ii (London: Printed for John and Paul Knapton, 1738), 657–7.

84 Martha K. Zebrowski, "Commanded of God, Because 'Tis Holy and Good': The Christian Platonism and Natural Law of Samuel Clarke," *Enlightenment and Dissent* 16 (1997): 10.

85 Gascoigne, *Age of Enlightenment*, 57.

86 Martha K. Zebrowski, "Richard Price: British Platonist of the Eighteenth Century," *Journal of the History of Ideas* 55, no. 1 (1994): 5; Zebrowski, "Commanded of God," 9.

87 Spellman, *Latitudinarians.*
88 Ditchfield, "Joseph Priestley," 146, 150.
89 Ditchfield, "Joseph Priestley," 147; Fitzpatrick, "Latitudinarianism," 211.
90 John Disney, *Sermons*, vol. 2 (Cambridge: Printed for T. Payne; T. Cadell; J. Woodyer, 1771), 201.
91 See David L. Wykes, "The Contribution of the Dissenting Academy to the Emergence of Rational Dissent," in *Enlightenment and Religion: Rational Dissent in Eighteenth-Century Britain*, ed. Knud Haakonssen (Cambridge: Cambridge University Press, 1996), 127 for more on the teaching methods in the Dissenting Academies.
92 Quoted in Wykes, "Dissenting Academy," 128.
93 R. K. Webb, "The Emergence of Rational Dissent," in *Enlightenment and Religion: Rational Dissent in Eighteenth-Century Britain*, ed. Knud Haakonssen (Cambridge: Cambridge University Press, 1996), 36.
94 Wykes, "Dissenting Academy," 137.
95 Quoted in Martin Fitzpatrick, "Toleration and Truth," *Enlightenment and Dissent* 1 (1982): 4.
96 Joseph Priestley, "Essay on the First Principles of Government," in *Works*, vol. xxii, 1817, 131, 132–3.
97 Richard Price, *Four Dissertations* (Bristol: Thoemmes, 1990), 366.
98 Fitzpatrick, "Toleration," 5.
99 Joseph Priestley, "The History of the Philosophical Doctrine Concerning the Origin of the Soul, and the Nature of Matter with Its Influence on Christianity Especially with Respect to the Doctrine of the Pre-Existence of Christ: Being a Sequel to the Disquisitions Concerning Matter and Spirit," in *Works*, vol. iii, 1817, 388.
100 Joseph Priestley, "Letter to Dr. Kenrick," in *Works*, vol. iv, 1817, 143.
101 James J. Hoecker, "Joseph Priestley and the Reification of Religion," *Price Priestley Newsletter* 2 (1978): 46; Joseph Priestley, "An Appeal to the Serious and Candid Professors of Christianity," in *Works*, vol. ii, 1817, 384.
102 Hoecker, "Joseph Priestley," 51, 53.
103 Joseph Priestley, "Institutes of Natural Religion," in *Works*, vol. ii, 1817, 2; Hoecker, "Joseph Priestley," 49.
104 Fitzpatrick, "Toleration," 29.
105 John Jebb, *The Works, Theological, Medical, Political, and Miscellaneous of John Jebb with Memoirs of the Life of the Author by John Disney*, vol. II (London: Printed for T. Cadell, 1787), 34–5; 137–8; 178.
106 Hoecker, "Joseph Priestley," 48.
107 Quoted in Fitzpatrick, "Toleration," 7.
108 Fitzpatrick, "Toleration," 6.
109 Webb, "Emergence," 40.
110 Page, "Enlightenment," 56.
111 Fitzpatrick, "Toleration," 29.

4 The ethical cosmos

Natural theology, epistemic humility and the immutability of goodness

The previous chapter has shown that engaging in natural theology in eighteenth-century England was an act with weighty political connotations. Debates about reason and revelation were politically charged. When it comes to considering the aims of these arguments and assessing what worth they might have their context is of crucial importance, and it shows they have an irreducible ethical and political nature. What remains now is to consider the content of some the arguments themselves.

Not widely renowned for his natural theology today, Richard Price is of particular interest to this book because he represents the continuation in the mid-late eighteenth century of a tradition of physico-theology that has its roots in Plato, the Cambridge Platonists, Isaac Newton and Samuel Clarke. In his *Dissertation on the Being and Attributes of the Deity*, published in 1787 as part of the third edition of the *Review* but written years before, Price presents two arguments for the existence of God: an argument from the contingent nature of the world and an argument from design.

A consideration of these arguments brings several things to light. First, the central characteristic of his natural theology must be recognised as its ethical nature. Due acknowledgement of this aspect of the tradition of natural theology of which Price is a part guides us towards a re-conception of natural theology as innately ethical and political. Second, Price's arguments have what Colin Crowder has identified as an ambiguity. They express elements of both a natural theology (seen particularly in the argument *from* design) and a theology of nature (in the argument *to* design). There is a tension here, and there is evidence of what has been called a turn to a harder rationalism, something also present in other natural theologies of this century.[1] What is of most importance in considering these arguments, however, is the recognition that this tradition of natural theology put ethical concerns at the forefront. The tension inherent in the arguments should be seen as the result of an account of reason that tries to embody a *via media* between deism, enthusiasm and Biblical fundamentalism emerging from a High Church hostile to Newton. This was held together with a commitment to a divinised universe, based not so much on rational argument but on intuition. Vital to these arguments, as part of their commitment to reason, was the prioritisation of epistemic humility. The result of all this is that they point towards a model of a theology of nature that is to be valued for the new insights it gives rise to, rather than for the metaphysical claims it tries to prove rationally.

A cosmology of divinised nature

Design and providence: natural theology and the theology of nature

Price presents two different versions of the design argument in his writings. The first type is an argument *from* design occurring in his *Being and Attributes of the Deity* and in the *Four Dissertations*, and the second type is the argument *to* design found in the *Review*. The first type attempts to infer a designing cause from the order perceived in nature. As far as he sees it, 'It is impossible to survey the world without being assured, that the contrivance in it has proceeded from some contriver, the design in it from some *designing* cause and the art it displays from some artist.'[2] He spends very little time on the argument in the *Being and Attributes* regarding it as immediately intuitive or self-evident. The *Four Dissertations* give it more of an airing. The argument is set within a larger discussion of providence, and it is contrasted in explanatory terms with mechanistic philosophy. It seems clear to Price that the phenomena of nature cannot be explained purely by mechanistic powers. He speculates that the primary causes of things surely ought to be some sort of power or principle, not something mechanical. There are many different creatures, he argues, all placed in circumstances adapted to their natures. This not only signals for him that there is some sort of plan or constitution of nature by which all created beings are provided for but also that there is an influence of the Deity *continually* in effect to maintain this ordered constitution. He thus infers from the cosmos a higher degree of wisdom, power and goodness in the Creator than that exhibited in creation itself.[3]

In the *Review*, he presents an argument *to* design. This is not an argument based on any sort of inference or explanation but one that advocates consciously a Platonic account of a value-laden universe. Plato's Demiurge of the *Timaeus* models creation on the archetypal ideas, part of the divine nature.[4] Price took this theology, as did the earlier Platonists, as an ethical argument: the cosmos is infused with divine value modelled on ethical archetypes. Morality is not only existent but also part and parcel of the physical constituents of the cosmos. The design argument was well known and widely accepted in the mid-eighteenth century. The formulations of it articulated before Paley's 1802 version rested on the analogy of human and divine contrivance and argued for a final cause for both. Paley's more (in)famous later version sought a similarity between natural and artificial mechanism and tried to establish the same kind of mechanical principles in human and divine contrivances.[5] The earlier version, however, has a long history, presented by Cudworth in the *True Intellectual System*, by More in his *Antidote against Atheism* and by Stillingfleet in *Origines Sacrae*.[6] John Wilkins later took up the argument, which he may have inherited from More – or possibly Stillingfleet – in his *Of the Principles and Duties of Natural Religion*, where he articulates a simpler and, for this reason, much more popular version of it.

The nub of Cudworth's argument, which is inherited in the versions articulated by these aforementioned Latitudinarians and in Price's later argument, is about the nature of knowledge and value. Cudworth is concerned to avoid two diametrically opposed positions: the first that chance is responsible for the order of matter (as Epicurus and Democritus suggested) and the second that God acts immediately on creation (as in Descartes's mechanism). It is impossible for Cudworth that 'dead and senseless matter' can form any sort of orderly system. In response, his design argument appeals to final causes in nature and envisages the only proper explanation for any event in nature as one that involves a final cause for ends (principally goodness). This, for Cudworth, is perfectly in keeping with Aristotle's own explanations of things in terms of final causes and his opposition to Democritus. The form of each animal, and the system of the world as a whole, are marked by regularities, and they act as if directed by wisdom. As he sees it, 'mere fortune and chance' could never have given rise to this, as the 'divine Mind and Wisdom' has 'printed its seal' on the matter of the corporeal world.[7]

The atheists, therefore, are mistaken according to Cudworth. They are not wrong just because they posit the wrong cause (chance) as an explanatory principle, however, but because they invert the meaning of *telos*. They argue that things are not *designed* for their uses but come into being *through* their use.[8] What is at issue here is not also an argument against atheists who deny the reality of a designing cause but also against anyone who would deny the reality of ethical value and reject knowledge and truth as existing outside of the knower. The problem with the atheists' account is principally relativism, not unbelief. Knowledge according to the atheist can only come into existence with a knower. For Cudworth, however, knowledge is not ectypal but archetypal: it is older than the world and the maker of all things.[9] Final causes, and the direction of the universe by the wisdom of God, are what ensure the underpinning of the natural world with transcendent value. This is a theology apparent in Plato's *Timaeus*, but it also coheres with the philosophy of Aristotle. A chance universe is one that leaves ethics in distinct peril and opens the door to the relativistic manipulation of value. This explains why Descartes's mechanism omits what Cudworth sees as the most pressing question: has God made anything for ends and good? The Cartesian argument in ignoring the 'organisation and formation of the bodies of animals' gets rid of final causes.[10] The most important investigation, for Cudworth, is not one about ends in the sense of drawing conclusions about what ought to be, but one that addresses whether things are made by God for good rather than coming into being by chance.[11]

Within Cudworth's *True Intellectual System* then, there is an argument *from* design and one *to* design, and both are held together out of concern to safeguard the physical universe as a moral universe. Nature itself is full of reasons, power and order. It is not dead and mechanical but, as Proclus asserts, proceeds from 'that supreme goddess, the Divine wisdom, which is the fountain of all life' both intellectual life and the life within matter.[12] Cudworth's vision of the natural world is of something infused with the divine life, making what is effectively an argument *to* design perfectly intuitive to him. The boundary between this argument and the one that seeks to argue *from* the natural world to a divine being is ambiguous. True philosophy, Cudworth remarks, is the knowledge of causes, and this leads necessarily to God.[13] This is not quite as simple as just reading off evidence of a divine designer from the natural world, however. Both types of argument are concerned primarily with the nature of morality. It is an appreciation for final causes – in other words, for the moral basis of the cosmos – that leads to the divine being. True philosophy is thus a moral enterprise. This particular argument from design is therefore one that cannot function aside from a consideration of the universe's moral nature. The drive behind Cudworth's argument is the conviction that nature is not 'dead' but rather replete with value. Chance cannot give a full explanation and nothing in nature can be explained without considering design 'or intention for ends and good,' which means that the mechanical world view of the atheists cannot explain natural justice and morality.[14]

The design argument is therefore an argument about the nature of ethical value, and it should be read in the context of Cudworth's anti-voluntarism as outlined in the previous chapters. It is concerned first and foremost with a defence of the immutability of value perceived as infusing the physical cosmos. This physico-theology gives the natural world a value and reality of its own, not determined solely by us.

The Cambridge Platonists' concept of plastic nature is articulated within this ethical framework. The plastic principle is a cause of production and generation, which acts for ends and it is used to defend the reality of final causes in nature, transfusing divine final purposes into nature. This doctrine enabled a middle way between the extremes of seeing God as acting immediately on nature (as in the case of a miracle) and the conception of matter as senseless.[15] Nature is in this way given an independence from the divine dictates. The principle of plastic nature safeguards the possibility of the contemplation of nature in the face of Descartes's voluntarism and its conception of arbitrary nature. If the whim of God's will can cancel or amend the laws of nature at any point, as Descartes suggested, it would be an impossible undertaking to contemplate nature. As Descartes saw it, we cannot even try to contemplate divine purpose in the natural world. If this is the case, all that is left is human projection onto nature. Plastic nature thus grants nature a degree of autonomy, which enables it to be self-producing and therefore free from the arbitrary impulses of God's will.

The ethical character of the Cambridge Platonists' philosophy shaped the English physico-theology that came after it in the late seventeenth and early eighteenth centuries. The ethical nature of the design argument is evident in John Wilkins's restatement of it, as part of his attempt to challenge the free-thinkers by showing the necessary connection between religion and ethics.[16] Thomas Wise's *A Confutation of the Reason and Philosophy of Atheism* (1706), condensed the *True Intellectual System* and utilised Stillingfleet's and Wilkins's arguments to support Cudworth's philosophy against Cartesian mechanism.

Price's argument inherits this tradition of ethical physico-theology, and it bears much closer similarities with Platonic forms of the design argument than with the deistic formulations of natural theology that became more widespread as the eighteenth century wore on. The first Dissertation presents an argument from design within the context of a discussion of providence as part of an attempt to urge theological reflection on continuous divine providential action in the general course of nature (as opposed to both occasional miraculous events and to action as initial first cause).[17] The express purpose of his argument is to defend an omnipresent God who is active in the world and who cares for it. His starting point is book ten of Plato's *Laws*, and the discussion is set within a context of reflection on Matthew 6:28.[18] God's care extends to all creatures of the cosmos, including the lilies of the field and the birds of the air. Creation itself should, therefore, be read as continuous, not restricted to one initial creative act.

Price expresses surprise at the evident human obsession with miraculous events, which ignores contemplation of the normal functioning of nature. Consider the organisation of any flower or herb of the field, or the structure of the human body, he asks, and then consider whether it is credible that the maker of these things does not have wisdom? For Price, it is the organisation of a flower rather than a spectacular miracle that should grab our attention.[19] The discussion about providence is clear enough in its central message: the Deity pervades and actuates the entire material world. He is trying to shift the philosophical gaze onto the flower as it is, rather than maintain a focus on individual instances of miracle. The act of creation was not merely the imposing of a template in one initial creative act, but rather it manifests itself continuously: every new creature he states is the production of divine power.[20] This is a doctrine of continuing creation, the constant assertion, as he puts it, of divine power throughout all of nature. What he points towards is a model of God's action as sustaining and upholding rather than a deistic first cause or *deus ex machina*.[21]

The result is a natural theology that arises to a significant extent from a Platonically inspired account of divine action and creation. Price's suspicions about plastic nature, however, see him assert a model of God's action instilling final causation in the cosmos *directly*. Much of this is due to his courting of a Newtonian metaphysic. He follows Samuel Clarke in denying that even God could add the power of thought to matter. Both Price and Clarke could only countenance mind or immaterial soul as capable of thinking and acting freely.[22] Price's commitment to the inactivity of matter leads him to worry that plastic nature is a threat to the argument for design because it implies an unintelligent agent can act to produce regularity in nature.[23] He embraces instead the Newtonian theology of God's immediate direct action on nature. What Price has in common with the Cambridge Platonist account of plastic nature, however, is an emphasis on a continually pervasive providence. The tone of the argument is distinctly anti-deistic.

Price's argument *to* design in the *Review* results from his moral philosophy and is an integral part of his Platonic epistemology, sitting in harmony with the anti-voluntarism essential to Cudworth's case. The embrace of reason had (as Chapter 3 has argued) distinct political overtones, and Price's argument is one that is concerned to defend the absolute nature of value and the supremacy of goodness over will. The argument rests on the *Review's* positing of moral ideas as archetypal: present to the divine mind but independent of God's will. Price's Platonic epistemology, Zebrowski argues, forms what is in essence a Platonic argument to design that follows the depiction Plato gives us in the *Timaeus* of the Demiurge as the best of causes modelling the cosmos on the best of archetypes. The demiurge uses the archetypes as both foundation and guide and, given the perfection of the model, the cosmos could not be shaped in any other way.[24] Immutable morality is, for Price, 'the source and guide of all the actions of the Deity himself, and on it his throne and government are founded.'[25]

The created world is, therefore, underpinned by its inescapable moral nature, and its integrity as an archetype in the philosophy of both Plato and Price is absolute, thus remaining steadfast regardless of the direction of the divine will. As Zebrowski states, the archetypal truth 'is compelling to the perfect God, the necessary design of his intentional creation in all of its moral and material aspects.'[26] These elements of the argument *to* design underpin the argument in the *Four Dissertations* too. In the context of his discussion of Plato's *Laws*, he affirms Plato's argument that the universal mind, which 'actuates all things' is 'possest of all perfection.'[27] From here, Price argues for God's care of all things, however great or small. God's perfection is necessarily benevolent. The argument cannot work, however, without a commitment to the universe as, in a deeply Platonic sense, both underpinned and suffused with value: value that is entirely independent of divine or human will and power. The Deity's 'goodness will as certainly engage him to direct [all things] agreeably to the ends of goodness, as his wisdom and power enable him.'[28]

What this gives us is a conception of design that holds two very different arguments together. Colin Crowder suggests these two types of argument make Price's argument essentially ambivalent.[29] It struggles with two opposing poles: one that embraces a standpoint of faith that might be called more accurately (to use the terminology of Pamela Sue Anderson, Ian Barbour and others) a theology of nature and another that has as its goal rational justification. For Price, the argument *to* design is from the standpoint of commitment to a divinised cosmos – a standpoint of faith from which theology reflects on value-laden nature. The inference of the divine *from* the existence of apparent adaption reveals the impetus to provide rational evidence for religious belief, which stands in some contrast with the intuitive certainty of God's existence: an intuition that Price appeals to in the Dissertation on Providence while directing his readers to the *Review* and its arguments from reflection on the nature of truth and morality.[30] The argument in fact, however, does not offer a straightforward inference of God's existence on the basis of apparent design but rather rests on the possibility of inference grounded implicitly in the cosmos as ethically conceived. The argument from design cannot work properly without an argument to design. That Price, together with others in this physico-theological tradition, cannot conceive of natural theology without revelation means that he cannot have intended the argument from design to work entirely independently. The argument *to* design is the one that forms the bedrock of his natural theology.

Contingency, space and a cosmology of sacred places

Price opens his *Dissertation* with a summary and endorsement of the consensus between all those who use the argument from contingency:

> The existence of all beings is either *contingent* or *necessary*. All beings exist *contingently* whose non-existence is *possible*; and the non-existence of all beings is *possible*, whose non-existence implies no contradiction. Our own existence and the existence of the whole visible world is *contingent*. All that exists contingently; and which, therefore, might or might not have existed, requires a reason or cause of its existence. There must, therefore, be a cause of our own existence and of the existence of the world.[31]

As D. O. Thomas points outs, the argument can only hold water if 'the world necessarily has a cause' is confused and equated with 'the world has a necessary – non-contingent – cause,' but Price offers no argument that the ultimate cause must be a cause of its own existence.[32] Price, however, is not satisfied with the argument as it stands here because it does not give a clear enough account of the nature of necessary existence. It is the attribute of necessary existence that marks the ontological distinction between God and everything else in existence, and which forms the basis for the rest of God's attributes. The focus of the *Dissertation* is geared, therefore, towards unpacking this complicated and, according to Price, much misunderstood concept.

The main inspiration for Price's treatment of necessity is Samuel Clarke. In Clarkean language, he distinguishes God's necessity from 'relative' and 'consequential necessity,' which is explained as a mere inference of cause from effect.[33] Rejecting the formulation of the cosmological argument that infers the existence of God as necessary cause from the existence of the cosmos as effect, Price goes on to claim instead that God's necessary existence is self-evident: it is 'not grounded upon or deduced from any facts or arguments' because God's non-existence is 'an impossibility appearing *immediately*, and carrying its own evidence with it.'[34] It is Samuel Clarke's argument that forms the substance of Price's discussion, and although he wished to correct what he saw as Clarke's misleading language of necessity, he embraces Clarke's attempt to argue for the necessity of God's existence.

There are several arguments presented. The first is that God's 'non-existence cannot be *conceived* without a contradiction,' for otherwise God's non-existence would be possible. Everything that is, is conceivable and cannot imply a contradiction. Price continues by arguing that God's existence is necessary for the 'very *conception* of all other existence.'[35] Again, this argument is drawn consciously from Clarke. Nothing can be conceived to exist without God, so God is necessary for the conception of anything. Price appeals to the authority of Clarke's first letter to Joseph Butler to argue that whatever exists necessarily has to be supposed in the conception of anything else. For Clarke, 'the existence of *any thing whatever*, includes necessarily a *Presupposition* of the existence of *Space* and *Time*,' and Price concurs that we cannot conceive of the material world without space and time, hence they are necessary.[36] Abstract duration and space are necessary to the conception of all existence. The argument is one that rests on the assumption not only that space and time are necessarily to be presupposed for the conception of anything but also that space and time are properties of the self-existent substance, God. God is, therefore, regarded as the 'substratum' of space and time, 'the *Ground* of the Existence of *Space and Duration itself*.'[37]

Price acknowledges the argument that God constitutes infinite space; duration is not original to Clarke but is proposed before him by Newton. This particular English tradition of physico-theology is identified by Buckley as a supplement to the Cartesian-Spinozan tradition that usurps faith for reason and inaugurates the self-alienation of reason. The natural theology of Newton and Clarke is for Buckley a philosophical approach to religion that replaced personal involvement with inferential knowledge, the commitment of faith with rationality, and the God of the theologians with a hypothesis. 'Christianity' at this time, he protests, 'would not accept the scepticism of the fifteenth and sixteenth centuries as its canonical appraisal of the human intellect, and then affirm the divine existence through an irrational faith glorying over epistemological ruins.'[38]

A closer look at this tradition reveals, however, that it rests on a theology of a divinised cosmos. As with the arguments concerning design, natural theology cannot easily be separated from a theology of nature. It must be acknowledged that in his treatment of space, Newton did introduce what is essentially a god of the gaps to satisfy his physical system, but in Clarke's hands, the argument is set within the framework of the *Euthyphro* dilemma in which power is curbed by wisdom. For both writers, the argument would not work without a prior faith commitment to a divinised cosmos with God as the ground of value. As with the design argument, Clarke's argument about contingency is most fundamentally one about ethics.

Newton presents a theology of God-space, and it underpins the argument from contingency. He describes space as a 'disposition' of a being '*qua* being' in that 'no being exists or can exist which is not related to space in some way.' He favours the use of the term 'disposition' or 'attribute' of space to distance his language from the baggage associated with the terms substance and accident, and by his preferred terms, he seems to mean a property necessary for a being's existence (as opposed to an 'accident'): if any being is postulated, then space has to be postulated. Space is thus an attribute or affection of all being. 'God is everywhere, created minds are somewhere, and body is in the space that it occupies.'[39] Space is distinct from substance because it cannot 'act upon things,' but it is not an accident either. The same, Newton asserts, can be said of duration. God is everywhere and eternal, and so all other beings must partake in God's extension and eternity.[40]

The account of God and space presented by Newton and Clarke rests on a distinction posited between two types of extension: spiritual and material, which owes much to Newton's tutor at Cambridge, Henry More.[41] Rejecting Descartes's insistence that spirits have no extension, More – in common with Hobbes on this particular matter – could not imagine anything existing without extension. The natural consequence of this philosophy for Hobbes was materialism. More, however, could never have swallowed this outcome and refused to assign extension solely to matter, proposing instead the reality of incorporeal substance: extended spirits.[42] The extension of incorporeal spirit was different, however, to the extension of corporeal matter because it is infinitely extended. In his *Antidote against Atheism*, More argues that matter cannot exist eternally. God must be a perfect being with the attributes of perfection (self-subsistency, immateriality, essence of infinity and duration, immensity of goodness, omniscience, omnipotence and necessary existence).[43]

Space, however, is different. Space is not identical with matter, and yet we recognise it as a real thing. Furthermore, we recognise that it reaches out infinitely in all directions. If it isn't 'nothing,' but it isn't matter, it must be something containing the properties of incorporeality and eternal self-existence. Building on the idea of a perfect being, More proposes that space must be identical with God. The same is true of time too. Duration can have no beginning or end and is likewise distinct from matter. This 'eternal uninterrupted and never-fading duration' must therefore belong to God.[44]

The *Enchiridion Metaphysicum* proposes an a priori argument for God-space on the grounds of this philosophy of space. Space must exist, or God could not have created finite matter because finite matter would be impossible if there was no space in which it was contained. The first step in More's argument is to show that there is at least one infinite incorporeal substance in the universe (space). Given God's perfection, space cannot be anything other than God. We know this when we consider God's moral attributes. Reflecting on the nature of space leads us to realise it is a 'mode' of God.[45] Space is not only real but also divine. He considers his argument as a firm proof of the divine existence because there cannot be a perfect being if anything eternal, necessary, infinite and immense exists apart from God.[46] The true idea of God contains in itself all possible perfection, and so it must contain necessity of existence. From this can be inferred space's identification with God.

Newton adopts More's idea of extension as an attribute of God, and it leads him to insist that extension (as opposed to bodily substance) cannot be understood independently of God.[47] Space is neither substance nor accident but, like absolute time, has a mode of being presupposed by all other forms of being. It is uncreated and eternal, and is the receptacle within which all other created beings come into being. It also contains an inherent structure of geometrical solids that are limitless in their number and size, and which constitute all varieties of shapes.[48]

Newton's theology of God-space is a development of the demiurge of the *Timaeus* who imposes geometric form on chaotic matter. Newton replaced the dominant Aristotelian account in which potentiality becomes actuality, with a conception of space as a receptacle through which bodies come into being via the direct action of God. As McGuire points out, Newton's account of space makes for a theology of divine creation on a par with the *Timaeus*. Space serves as the receptacle in which God acts to impose the form of matter. This is not simply a theory about how bodies become corporeal through God's will but rather a story of how the physical cosmos is made manifest in space that, borrowing from Henry More's philosophy, is envisaged as sacred. It presents, as McGuire puts it, a cosmology of sacred places.[49] God's action, by 'informing' space infuses divinity into infinite space and the result is a creation that is inherently divinised. The action of God creates physical reality in space, which is why Newton can think that limitless space '*is* the sacred field of God.'[50]

This account of space emerges out of the tradition of commentary on the *Timaeus* which includes Proclus, Chalcidius, Philoponus and Patrizi, and it leads Newton, along with Pierre Gassendi, Walter Charleton, Cudworth and Blaise Pascal, to envisage space and time as 'prior ontologically to the way of being of other created things.'[51] Space is distinguished from bodily things because, unlike space, corporeal things exist by divine will. In Newton's ontology, bodies have active powers endowed to them by divine will, and through such powers, they can affect other physical bodies and give rise to perceptions in the mind.[52] The Scholastic Aristotelian ontology of material substance consisting of matter and form is replaced by infinite extension.

McGuire speculates that the idea of a spiritualised *tonos* that acts as an omnipresent force penetrating, binding together and keeping in harmony all the parts of the cosmos might be the argument for God that Newton refers to Bentley about, with the reservation that he wished to stay silent about it 'till the Principles on which it is grounded are better received.'[53] Further weight is given to this suggestion by the fact it is the exact same argument proposed later by Price who expressed general approval towards the idea. If it was indeed Newton's argument, it can be traced back at least as far as Justin Martyr who adopted two Pythagorean models that Newton assimilated: one of God as spirit inherent in all the cosmos and one of God as artificer who orders everything harmoniously.[54] Justin's Christianisation of Pythagoras saw him declare that God 'is not, as some think, outside the world, but in it. . . He is the blending agent of all ages; the executor of His own powers and deeds; the first cause of all things.'[55] The first model, positing a God penetrating all things, is present in Henry More but would also have been familiar to Newton through Cicero's *De natura deorum* and Virgil's *Georgics*. Furthermore, another two important influences on Newton were Philo Judaeus's *Allegorical Interpretation of Genesis* and possibly Justus Lipsius's *Physiologiae stoicorum*.[56] All these sources led Newton to a model of nature animated and infused by God.

Newton's theology of God-space was informed to a significant degree by ancient Jewish writings. He searched them relentlessly for original wisdom that he believed had become corrupted. In them, he found the Hebrew *mak om* 'place' that he used to try to convey his belief that space itself is not necessarily a property of God, even if God might be said to dwell *in* space. This theology was also in keeping with the way the ancients modelled their temples on the heavens to express the belief that God dwells in all bodies just as in the temples and given his understanding of it, the temptation to take Newton's conception of God-space too literally should be resisted.[57] He was well aware of the misunderstandings that could arise from speaking of God as space. He expresses dissatisfaction with the implications of Clarke's exchange with Leibniz, and he issues a warning that although the Hebrew *makom* and the book of Acts 17:27–8 tells us that God is not far from any of us this does not imply literally the Deity is in *all* place. The scriptures use allusions and figures of speech for want of proper language, and for this reason, he invites us to interpret Clarke's use of 'quality' and 'property' as merely figures of speech that 'signify the boundless extent of God's existence with respect to his ubiquity and eternity.'[58]

Informed by ancient concepts of spatial divinity as it was, Newton's theology of God-space adopted and developed More's suggestion that God should be seen as part of the explanatory order of things. Despite Newton's aim to keep metaphysics distinct from physics and to keep religion out of his scientific investigations he had one exception: space.[59] That Newton was committed to a metaphysic in which God pervades all space and in which the divine and corporeal are necessarily diffused meant that for him, especially in his later works, positing God as the cause of gravity was the obvious thing to do.[60] Later editions of the *Principia* show the identification of God and absolute space come out into the foreground of his thought at the beginning of the eighteenth century.[61] Why then did Newton feel the need to introduce God into his scientific writings? McGuire gives a helpful suggestion: the theory of divinised absolute space and time gave his cosmology a completeness that it would have lacked otherwise, and it also gave a much sought after theological justification of his mechanics and mathematical physics.[62] The effect of this development, however, was to consolidate the place More gave to God as an identifiable cause in the physical realm. Scientific explanation and theology come together on the same plane, with the result that God plugged a discernible gap in the new mechanistic scientific knowledge.

For Clarke and Price, however, the theology of God-space is first and foremost a commitment to the supremacy of God's goodness over God's power. The argument is both anti-deist and anti-voluntarist. As Harrison suggests, Newton himself was not a voluntarist when it came to the Euthyphro dilemma. He certainly believed the universe was dependent on the divine will, but this does not necessarily make him a voluntarist. Newton did not think the divine will has primacy over the divine intellect as God's will is continually constrained by goodness and wisdom.[63] In this, he is at one with the anti-voluntarist stance of Cudworth and Clarke. The arguments of Clarke's Boyle lectures were not only anti-materialist but also anti-voluntarist, targeting most notably the followers of Hobbes, Descartes and Spinoza. Through his theology of God-space, Clarke responds to issues of being and creative power that are first set forth in Plato's *Timaeus*.[64] Like More and Newton, he denies that matter can exist necessarily of its own nature. If it could, it would be a contradiction to suppose it might not exist. He then asserts that there must be some being in the universe that exists necessarily. If we try to suppose

> that there is *no Being* in the Universe that exists Necessarily; we always find in our Minds . . . some Ideas, as of *Infinity* and *Eternity*; which to remove . . . is a Contradiction in the very Terms.[65]

Modes and attributes are examples of these ideas, as they exist only by the existence of substance to which they belong. We might be able to imagine the material world not existing, but we cannot conceive of eternity or immensity not existing. Unlike material substances, space and time are two things that must exist: beings which exist in time and space must presuppose time and space. They are needed for the existence of everything else.

For Clarke as for Newton, time and space are real things not just relations between two bodies. They are also unbounded because of the fact that anything attempting to limit them will itself take up space and time. The being that '*makes*' duration and space must also, he says be infinite and eternal thus showing that 'Necessary substance' must exist and it cannot be matter, so therefore must be immaterial i.e. God.[66] When Price picks up this argument, he follows Clarke entirely. It is important to note that the argument is not first and foremost about God as efficient cause but about God as necessary to the conception of all existence.[67]

Space is not 'nothing' for Clarke (again following More and Newton) – it must be something – but it is not strictly speaking a substance but rather a 'property' or 'mode' of the self-existent substance. All other substances are *in* space but the self-existent substance is not in space. It is rather the 'substratum' of space. Space and duration are necessary but not themselves substances, so they are best conceived as properties or modes.[68] Clarke insists that his doctrines of space and time do not reduce the Deity to an existence within the confines of the temporal world. Space is not an 'eternal and infinite being'; God 'does not exist in space, and in time; but his existence causes space and time' in the sense that *in* space and time, all other things exist.[69] Price too picks up on this caution about literal misunderstanding. None of the expressions that can be used, he insists, including *substratum*, are strictly just.[70] They are not proposed literally and are difficult to grasp.

Necessary existence for Clarke, as later for Price, grounds the possibility of all other existence. What is necessary (what cannot not be) is that without which nothing can be conceived. When Price picks this up in the *Dissertation*, he goes on to claim that whatever is necessary for the conception of all existence is an attribute of God. This includes time, space, wisdom, power and knowledge.[71] As Clarke had argued for space as a mode of God, Price perceives all truth as a *'mode of a substance'* in other words, 'the *essential wisdom and intelligence of the one, necessary Being.'*[72] There are difficulties here, as Thomas suggests, because Price attributes *unlimited* perfection to God while at the same time constraining God to the moral law by limiting God by rectitude. It is hard for Price to maintain that 'Necessity of existence admits of no *limitation* or *imperfection*' while simultaneously holding that God's power is limited by rectitude.[73]

That Price attempts to hold the two together in tension is best seen as a legacy of his Platonism, shaped not only by Cudworth's account of God's nature and God's will but also by Clarke's distinction of God's moral power and moral perfection. Price himself would probably have seen no tension in this. Clarke's model of God in which knowledge of what is good determines infinite power is one grounded in the *Timaeus's* discussion of the relationship between the demiurge and the real, immaterial being.[74] The creative power of the demiurge is subordinated to real being. This is once again the dilemma of the *Euthyphro*. The same problem raised by Plato was at the heart of Christian doctrine as Clarke saw it. The *Timaeus* has the demiurge model the cosmos on real being that is separate from him and from this point onwards, philosophy is left grappling with the problem of how the eternal rational model of archetypes relates to the demiurge who actually creates. As Zebrowski argues, it is this problem – one about the relationship between real being and creative power – that Clarke is addressing in his philosophy of religion.[75] This is the problem of the relationship between goodness and power, and it is the *Euthyphro* dialogue that goes on to become Clarke's defining text. The law of nature is superior to the authority of all human beings and is antecedent to the will of God. In matters of natural reason and morality, that which is holy and good, he says, is not holy and good because it is commanded, but commanded precisely because it is holy and good.[76]

The argument is anti-voluntaristic and for Clarke it is anti-Hobbesian. The suggestion that obligation in civil society might depend only on the will or dictates of governors is anathema to Clarke. In his *Discourse,* the second Boyle lecture, he takes issue with Hobbes's assumption that human individuals are continually seeking dominance over each other and that we are constantly jealous and suspicious of one another. The supposition here is that morality only comes into being with the social compact. Hobbes might as well have said, as Clarke points out, that human laws and constitutions have the power to turn light into darkness and sweetness into bitterness.[77] There is more than an echo here of Cudworth's accusation of circularity. If obligations depend on the social compact, what is the compact based on? God's authority is not one of sheer power and dominion but one of moral righteousness based on justice and goodness.[78]

A Platonic response to the *Euthyphro*'s question thus frames Clarke's distinction between infinite power and moral perfection. God uses power only in accordance with wisdom, which is how God can be said to have moral necessity. Divine power is subordinated unequivocally to divine wisdom.[79] God is infinitely wise and therefore the world and everything in it must be the effect of infinite wisdom. It is in this way that all things depend on God and receive their being from God, and it is this, Clarke states, that constitutes an a priori argument for God's existence.[80]

This is the thinking that lies behind Price's account of the attributes of God's power and knowledge of the good. Price had read Plato for himself, but the Platonism of Clarke's *Demonstration* accords perfectly with Cudworth and More's submission of God's power to knowledge of the good, and Price's natural theology effectively brings this together with a Newtonian metaphysic. The unifying philosophy is that of the *Timaeus* and its account of a cosmology of sacred places modelled on a real immaterial being as the archetype of ethical value. Thus Price insists that God is not 'in' space or time but rather 'is' space and time in the same way that God 'is intelligent, not by the *apprehension* of truth, but by *being* truth; and *wise*, not by knowing all that is knowable, but by being that intellectual light which enlightens all other beings, and which makes them wise and knowing.'[81] It is in this sense that God is exalted as wisdom, reason, eternity, immensity and power, and it is in this way that the cosmos for Price, such as Newton, becomes a sacred place.

The importance of the ethical nature of this argument cannot be underestimated. The conclusion that the whole of Price's *Dissertation* is geared towards establishing is not that God exists but that God is a morally excellent being.[82] D.O. Thomas is right that D.D. Raphael underestimates the extent to which Price borrows from Clarke in his account of God as truth and reason, and the debt to Platonism is even more evident in the antivoluntarist implications that Price draws out of this conclusion. As Thomas points out, Price is not only proposing that reason, independently of revelation, can perceive the content of morality (or, we might add, fundamental truths about the attributes of God) but also asserting a more radical anti-Calvinist position that subordinates the supremacy of God's will to the binding nature of morality.[83] Descartes and Spinoza are obvious targets but Price singles out Richard Cumberland, William Warburton and adds, in the third edition of the *Review*, William Paley.[84] A Clarkean God-space theology, together with the argument from contingency, is used as a direct response to the threat of voluntarist conceptions of the divine.

The arguments about design and contingency are thus primarily ethical arguments and they rest on an ontology of a divinised cosmos. Natural theology and ethics are inextricably linked, and the belief that reason can attain fundamental truths about God is grounded in a basic theological commitment to a divinised ethically significant universe. Zebrowski makes the case for appreciating Clarke's method of natural theology as founded on Paul's words to the Romans, 'when the Gentiles, which have not the Law, do by nature the things contained in the Law . . . the work of the law is written in their hearts.'[85] As she points out, exactly the same can be said for Price. Reasoning about religion leads us, most crucially, to an appreciation for the reality of the ethical universe and for the absolute nature of moral truth. Theirs is not a vision of reason usurping faith but of a sacred cosmos imparting something of the divine wisdom.

The cosmos is in fact so much a sacred place for Price that God's existence is often missed: 'we meet him in every truth we contemplate, in every idea that passes through our minds, and every instant that measures our existence: And for this very reason we overlook him.'[86] One important consequence of this metaphysic is that there can be no clear signs of divinity in nature if the whole of nature is suffused with divinity. This explains Price's lack of interest in the miraculous and the primacy he gives to providence instead. The argument for necessary existence should be read in the same spirit as Price's appropriation of the design argument: it is God's essence, not God's influence, that the conception of God's necessary existence is primarily intended to portray.[87]

The necessary existence of God, and God conceived of in terms of space and time, represent a stance against God conceived of primarily as first cause and towards God as sustainer and upholder of the cosmos. The result is an argument for necessary existence that is given religious significance by a commitment to the theology of Acts 17:27–8, 'in him we live and move and have our being.'[88] Price adheres to this belief because, like Clarke and Newton before him, the world is precisely *not* a machine. The argument is one about ethics; it is a theology of nature, and it is anti-deistic. As Clarke puts it, 'The Notion of the World's being a great *Machine*, going on *without the Interposition of God*, as a Clock continues to go without the Assistance of a Clockmaker; is the Notion of *Materialism* and *Fate*.'[89] In his eyes, God's providence must be continuous, not restricted to one creative causal act, and only this theology can guarantee the reality of moral goodness and a cosmos that has a non-relative value.

Deism and fundamentalism: natural theology as *via media*

The natural theology of the physico-theological tradition discussed earlier is anti-deistic. It is also anti-enthusiastic in its stance against voluntarism and the supremacy of will. In addition to this, it should also be recognised as an alternative to High Church Laudianism and the rise of eighteenth-century Biblical fundamentalism that emerged from High Church theology. As suggested in the last chapter, the way the Latitudinarians and Rational Dissenters responded to the threat of atheism was very different from the approach of those adopting a more elevated Anglican position. The arguments of Clarke and Price are also characterised by an appeal to mathematics that implies a harder rationalism than that present in the Cambridge Platonists. Clarke wished to reduce all argument to the one method which 'should be as near mathematical, as the nature of such discourse would allow,'[90] and Price follows him by promoting a mathematical method for the investigation of religion. This move, however, represented a middle way in the eighteenth century between deism, enthusiasm and fundamentalism. When Price advanced a mathematic method, it was to promote the cause of epistemic humility in keeping with the physico-theological tradition he was drawing upon. This humility was badly needed in differing ways in the deistic, enthusiastic and fundamentalist traditions he was actively distancing himself from, and his turn to a mathematical rationalism is in contrast to the turn to a more literalist fundamentalism by those sympathetic to High Church concerns. Instead of pointing towards a dispute between reason and revelation, the context of this debate points towards what was a theologically pressing question of Biblical hermeneutics.

Not the light of nature alone: deism and natural theology

The previous three chapters have drawn attention to the central place of revelation in Price's theology. This is partly an inheritance from his Non-conformist Protestant roots, but the model of natural theology from which he drew bolstered it. Despite assumptions that have been continually levelled to the contrary, this tradition of natural theology is a long way from deism. James Force has done much to argue that Newton's scriptural theology places him at odds with deism. In the writings of a deist such as William Wollaston, revelation is divorced from what is most truly the '*religion of nature* or *natural religion*' and faith is based entirely on reason.[91] That Newton should be interpreted as a deist has been the dominant opinion since the eighteenth century but it is at odds with Newton's belief in the divine origin of revealed scripture, which must be properly interpreted. In contrast to a deist like Tindal, he refused to reject scripture for a religion of reason and his theology is profoundly Biblical.[92]

Clarke also shared Newton's attitude towards the scriptures. Chapter 3 has shown how for Clarke the light of nature alone is not enough. His natural theology in no way represents a deistic usurping of scripture for rational arguments but a combining of scriptural authority with rational inquiry. He was outspokenly critical of the deists in his Boyle lectures for disregarding revelation and for assuming that reason is sufficient and universal. Rational arguments, he stated, lead to religion both 'natural *and* revealed.'[93]

The ambivalent nature of the eighteenth-century arguments concerning design and contingency identified earlier is actually lessened when the centrality of revelation for Newton, Clarke, Price and Cudworth is considered and when their distance from deism is fully acknowledged. If natural theology is defined as anterior to or apart from revelation, it would essentially amount to what Clarke defines as deism. Clarke gives four definitions of deism. Two of them – belief in a God who either has no concern for the world at all or no concern for the moral actions of human beings – are familiar to more contemporary definitions. A third denies any future state after death (and therefore denies moral justice), whereas a fourth acknowledges the existence of a powerful eternal God of justice but only 'by the light of Nature alone' with no recourse to revelation. For Clarke, the suggestion that rational argument can be separated from revelation is deistic and it is something he forcefully rejects. As the previous chapters of this book have shown, revelation through scripture is just as central for the Rational Dissenters, including Price. For the thinkers in this physico-theological tradition, therefore, rational inquiry and analysis cannot judge the worthiness of scripture and natural theology is, in effect, inseparable from a theology of nature.

Biblical fundamentalism, anti-Newtonianism and the Hutchinsonians

The intellectual atmosphere of the last decade of the seventeenth century was dominated by two events: the Glorious Revolution of 1688 and the rise of Newtonian science. Newton's *Principia* was published in 1687 just one year before the Glorious Revolution. Both events were followed by decades of turmoil in the Anglican Church. Tensions between High and Low Anglicans and the dispute about the legitimacy of the Revolution meant that threats from freethinkers, deists and enthusiasts could not be met by a united Anglican front. By the turn of the eighteenth century and Anne's reign, the political struggle between Whig and Tory had enveloped every aspect of the Church of England. The vast majority of Anglican clergy between 1689 and 1720 were High Churchmen. Having given up on the Crown for support after William III, (among other things) presided over the spread of Dissenting Academies and demonstrated a clear dislike of the sacramental test, they sought support in Parliament instead with the hope for a long period of Tory supremacy.[94]

On the other hand, the Glorious Revolution and Newton's natural philosophy were mutually reinforcing for the Latitudinarians. Both gave vital support towards a stable Christian state with an established broad and narrowly tolerant church and a constitutional government.[95] The discovery of laws that determined the behaviour of the physical world demonstrated to Clarke, Boyle and Wilkins among others that nature is ordered to a particular design. This had social and political implications because it meant God had providentially ordained the order in society. The emerging science could deal a double blow both to Hobbesian materialism and to the instability of the Interregnum. Whereas deists such as Toland used Newtonianism to defend freethinking radicalism on the grounds that matter was active with an inner energy which justified political radicalism in opposition to the moderate settlement of 1688, for the Latitudinarians the laws of Newtonianism were a sharp contrast to 'arbitrary and capricious will' and they served as a bulwark against both Hobbesian materialism, and enthusiasm.[96] Furthermore, by uncovering truths that were discovered entirely independently of both revelation and tradition, Newton's natural philosophy was used by many Latitudinarians to bolster the claim for the natural light of reason.[97] As the century progressed, the followers of Newton continued in their tendency to be Whig and – when in the Anglican Communion – Latitudinarian.[98]

The result was a significant degree of interdependence between Whiggism, Newtonianism and Latitudinarianism, one furthered by the fact Newton was Lucasian chair of mathematics in Cambridge where the Latitudinarian Whig Richard Bentley (1662–1742) – also tutor to Stillingfleet and the first Boyle lecturer – was Master of Trinity College. The relationship between Whiggism, Latitudinarianism and Newtonianism was mutually beneficial as Newton's physics affirmed the validity of human reason and the Latitudinarians helped to promote his physics by affirming it in the lectern and pulpit.[99] Newtonianism remained suspicious in the eyes of the High Church, however, for its perceived radicalising tendencies and its rationalism. By the mid-late eighteenth century, many High Church Anglicans were vocally anti-Newtonian. Those most vehemently anti-Newtonian identified with the movement called Hutchinsonianism. Things came to a head between the Hutchinsonians, Latitudinarians and Rational Dissenters in the second half of the eighteenth century in a bitter dispute about subscription.

In 1771, a group of moderate Anglican clergy met at the Feathers Tavern on the Strand and organised a petition to replace subscription to the Thirty-Nine Articles and 'forms of worship composed by fallible divines, and enjoined by human authority' with a declaration of belief in the scriptures.[100] Primarily concerned with Anglican divines and those attending university, the petition was grounded in the argument of Francis Blackburne's

Confessional (1766) that no Protestant minister should be required to sub-scribe because general assent to the scriptures is enough. Theophilus Lind-sey became its 'Principal Conductor' and signatures were obtained from 200 clergy and 50 laymen whereupon it was presented to Parliament in February 1772. Its defeat was comprehensive. A huge majority of MPs in the House of Commons rejected it, and by so doing, they defined Anglican orthodoxy in terms of adherence to doctrine and the Articles, rather than belief in the scriptures.[101]

The reverberations of the failure of this petition were long lasting. It caused a momentous split within liberal Anglicanism. When the petition failed, many of the signatories, including John Jebb, Lindsey and John Dis-ney abandoned Anglicanism altogether in favour of Rational Dissent. They felt their position in the established church had become untenable. Oth-ers including Edmund Law and William Paley did not sign, although they were supportive of the principle of relaxing subscription. The petition was a watershed and brought into sharp relief the difference between the Church of this particular decade and the one in existence in the early eighteenth century, which, as William Gibson points out, had found space within it to accommodate thinkers such as Samuel Clarke and Stephen Nye who shared similar views to Blackburne. In the latter half of the eighteenth century, the Church came to be defined by a growing conservatism and its definition of orthodoxy, and even those who considered themselves people of latitude insisted on the necessity of subscription.[102]

Despite the 1772 failure, hopes were high that another petition, this time on behalf of the Rational Dissenters, would be more successful. Lord North had spoken out encouragingly about their chances despite the fact the Feathers Tavern campaigners had failed. The issue was pressing for Rational Dissent. The Corporation and Test Acts were still in place and although official prosecutions were virtually unheard of, tolerance of Dissent was uneasy, resting on a significant power imbalance with the background threat of mob violence (a fear that proved well grounded when it turned into an alarming reality for Priestley and other Rational Dissenters at the end of the eighteenth century). The Dissenters were quick off the mark at responding to North's positivity. An extraordinary meeting of the General Body of Dis-senting Ministers was called which went on to appoint a committee that would apply for relief from subscription. Price became a member of this committee and an active campaigner in favour of religious freedom. A bill was presented in April 1772, but despite passing with a significant majority through the House of Commons, the bishops of the House of Lords refused it. A subsequent bill in 1773 was also heavily defeated in the Lords.

The Feathers Tavern petitionaries and the Rational Dissenters had both a common cause and a common argument. They denied that the state had any right to enforce conformity regardless of whether or not its theology was correct. Their claim to freedom of conscience thus took precedence over theological truth claims enforced by an established church and guaranteed only by what they saw as mere human authority. The previous chapters have highlighted how for the Rational Dissenters and the Latitudinarians, reason was the primary tool to challenge voluntarism and arbitrary power. It helped to consolidate the value of freedom against the constraints of prescribed religion. Rational Dissenting confidence in reason was in no doubt a direct consequence of the socio-political context. As Mark Philp argues, the eighteenth century was certainly a period of enlightenment for the Rational Dissenters but not in the sense of the normal understanding of the term 'Enlightenment.' It meant release from the iron grip of an establishment church and the alliance of church and state.[103] Their rationality has thus been called for good reason an 'enlightened version of Puritanism' for its commitment to obedience of conscience.[104] 'Enlightenment' on this understanding meant the freedom to pursue one's conscience in an atmosphere of increased religious toleration. The Rational Dissenters thus represented a development rather than a hiatus from the rationalising tendencies of both Puritanism and Latitudinarianism.

The response to the petitions of the early 1770s from those loyal to High Anglicanism was swift. George Horne, Bishop of Norwich and the most well-known High Church Tory, was appalled at the claim for freedom of conscience. To the Rational Dissenters' suggestion that doctrine was not relevant to their petition for freedom of conscience, Horne's curt response was dogmatic: 'orthodoxy and heterodoxy are but other terms for right and wrong, applied to the doctrines of religion.'[105] This was a position with a theological basis in a commitment to tradition. For Horne the truth of Christianity resided only in the Anglican Church in the doctrines handed down in the tradition of the Fathers, safeguarded by the rituals and sacraments, and from where he was standing Anglican doctrine and liturgy were all that was needed to promote faith.[106]

Horne was a Hutchinsonian: one of a group of thinkers who championed the theology of the anti-Newtonian John Hutchinson (1674–1737). C. B. Wilde informs us that whenever there was debate between High and Low Anglicanism throughout the eighteenth century the Hutchinsonian presence can be detected.[107] It was a theology unpopular with the more Latitudinarian bishops but avidly embraced by many who defended High Church ideals. Hutchinson himself had aimed his energies at Newton's theological system, but in the second half of the eighteenth century, the Rational Dissenters, especially Price and Priestley, began to draw the Hutchinsonians' fire.[108] William Jones of Nayland, Horne's friend and later his chaplain, was a Hutchinsonian who spent some considerable time undermining Newtonianism and the petitioners' cause. *The Fable of the Rats* was his stiff retort to the attempt to abolish subscription. The petitioners were depicted as rats eating away at the foundations of their own house, their incessant nibbling endangering the fabric of the very edifice they relied upon.[109] Subscription was a political issue ensuring the safety of the state. Of his own kind, however, Jones proclaimed, 'When we are describing Hutchinsonians, it would be unjust to forget, that they are true churchmen and loyalists; steady in the fellowship of the apostles, and faithful to the monarchy under which they live.'[110] The politics of subscription and the theology of church tradition were inseparably intertwined.

The Hutchinsonian presence cannot be ignored when considering eighteenth-century debates about the scope of natural theology. Hutchinson was unremittingly anti-natural theology. Newton's theology of God-space, he thought, was an affront to God's power: 'He who says that there is a power, motion, or gravity which is not from Him and at His command, does he not set up another god?'[111] Hutchinson denied the theory of gravitation outright and proposed that the Old Testament contained the correct theory of natural science. Knowledge of the natural world is to be found, he argued, not in Newton's mathematics but in the scriptures as dictated by God. He was a Biblical fundamentalist with a steadfast commitment to the literal truth of every part of the Hebrew Bible. The Hutchinsonians were the forerunners of later nineteenth-century fundamentalism.

The Hutchinsonians appealed to a doctrine of analogy based on an epistemology of sensation. The epistemology behind this was Lockean but Hutchinsonianism went beyond Locke in dismissing even reflection as a source of knowledge.[112] We have no knowledge of spiritual things immediately they thought, only as they are mediated by analogy with what we can know through our senses. That ideas can only enter the mind through the senses meant for the Hutchinsonians that we can have knowledge of revelation only by analogy with whatever is perceived by our senses. Divine truths must be apprehended through what is material. For Hutchinson, every character of the Hebrew Bible referred to a sense object (animals, trees, elements etc.), and they all have a spiritual significance.[113] Using his method, he saw scripture as the sole fountain of knowledge finding not least signs of the Trinity throughout the Old Testament (especially in the cherubim).[114] With this method of interpretation, he made Trinitarianism strictly Biblical.

Hutchinson's Hebraic literalism set up a sharp contrast between inferential knowledge of the divine and scriptural revelation. He denied mathematical reasoning could produce knowledge about the world. Jeremiah 31:37 instructs that whoever attempts to measure the heavens or the foundation of the earth will be cast off from God.[115] The was clear evidence for Hutchinson that Newton had gone about things entirely the wrong way by trying to develop a model of how the universe works on mathematical principles. He has put, Hutchinson said, the cart before the horse, and he should have begun with the scriptural depiction of the cosmos and then described it in mathematical form.[116] Only the scriptures can be the source of knowledge about nature and about God's nature. For the Hutchinsonians, scripture is the sole fountain of knowledge and every word is the perfect word of God, containing within it the truths of science. In the words of William Jones: 'Scripture is found to have a language of its own, which doth not consist of words, but of signs or figures taken from visible things.'[117]

The Hutchinsonians were not a million miles away from their Latitudinarian and Rational Dissenting targets in some key respects. They aimed to find a middle way between extreme rationalism and the enthusiastic prioritising of private judgement. What they called 'right reason' aimed to be a balance between the two.[118] The Latitudinarians and the Rational Dissenters could in fact agree with Horne that scripture, not mathematics, is where revelation is to be found and that the scriptures are sufficient for revelation. As Aston argues, however, the Latitudinarians and Rational Dissenters could not follow him in defending historic creeds.[119] This is where their common ground broke up. Unlike the natural theologians, the Hutchinsonians would not infer theology from the works of nature but intended instead to bring 'the volume of nature in aid of the volume of Scripture': all observed natural phenomena they thought confirmed the meaning of scripture.[120] Horne took this up to argue the point of philosophy was to assist not just faith but more precisely Anglicanism.[121] For their method of analogy, the Hutchinsonians saw themselves, together with the Nonjurors, as the true continuation of the tradition of the Church Fathers.

The debate about the place of reason in religion and the legitimacy of natural theology was therefore a matter of Biblical hermeneutics and the authority of tradition. As far as Hutchinson was concerned, a correct reading of the Bible is able to demonstrate that the scriptures and the natural world prove the Trinity. His literalism led him to deny that fallen human beings could make inferences from the natural world to God, and for this reason, all natural theology was refused on the grounds of it being the 'religion of Satan, or Antichrist.'[122] This theology fitted neatly with a Nonjuror world view and saw the Bible as containing, as Horne's tutor George Watson put it 'the sacred repositories of all true knowledge.'[123]

In contrast to Hutchinsonianism, the champions of Newtonian science gave God's work the same status as God's word and thus moved away from literal interpretations of the Bible.[124] Theirs was a natural theology inoperable without revelation but what it *did* reject was the belief that every bit of the Bible is true. Reading Newton and Clarke as deist and locating all the Rational Dissenters, including Price, in a tradition that reduces faith and revelation to rational investigation, therefore, papers over the pressing question of Biblical interpretation, which lies at the heart of the debate between the Newtonian physico-theology and the Hutchinsonians. When Price adopted Clarke's mathematical model of rationalism it was in direct contrast to the Hutchinsonian empiricist method. Hutchinson was not against reason per se, but the only role it could have was what he called 'deduction' by which reason could infer knowledge from the scriptures.[125] Price's use of intuition, his much higher view of reason and his theology of nature made for an alternative to this Biblical fundamentalism. It was ultimately the Hutchinsonian insistence on a harmony between the natural world and the Bible that shaped the Bridgewater Treatises,[126] not the physico-theology of Cudworth, Newton, Clarke and, later, Price. Their natural theology in fact marks a middle way between the extreme rationalism of deism, the fideism of enthusiasm and the fundamentalism of High Church Hutchinsonianism.

The search for truth and the limits of knowledge

Hutchinsonianism reached its peak in the mid-eighteenth century but had a strong presence within the High Church until the end of the eighteenth and even into the nineteenth century.[127] It continued to offer loud objections against natural theology, particularly the Newtonian form of it and it entrenched the division between the Whig defence of reason and the High Church objection to it. Henry Dodwell (*Christianity not Founded on Argument*, 1742) and Charles Leslie (*Short and Easy Method with the Deists*, 1697) were two of the most important Nonjuror theologians, and they attracted significant support from the Hutchinsonians. They refused what they saw as the alien import of philosophy into theology and were accused by their Latitudinarians detractors of setting up a false dichotomy, 'depressing Reason, the better as they assume to advance Revelation, and who labour with all their might to destroy Natural Religion, as the best and only means of supporting Revealed.'[128]

The theology defended by the Hutchinsonians and those of a High Church persuasion was of an Augustinian character and gave primary significance to the doctrines of original sin and redemption.[129] Adam's assertion of his own will against God's resulted in original sin and rendered human reason destitute. God's grace is then made the only salvation and faith becomes the only valid human response. The doctrines of Augustinianism (primarily incarnation, fall and atonement) cannot be defended or articulated through reason, only justified through revelation and tradition.

With Hutchinsonianism came a conviction in theological certainty. Hutchinson sought to 'knock down Newton and set up Moses as the infallible guide to the natural and spiritual system of the universe.'[130] For Horne, likewise, there was no need to be sceptical about any aspect of the creeds or the Anglican liturgy, 'Scepticism in a Christian is a most damnable sin since without faith it is impossible to please God & faith can no more stand upon uncertainty than a house upon the waves of the sea.'[131] Nigel Aston has pointed out that this was the matter on which Joseph Priestley and Horne were most diametrically opposed. Priestley could never have accepted that the creeds, liturgy or Articles of the Church were a matter of certainty and proposed instead the certainty of reason as a hermeneutical tool thereby rejecting the association of church and state. As he saw it, 'Civil power is an inflexible thing, and is deaf to all individuals of argument and persuasion; so that truth has no chance where it prevails.'[132] For the Rational Dissenters this lack of certainty is the basis for freedom of conscience. For the Hutchinsonians, no freedom of conscience is necessary if there is no doubt.

Despite the fact Priestley could never have accepted Horne's lack of scepticism towards the creeds, his own rationalism is characterised by a great confidence in reason, as Chapter 2 has illustrated. Whereas for Priestley, reason is the way to demonstrate the corruptions of established beliefs, Price adopts much more caution about reason's abilities. Central for Price is a commitment to epistemic humility. In adopting the natural theology that he did, he was preserving a belief in the limits of knowledge. This puts him in contrast with the certainty of the Hutchinsonians but also the enthusiasts, Socinians and the deists, all of whom appealed to some sort of infallible authority.

As suggested earlier, the two poles of Price's argument – a natural theology and a theology of nature – mean that on the one hand Price is theologising from his perspective of a sense of the divine in nature (a perspective he holds intuitively as a result of his religious world view) whereas on the other hand he is drawn to the requirement for evidence and inference as part of his attempt to defend the integrity of individual conscience. The theology of nature is certainly fundamental for Price and grounds the argument of his natural theology. What is also of crucial importance in his rational arguments, however, is the idea of epistemic humility.

Introducing his arguments in the *Dissertation*, Price ventures that the conviction of the existence of a creator of the world is not left to depend on 'abstruse reasonings and deductions' but is apprehended through 'immediate and irresistible perception.'[133] The visible universe he sees as *self-evidently* an exhibition of the power and wisdom of a powerful and wise cause. The intuition Price speaks of when he talks of immediate apprehension and self-evidence is not a rational concept divorced from spiritual experience, however. It is, instead, best read in terms of Joseph Butler's natural theology articulated in his *Analogy*. In the preface to the first edition of the *Review*, Price states that he is more indebted to Butler than to any other writer. He did, however, omit this preface in the third edition. Raphael ventures that this might have been because in fact he realised his debt was not actually as formative as he had thought.[134] He certainly disagreed with Butler on Christology, and the influence of Butler on his moral epistemology is not as great as Cudworth's, but his moral psychology bears Butler's stamp, as does his account of the intuition of the insights of natural theology. When it comes to the philosophy of religion, Price fuses a Butlerian understanding of intuition with his Cudworthian and Platonic account of epistemology.

Reason, according to Butler, 'almost intuitively' bears witness to the truth of the moral system of religion, by which he means the conviction that things are under the direction of a good God revealed through scripture. It is intuitive reason that apprehends the ethical nature of a cosmos made good through God's providential care. But not only that, as intuition is what Butler means when he uses the term 'natural religion' opposed to the darkness of superstition. The true natural religion, which Butler sees himself recovering, is 'scarce discernible at all, in the religious establishments of the most learned, polite nations,' forgotten by the tradition of superstition that has overcome it.[135] Butler is at one with the Cambridge Platonists, Clarke and

Price here by pitting the natural religion against not only atheism but also the darkness of enthusiasm and the absolute authority of tradition. Latitudinarian rationalism was the foundation for Butler's philosophy and for this 'Whig nation-builder,'[136] as for other Latitudinarians, superstition is every bit as dangerous as atheism, primarily because of the human tendency to deceive ourselves and to let others deceive us.[137] The theological and ethical dangers detected in such intellectual hegemony give rise to his theology of conscience, formed as an affirmation of enlightened individual judgement.

Intuition in the way that Price and Butler promote the term does not refer primarily to a rationalist method of argument but rather it encapsulates aspects of an extra-logical grasp of the truth along the lines of the Cambridge Platonists' theology of the illumination of the soul (not all that far removed from their Puritan predecessors).[138] Cudworth explains that only a mind in touch with the reality of spirit can intuit a perfect mathematical figure such as does not exist and never has existed in material nature,[139] whereas for Butler, miracles to those who witness them are intuitive proofs of Christianity's truth. Intuitive perception comes only to those who embrace the divine life. Within Price's philosophy, it is a sense of the all-pervasive presence of God that gives him an immediate intuition of God's necessary self-existence. Price's design argument and his Clarkean argument for God's existence thus capture a sense of his living in a divine cosmos, granting a religious significance to a natural world that cries out with the inscriptions of divinity. It was the sheer power of this vision of nature that Hume and Kant appreciated when they accepted the *impression* of design, even after they rejected the argument.[140] Price's intuition of design and the reality of God-space represent his way of seeing the world in a particular way.

In tension with this religious intuition sits Price's probabilistic model of evidence and his suggestion that God's existence might be inferred from our experience of the world. The design argument and argument from contingency, if taken together, produce '*some degree* of *real* evidence,' and they make a foundation for reasoning about religion.[141] It is not proof that he is after, however, but rather the acceptability of the religious world view. He outlines two opposing paradigms: one of 'religion' and belief in the objectivity of goodness and the other of relativism and materialism. The 'evidence' of natural theology is meant to establish the reasonableness of belief in a good God who creates a world with a *telos* orientated towards happiness.

The kind of reasoning he uses is that which we use 'in the common course of life,' which 'explains to us the principles and grounds upon which we act in almost all our temporal concerns'[142] – i.e. 'moral' reasoning that cannot be certain. He appeals to Butler's *Analogy* for an application of this type of reasoning to the sphere of religious knowledge. In fact, he says, we often act on evidence that is much less than probable in everyday life. Butler contrasts probability with demonstrative knowledge because it admits of degrees. If an analogy can be made between the way we make everyday decisions and the way we assess religious claims, it can only serve to show us the limits of our knowledge. Butler's model of probability always entails a measure of doubt – sometimes significant levels of it – because occasionally we need to act on probabilities 'so low as to leave the mind in very great doubt which is the Truth.'[143] The probabilistic method is proposed, therefore, to ensure a mindfulness of epistemic humility.

In 1761 when the mathematician Thomas Bayes died, Price was asked by Bayes's family to sort through his papers. Coming across what was clearly an important but unfinished theory of probability, Price completed it and submitted it to the Royal Society. Besides bequeathing Bayes's theorem to the world Price's mathematic talent consolidated an interest in the relationship between mathematics and religious belief that would have been kindled in the first instance by his reading of Clarke. The endorsement of a mathematical method for the philosophy of religion is evident in the *Four Dissertations* in which Price extends Bayes's work to argue that the constitution of the universe could not have occurred through chance. Probabilistic reasoning is used to argue for the likelihood of the universe arising through the action of a providential God. What we see in Price is in many ways a furthering of Clarke's mathematizing of natural theology.[144] The methods of the sciences are applied to the subject of theological reflection.

Like Butler, however, Price uses probability to encourage appreciation of the limits of our knowledge, rather than aspiring to attain justification of belief. The proof of Christianity does not consist in a clear sum of arguments, but it 'is the *overbalance* of evidence that remains after every reasonable deduction is made on account of difficulties.'[145] He is concerned only, he states, with the fact that evidence should be used to 'give a chance for the truth of Christianity'[146] rather than offer any indisputable assurance. Despite his mathematical prowess, he remains unclear about whether Christianity is more probable than not or whether it can merely be shown to be reasonable. It is epistemic humility that probability guarantees for Price just as much as it does for Butler. Probabilistic arguments are used to check the tendency to be overly confident about one's own knowledge as much as to prove anything to one's opponent.

In this sense, Price shares the conviction of the seventeenth-century Latitudinarians that 'the impartial search for religious truth, not the final position reached, was the true mark of piety.'[147] This is the mark of the honest mind in action. As John Wilkins put it in his *Natural Religion*, when the evidence is 'less plain and clear,' it can give rise only to opinion and probability.[148] Newton's empiricism too was fully conscious of its own limits with James Force giving good reasons when he claims that 'Newton's epistemological caution is legendary.'[149] It is reflected throughout his theology not least in his advice to interpreters of prophecy not to attempt to necessitate God almighty by predicting in advance when or how God will chose to fulfil his promises. This same awareness of epistemic limits is there in Clarke as well, for whom the human understanding is 'dark and cloudy' requiring extraordinary and supernatural assistance 'which [is] above the reach of bare Reason and Philosophy to procure.'[150]

When it comes to analogy, the belief in an analogy between the natural world and the truths of theology was something the Hutchinsonians shared with Butler. Whereas for Butler, however, an argument based on analogy can only result in probable truth, the Hutchinsonians believed analogy to produce necessary truth because it is the divine method for bringing us to know the ultimate fitness of things.[151] The natural world was thus a direct analogy or image of the spiritual, and, in William Jones's words, the divine analogy 'opens a new and striking alliance between the theology of the Scripture, the Constitution of Nature, and the mythological mysteries of Heathenism.'[152] The refusal of certainty was something that Price inherited from Butler, and it was in keeping with the natural theology of the Latitudinarian tradition. The harmony Price sought between reason and revelation was one that fully acknowledged the scriptures as revealing things that could not otherwise be known.[153] Religion is certainly not a merely matter of inference for him and revelation is not subject to the dictates of reason but goes beyond it. Price's use of probabilistic argument, therefore, makes for a sharp contrast both with the deistic extolling of reason, the voluntarism of enthusiasm and the certainty of Hutchinsonianism. In fact, in many cases, he claimed, the more confident someone is of something, the more reason there is to doubt. With this, he expresses his hatred towards dogmatism as one of the greatest enemies to improvement and true wisdom and he insists his conviction on most points is only a preponderance to one side. Christianity, *if true*, he suggests gives an assurance of a resurrection from death to a happy immortality. Any degree of preponderance here is a ground for hope and comfort amidst the trials of this world.[154]

Ultimately, therefore, Price's account of reason shows a basic sensitivity towards the fact that the use of any evidence is problematic: the practice of candour discussed in Chapter 2 enabled him in one important respect to see that the way we look at the world and how we assess the so-called evidence of the book of nature is very much dependent on our prior convictions. There is a grasping towards an appreciation for the fact the gulf between believer and unbeliever involves more than one party incorrectly weighing up the evidence. This gulf is created at least in part by a different vision of the world, and, as Crowder explains, Price is perhaps not unaware of this as he struggles between the attempt to capture the sense of the religious believer who lives in a theistic world and the attempt to judge (more objectively) between belief and unbelief. This is directly related to the tension between the arguments to and from design. For one thing, he is certain that his version of rationality is preferable to that of the Socinians, and he maintains against the atheists and the enthusiasts that truth is objective, not based on power. This gives him a commitment to the rationality of religious belief, which he tries to hold together with his intuition of God's existence.

As to where this leaves the design and cosmological arguments themselves, the most fruitful suggestion is that offered by Crowder: the important kernel of the design argument must be that it is an attitude that generates new insights. The tradition of physico-theology that Price belonged to had an unwavering commitment to the reality of ethical value and to that value as infused throughout the natural cosmos. It showed an awareness that a different – more voluntaristic, or relativistic – ethic would result in a vastly different attitude towards the wider world. Value is thus defended as inherent, not projected, for this Platonic tradition of physico-theology. Different ways of seeing the world are affirmed as inevitably ethical. The focus is therefore shifted to our attitude towards the wider world, towards the inner orientation of the self. Hedley summarises the Platonists' prioritising of mind above matter succinctly: it is an ethical doctrine; one that realises our world is 'neither a collection of neutral facts nor a kaleidoscope of our projected fancies.'[155]

This throws the contrast between Price and Priestley into sharper relief. Price's rationality of epistemic humility and commitment to innate ideas and deiform reason put him at odds with Priestley's more materialistic thinking. Priestley's envisaging of spirit as emerging in nature from the powers of attraction and repulsion was one that Price saw as moving away from ethical realism and towards the relativism of hedonism. The soul's separate existence, Priestly proclaimed, is a grand error arising from those ancient philosophers who made 'the Supreme Mind the author of all good.'[156] Without this 'mind,' however, the author of good takes a step closer to becoming the human individual through the move towards a utilitarian ethic.

Price's natural theology, on the other hand, strives to maintain the ethical import of the Platonic distinction between mind and matter. When the Cambridge Platonists combined rationality, religion and ethics, they were offering a cogent argument against materialistic empiricism. This places them in a tradition that can be traced through Erasmus back to Plato's *Laws*.[157] What they are most concerned about is the danger that Stephen Clark perceives in reductionist materialism: that goodness and beauty can have no real existence. The same is true for Plotinus. It is the *ontological* priority of 'design' (by which we could say 'art') over 'chance' that characterises Plotinus's adoption of the argument of Plato's *Laws*, the target of which is the Epicurean model of the arbitrary movement of atoms.[158] For Epicurus the world is comprised of atoms in a void and the only thing worth living for is pleasure. What he abandons is the idea of an ordered world, and in this, there can be no good beyond the moment's joy.[159] It is this commitment to the reality of goodness and truth that sees the seventeenth- and eighteenth-century English natural theologians embrace rationalism. They could appreciate, as a result of their political context, that a response to Epicureanism based on mystery would only buy into the same relativist ethic they denied. Truth that is merely will or power is no truth at all, and contains within it the overwhelming likelihood of oppression.

As the eighteenth century drew to a close, political radicals began to use rational arguments to undermine not only High Church appeals to mystery or the authority of doctrine but also to challenge the very existence of the established order. The arguments of the French *philosophes* cohered with the arguments of extreme radicals like Thomas Paine who called for the complete abolition of the establishment. In Britain, this gave rise to political worries. Gascoigne explains how a military defeat, the Gordon Riots and an increasing hostility to the radical demands of Rational Dissenters such as Cartwright and Jebb were significant in depleting the appetite for Parliamentary reform.[160] At the same time, Samuel Horsley played a significant role in the decline of natural theology through his attacks on Hoadly the 'republican bishop' in the 1790s.[161] Horsley warned of the dangers of neglecting revealed religion and did much to add momentum to a reassertion of the distinctive nature of Christianity.

The result at the end of the eighteenth century, and the turn of the next, was a move away from natural theology towards an emphasis on revealed religion as beyond the limits of human reason.[162] William Paley represents a late flowering of natural theology in Cambridge, but he was soon eclipsed by divines who emphasised the priority of doctrine and the limits of reason.[163] If the truths of Christianity were not distinct from what could be ascertained through natural theology and through an unmediated grasp of the scriptures (which was the Latitudinarian conviction), then there was little need for the clergy with its privileges, or for the liturgy and traditions of the Church, all of which were proposed by the High Church to mediate between corrupted reason and revelation. It was very much in the interests of those highly critical of Latitudinarianism in the latter decades of the eighteenth century to follow William Jones and blast all forms of natural religion as 'but another name for Deism.'[164] The French Revolution cemented the connection between Anglican orthodoxy and the survival of the state and left Rational Dissent, and the arguments of the Latitudinarian natural theologians, out in the cold. As Gibson puts it, this resulted in a Hutchinsonian victory that inspired a generation of High Church bishops and their anti-rationalism well into the nineteenth century.[165]

Notes

1 Alan P. F. Sell, "Henry Grove: A Dissenter at the Parting of the Ways," *Enlightenment and Dissent* 4 (1985): 57; Alan P.F. Sell, "Samuel Clarke on the Existence of God," *Enlightenment and Dissent* 3 (1984): 67.

2 Richard Price, *A Review of the Principal Questions in Morals*, 3rd ed. (Oxford: Clarendon, 1948), 285.

3 Richard Price, *Four Dissertations* (Bristol: Thoemmes, 1990), 25, 27–8.

4 Martha K. Zebrowski, "Richard Price: British Platonist of the Eighteenth Century," *Journal of the History of Ideas* 55, no. 1 (1994): 35; Price, *Review*, 89.

5 Neal C. Gillespie, "Divine Design and the Industrial Revolution: William Paley's Abortive Reform of Natural Theology," *Isis* 81, no. 2 (1990): 216.

6 Isabel Rivers, " 'Galen's Muscles': Wilkins, Hume, and the Educational Use of the Argument from Design," *The Historical Journal* 36, no. 3 (1993): 577–79.

7 Ralph Cudworth, *The True Intellectual System of the Universe. . . with a Treatise Concerning Eternal and Immutable Morality*, ed. John Harrison, vol. ii (London: Thomas Tegg, 1845), 601–2.

8 Cudworth, *TIS*, vol. ii, 605.

9 Cudworth, *TIS*, vol. ii, 605.

10 Rivers, " 'Galen's Muscles'," 584.

11 Cudworth, *TIS*, vol. ii, 616.

12 Cudworth, *TIS*, vol. ii, 619.

13 Cudworth, *TIS*, vol. ii, 621.

14 Cudworth, *TIS*, vol. ii, 610.

15 Cudworth, *TIS*, vol. ii, 606.

16 Rivers, " 'Galen's Muscles'," 582.

17 Colin Crowder, "Berkeley, Price and the Limitations of the Design Argument," *Enlightenment and Dissent* 8 (1989): 7.

18 Price, *Four Dissertations*, 9.

19 Price, *Four Dissertations*, 56, 57; Crowder, "Berkeley," 22n.

20 Price, *Four Dissertations*, 53, 74.

21 Crowder, "Berkeley," 8.

22 Samuel Clarke, *The Works of Samuel Clarke*, vol. iii, iv vols. (London: Printed for John and Paul Knapton, 1738), see esp. 846.

23 Price, *Four Dissertations*, 47n.

24 Zebrowski, "Richard Price," 35.

25 Price, *Review*, 109.

26 Zebrowski, "Richard Price," 35.

27 Price, *Four Dissertations*, 9–10.

28 Price, *Four Dissertations*, 5.

29 Crowder, "Berkeley."

30 Price, *Four Dissertations*, 19.

31 Price, *Review*, 287.

32 D. O. Thomas, *The Honest Mind: The Thought and Work of Richard Price* (Oxford: Clarendon, 1977), 22.

33 Price, *Review*, 287.

34 Price, *Review*, 287.

35 All Price, *Review*, 288.

36 Joseph Butler, *Several Letters to the Reverend Dr. Clark from a Gentleman in Gloucestershire, Relating to the First Volume of the Sermons Preached at Mr. Boyle's Lecture; with the Dr's Answers Thereunto* (London: James Knapton, 1716), 11; Price, *Review*, 289.

37 Samuel Clarke, *The Works of Samuel Clarke*, vol. ii (London: Printed for John and Paul Knapton, 1738), 745.

38 Michael J. Buckley, *At the Origins of Modern Atheism* (Yale: Yale University Press, 1987), 348, 356, 359.

39 Isaac Newton, "De Gravitatione et Aequipondio Fluidorum," in *Unpublished Scientific Papers of Isaac Newton*, ed. A. Rupert Hall and Marie Boas Hall (Cambridge: Cambridge University Press, 1962), all 136; Edward Slowik, "Newton's Neo-Platonic Ontology of Space," *Foundations of Science* 18 (2013): 423.

40 Slowik, "Ontology of Space," 441.

41 Edwin Arthur Burtt, *The Metaphysical Foundations of Modern Physical Science: A Historical and Critical Essay* (London: Kegan Paul, Trench, Trubner & Co., 1925), 256, 279; David Leech, *The Hammer of the Cartesian: Henry More's Philosophy of Spirit and the Origins of Modern Atheism* (Leuven: Peters, 2013);

See also e.g. Max Jammer, *Concepts of Space: The History of Theories of Space in Physics* (Cambridge, Mass.: Harvard University Press, 1954).

42 Burtt, *Metaphysical Foundations*, 129; Henry More, *Henry More's Manual of Metaphysics: A Translation of the Enchiridium Metaphysicum (1679)*, trans. Alexander Jacob (Hildesheim: G. Olms Verlag, 1995), 118.

43 Henry More, *An Antidote against Atheism: Or, an Appeal to the Naturall Faculties of the Minde of Man*, ed. G. A. J. Rogers (Bristol: Thoemmes Press, 1655), 12.

44 More, *Antidote*, 334–5; Henry More, *Divine Dialogues* (London: Printed by James Flesher, 1668), 108; For an excellent discussion about More on space see Leech, *Hammer of the Cartesians*, 108, esp. 140.

45 More, *Manual of Metaphysics*, 172.

46 This interpretation follows that of Leech, *Hammer of the Cartesians*, 172, 174–5.

47 Newton, "De Gravitatione," 142; Slowik, "Ontology of Space," 435–6.

48 J. E. McGuire, "The Fate of the Date: The Theology of Newton's 'Principia' Revisited," in *Rethinking the Scientific Revolution*, ed. Margaret J Osler (Cambridge: Cambridge University Press, 2000), 279.

49 McGuire, "Fate of the Date," 282.

50 McGuire, "Fate of the Date," 282.

51 McGuire, "Fate of the Date," 280; Newton, "De Gravitatione," 140.

52 McGuire, "Fate of the Date," 281.

53 McGuire, "Fate of the Date," 287.

54 Betty Jo Teeter Dobbs, *The Janus Faces of Genius: The Role of Alchemy in Newton's Thought* (Cambridge: Cambridge University Press, 1991), 195.

55 Quoted in Dobbs, *Janus Faces*, 195.

56 Dobbs, *Janus Faces*, 205.

57 J. E. McGuire, "'Predicates of Pure Existence: Newton on God's Space and Time," in *Philosophical Perspectives on Newtonian Science*, ed. Phillip Bricker and R. I. G. Hughes (Cambridge, MA: MIT Press, 1990), 91–108.

58 Quoted in Frank E. Manuel, *The Religion of Isaac Newton: The Fremantle Lectures 1973* (Oxford: Clarendon, 1974), 35n.

59 Jammer, *Concepts of Space*, 96.

60 McGuire, "Fate of the Date," 285.

61 Jammer, *Concepts of Space*, 108.

62 Jammer, *Concepts of Space*, 115.

63 Peter Harrison, "Was Newton a Voluntarist?" in *Newton and Newtonianism: New Studies*, ed. James E. Force and Sarah Hutton (London: Kluwer Academic Publishers, 2004), 41.

64 Martha K. Zebrowski, "Commanded of God, because 'Tis Holy and Good': The Christian Platonism and Natural Law of Samuel Clarke," *Enlightenment and Dissent* 16 (1997): 4 makes this point. Clarke, *Works*, 1738, ii: 530.

65 Clarke, *Works*, 1738, ii: 527.

66 Clarke, *Works*, 1738, ii: 752–3.

67 Thomas, *Honest Mind*, 23.

68 Clarke, *Works*, 1738, ii: 745.

69 Clarke, *Works*, 1738, ii: 743.

70 Price, *Review*, 290n.

71 Price, *Review*, 290.

72 Price, *Review*, 88; Thomas, *Honest Mind*, 24.

73 Thomas, *Honest Mind*, 25; Price, *Review*, 289.

74 Zebrowski, "Commanded of God," 3.

75 Zebrowski, "Commanded of God," 18.

76 Clarke, *Works*, 1738, ii: 626–7.
77 Clarke, *Works*, 1738, ii: 633.
78 Clarke, *Works*, 1738, ii: 635; 636–7.
79 Zebrowski, "Commanded of God," 21.
80 Clarke, *Works*, 1738, ii: 569.
81 Price, *Review*, 290.
82 Thomas, *Honest Mind*, 26.
83 Thomas, *Honest Mind*, 26–7.
84 Price, *Review*, 114–16n; 283; Thomas, *Honest Mind*, 27.
85 Zebrowski, "Commanded of God."
86 Price, *Review*, 293.
87 Crowder, "Berkeley," 9.
88 Crowder, "Berkeley," 9.
89 Samuel Clarke, *The Works of Samuel Clarke*, vol. iv (London: Printed for John and Paul Knapton, 1738), 590.
90 Quoted in B. A. Gerrish "Natural and Revealed Religion," in *The Cambridge History of Eighteenth-Century Philosophy*, ed. Knud Haakonssen, vol. 1 (Cambridge: Cambridge University Press, 2006), 654.
91 Diego Lucci, "William Wollaston's Religion of Nature," in *Atheism and Deism Revalued: Heterodox Religious Identities in Britain, 1650–1800*, ed. Wayne Hudson, Diego Lucci, and Jeffrey R. Wigelsworth (Farnham: Ashgate, 2014), 130.
92 James E. Force, "Samuel Clarke's Four Categories of Deism, Isaac Newton and the Bible," in *Scepticism in the History of Philosophy*, ed. Richard H. Popkin (London: Kluwer Academic Publishers, 1996), 63.
93 Clarke, *Works*, 1738, ii: 605; Force, "Four Categories of Deism," 56; Lucci, "Religion of Nature," 130.
94 Geoffrey Holmes, *The Trial of Doctor Sacheverell* (London: Eyre Methuen, 1973), 43.
95 Margaret C. Jacob, "The Crisis of the European Mind: Hazard Revisited," in *Politics and Culture in Early Modern Europe: Essays in Honor of H. G. Koenigsberger*, ed. Phyllis Mack and Margaret C. Jacob (Cambridge: Cambridge University Press, 1987), 265; Margaret C. Jacob, *The Newtonians and the English Revolution, 1689–1720* (Hassocks, Sussex: The Harvester Press, 1976).
96 David Kubrin, "Newton's Inside Out! Magic, Class Struggle, and the Rise of Mechanism in the West," in *The Analytic Spirit: Essays in the History of Science*, ed. Harry Woolf (London: Cornell University Press, 1981), 115; Jacob, "Crisis of the European Mind," 265.
97 C. B. Wilde, "Hutchinsonianism, Natural Philosophy and Religious Controversy in Eighteenth Century Britain," *History of Science* 18 (1980): 9.
98 Patricia Fara, "Marginalized Practices," in *The Cambridge History of Science, Volume 4: The Eighteenth Century*, ed. Roy Porter (Cambridge: Cambridge University Press, 2003), 503.
99 Hiram Caton, *The Politics of Progress: The Origins and Development of the Commercial Republic, 1600–1835* (Gainesville: University of Florida Press, 1988), 201.
100 Francis Blackburne, *Proposals for an Application to Parliament for Relief the Matter of Subscription to the Liturgy and Thirty-Nine Articles of the Established Church of England* (London: Sold by B. White, 1771), 1.
101 William Gibson, *The Church of England 1688–1832: Unity and Accord* (London: Routledge, 2001), 99.
102 Gibson, *Church of England*, 99–100.

103 Mark Philp, "Rational Religion and Political Radicalism in the 1790s," *Enlightenment and Dissent* 4 (1985): 37.

104 Martin Fitzpatrick, "Toleration and Truth," *Enlightenment and Dissent* 1 (1982): 23.

105 Quoted in Anthony Page, *John Jebb and the Enlightenment Origins of British Radicalism* (London: Praeger, 2003), 108.

106 Gibson, *Church of England*, 101.

107 Wilde, "Hutchinsonianism," 10.

108 Jeremy Gregory, *Restoration, Reformation and Reform, 1660–1828: Archbishops of Canterbury and Their Diocese* (Oxford: Clarendon, 2000), 59.

109 William Jones, *The Theological and Miscellaneous Works of the Rev. William Jones* (London: Printed for C. and J. Rivington, 1826), 396–9.

110 William Jones, "Preface," in *The Works of the Right Rev. George Horne*, vol. 1 (London: Printed for J. Johnson, 1818), xxvii.

111 Quoted in Albert J. Kuhn, "Glory or Gravity: Hutchinson Vs. Newton," *Journal of the History of Ideas* 22 (1961): 310.

112 C. D. A. Leighton, " 'Knowledge of Divine Things': A Study of Hutchinsonianism," *History of European Ideas* 26, no. 3–4 (2000): 162–3.

113 Kuhn, "Glory or Gravity," 307.

114 Kuhn, "Glory or Gravity," 308.

115 John Hutchinson, "A Treatise of Power Essential and Mechanical: Wherein the Original, and That Part of Religion Which Now Is Natural, Is Stated," in *The Philosophical and Theological Works of John Hutchinson*, vol. 5 (London: Printed for James Hodges, 1748–9), 226.

116 Geoffrey Cantor, "Revelation and the Cyclical Cosmos of John Hutchinson," in *Images of the Earth: Essays in the History of the Environmental Sciences*, ed. Ludmilla Jordanova and Roy Porter (Oxford: British Society for the History of Science, 1997), 32; John Hutchinson, "Moses's Principia. Part II: Of the Circulation of the Heavens; of the Cause of the Motion and Course of the Earth, Moon Etc. In Confirmation of the Natural History of the Bible," in *The Philosophical and Theological Works of John Hutchinson*, vol. 2 (London: Printed for James Hodges, 1748–9), xxix – xxx.

117 Kuhn, "Glory or Gravity," 318.

118 Kuhn, "Glory or Gravity," 318.

119 Nigel Aston, "Horne and Heterodoxy: The Defence of Anglican Beliefs in the Late Enlightenment," *English Historical Review* 108, no. 429 (1993): 900.

120 Kuhn, "Glory or Gravity," 319.

121 Gibson, *Church of England*, 101.

122 William Jones, "The Life of Bishop Horne," in *The Theological and Miscellaneous Works of the Rev. William Jones*, vol. 6 (London: Printed for C. and J. Rivington, 1826), 16.

123 Quoted in Aston, "Horne and Heterodoxy," 900.

124 Jacob, "Crisis of the European Mind," 269.

125 Cantor, "Revelation," 21.

126 Gregory, *Restoration, Reformation and Reform*, 59.

127 Leighton, "Knowledge of Divine Things," 172: its significance has been debated but Leslie Stephen and Leighton, among others, argue for its enormous importance throughout the eighteenth century.

128 Ralph Heathcote, *The Use of Reason Asserted in Matters of Religion: Or, Natural Religion the Foundation of Revealed* (London: Printed for Thomas Payne, 1756), 3.

129 For this argument, see Wilde, "Hutchinsonianism," 6.

130 Kuhn, "Glory or Gravity," 306–7.

131 Quoted in Aston, "Horne and Heterodoxy," 900.
132 Joseph Priestley, *Letters to the Author of Remarks on Several Late Publications Relative to the Dissenters, in a Letter to Dr. Priestley* (London: Printed for J. Johnson, 1770), 16.
133 Price, *Review*, 285.
134 D.D. Raphael, "Editor's Preface" in Price, *Review*, vii.
135 Joseph Butler, *Fifteen Sermons Preached at the Rolls Chapel. . . to Which Are Added, Six Sermons Preached on Publick Occasions* (London: Printed for John and Paul Knapton, 1749), 320 c.f. 319.
136 Bob Tennant, *Conscience, Consciousness and Ethics in Joseph Butler's Philosophy and Ministry* (Woodbridge: The Boydell Press, 2011), 4.
137 Butler, *Sermons*, 339.
138 Samuel I. Mintz, *The Hunting of Leviathan: Seventeenth Century Reactions to the Materialism and Moral Philosophy of Thomas Hobbes* (Cambridge: Cambridge University Press, 1970), 150.
139 Ernst Cassirer, *The Platonic Renaissance in England*, trans. James P. Pettegrove (New York: Nelson, 1953), 152.
140 Norman Kemp Smith, "Is Divine Existence Credible," in *Religion and Understanding*, ed. D. Z. Phillips (Oxford: Basil Blackwell, 1967), 114.
141 Price, *Review*, 273.
142 Price, *Review*, 273.
143 Joseph Butler, *The Analogy of Religion, Natural and Revealed, to the Constitution and Course of Nature* (London: Printed for John and Paul Knapton, 1736), iv.
144 Crowder, "Berkeley," 4.
145 Price, *Four Dissertations*, 366.
146 Price, *Four Dissertations*, 461.
147 B.J. Shapiro, "Latitudinarianism and Science and Seventeenth-Century England," *Past and Present* 40 (1968): 30.
148 John Wilkins, *Of the Principles and Duties of Natural Religion* (London: Printed for R. Chiswell, 1710), 10–11.
149 Force, "Four Categories of Deism," 63.
150 Samuel Clarke, "A Discourse Concerning the Unchangeable Obligations of Natural Religion, and the Truth and Certainty of the Christian Revelation," in *The Works of Samuel Clarke*, vol. ii (London: Printed for John and Paul Knapton, 1738), 666.
151 Kuhn, "Glory or Gravity," 305.
152 Quoted in Kuhn, "Glory or Gravity," 305.
153 Price, *Four Dissertations*, 362.
154 To the Marquis of Lansdowne September 13, 1789 Richard Price, *The Correspondence of Richard Price*, ed. W.B. Peach and D.O. Thomas, vol. III (Cardiff: University of Wales Press, 1994), 256.
155 Douglas Hedley, "Imagination and Natural Theology," in *The Oxford Handbook of Natural Theology*, ed. Russell Re-Manning, John Hedley Brooke, and Fraser Watts (Oxford: Oxford University Press, 2013), 549.
156 Joshn Money, "Joseph Priestley in Cultural Context: Philosophic Spectacle, Popular Belief and Popular Politics in Eighteenth-Century Birmingham," *Enlightenment and Dissent* 8 (1989): 71; Joseph Priestley, *The Theological and Miscellaneous Works of Joseph Priestley*, ed. John Towill Rutt, vol. 3 (London: R. Hunter, 1817), 219.
157 Douglas Hedley, "Real Atheism and Cambridge Platonism: Men of Latitude, Polemics, and the Great Dead Philosophers," in *Platonisms: Ancient, Modern, and Postmodern*, ed. Kevin Corrigan and John D. Turner (Leiden: Brill, 2007), 160.

158 Hedley, "Real Atheism," 166.
159 Stephen R.L. Clark, *Biology and Christian Ethics* (Cambridge: Cambridge University Press, 2000), 119.
160 John Gascoigne, *Cambridge in the Age of Enlightenment: Science, Religion and Politics from the Restoration to the French Revolution* (Cambridge: Cambridge University Press, 1989), 213.
161 Gascoigne, *Age of Enlightenment*, 249, 269.
162 Gascoigne, *Age of Enlightenment*, 238.
163 Gascoigne, *Age of Enlightenment*, 239.
164 William Jones, *An Essay on the Church* (London: Printed by R. Raikes, 1787), 77.
165 Gibson, *Church of England*, 102.

5 Casting out Hagar and her children
Deiformity, liberty and politics

The year 1785 saw the president and fellows of Harvard University hail Richard Price as 'a patron of humanity, a benevolent assertor of the civil and religious liberties of mankind, and a warm friend to the United States of America.'[1] This sentiment was not untypical of those addressed to Price by his American contemporaries: they followed an official request (put forward by John Adams, Arthur Lee and Benjamin Franklin on behalf of Congress) to make Price a citizen of the United States in recognition of the encouragement and support given by Price to the American rebels in their struggle for independence from Great Britain.

Although Price's influence is little debated today, especially in Britain, to Washington's 'revolutionists,' it seems, he only had to speak to be heard.[2] Much of his influence was channelled through three pamphlets published between 1776 and 1784: *Observations on the Nature of Civil Liberty, Additional Observations on the Nature and Value of Civil Liberty, and the War with America* and *Observations on the Importance of the American Revolution and the Means of Making it a Benefit to the World*. More than 17 editions went to press in Britain, the United States and Europe, making Price one of the most widely read supporters of the American colonies. The first pamphlet, *Observations on the Nature of Civil Liberty*, was regarded by some as the 'most famous British tract on the war with America,'[3] and his political works sparked furious replies from, among others, Edmund Burke and John Wesley. Given the model of democratic ecclesiology espoused by eighteenth-century Rational Dissenters, and their role in encouraging support for a more participatory government, it is perhaps unsurprising that the cause of the colonists found such a sympathetic defender in Price. Although the Rational Dissenters were in the minority among the promoters of American liberty, they made a significant contribution to the ideology of independence, and were able to give considerable impetus to the campaign.

At first glance, Price's political philosophy seems to espouse a classic liberalism in Lockean form. He himself states, 'The principles on which I have argued . . . are the same with those taught by Mr. Locke and all the writers on civil liberty who have been hitherto most admired in this country.'[4] Commentators have thus assumed Price has a Lockean account of liberty despite

Zebrowski's warning that Price never explains how liberty is grounded in reason and he gives no argument that his rationalism is that of Locke's.[5] This chapter argues that in fact Price's highly theological model of liberty, upon which his political philosophy is built, is one substantially informed by Platonic thought, including Cambridge Platonism. Although the basic political *principle* of liberty Price upholds is similar in essence to that of Locke's; his reason for holding it is fundamentally Platonic rather than Lockean and is grounded in a Platonic metaphysics.

This observation will lend support to the claim that Price represents the spirit of the Platonic tradition in eighteenth-century thought.[6] Through its influence on Richard Price, therefore, the Platonic tradition should be recognised as having significance for the shaping of the vision of the American struggle for independence. A further conclusion follows from this. A consideration of Price's political ideas challenge conventional conceptions of what liberalism actually is – a point of some importance when it is often assumed to be part and parcel of the project of modernity and thereby inherently anti-Christian.[7] A Rawlsian account of liberalism, for example, prioritises the right over the good and has no strong conception about the real purpose of human freedom. Central to mainstream definitions of liberalism is, therefore, a commitment to a negative conception of liberty – a *freedom from* external constraint. It is neutral with respect to how one should live one's life. As Isaiah Berlin proposed, the core meaning of liberty on this understanding is freedom from coercion.[8]

Such a definition underpins the assumption that it is inevitably both secular and nihilist, part of an Enlightenment that was anti-theological at its core.[9] Jonathan Israel's distinction between the moderate and radical Enlightenments gives weight to this account. As stated in Chapter 2, he depicts values of religious toleration together with values of equality, democracy, freedom as part of a 'package logic' of materialism and monism, part of the radical Enlightenment and completely distinct from its more moderate theological counterpart.[10] The preceding chapters have gone some way towards challenging the neatness of these Enlightenments, and by examining Price's political thought, this chapter will advance the argument further. Price presents a Platonically informed model of freedom based on a perfectionist anthropology, and liberty is not the primary good for him. His politics forces a rethink of Platonic political philosophy, suggesting it is not as totalitarian and antidemocratic in some of its potential practical applications as has so often been thought. In addition to this, his Platonic metaphysics encourages a reconsideration of the understanding of classical liberalism itself, challenging its necessary connections with an anti-theological tradition.

Moral liberty in the healthy mind and the well-ordered state

There is an anomaly in viewing Price's political philosophy as Lockean. Price's *A Review of the Principle Questions in Morals* is concerned to deconstruct Lockean epistemology and defend in its place a Platonic account of innate ideas. As argued in Chapter 1, the understanding as a source of new ideas is vital for Price's moral epistemology, grounding his rejection of relativism and related voluntarism. The *Review* makes a direct link between an empiricism that grounds all ideas on sense experience and Protagorean relativism.[11] Likewise, any form of voluntarism that establishes the laws of morality on God's will rather than God's nature (including that of Locke's) would leave morality open to the charge of relativism and subjectivism. Why then would Price, who expends so much energy refuting the inherent dangers he perceives in a Lockean moral epistemology, adopt Lockean political principles, especially given the acknowledged moral foundation of his political theory? This apparent incongruity may be resolved by understanding Price's political idea of liberty as arising primarily from his Platonic metaphysics.

During the latter part of the eighteenth century, liberty became a central concept in arguments both for and against American independence. Those on both sides of the debate were agreed that liberty was a fundamental moral good, but disagreements centred on whether this liberty was best protected by governance under the 'mother' country or by total independence. For those concerned to safeguard the supremacy of Britain, an organic model of church and state was seen to justify the subordination of the members under one governing body; as the human body is governed by the head, so too is England an empire governed by a supreme king to which the body politick ought to be obedient.[12] This organic model underpinned the force of Burke's insistence that God willed the state with the king as its head – a philosophy grounded on a Trinitarian Christology in which a fully divine and fully human Christ is the head of the body of the Church. On the other hand, liberty defined in terms of self-government was the definition commonly accepted by both Rational Dissenters and Whigs, and it was this conception that did much to aid the cause of the American rebels. 'Civil liberty' and 'political liberty' were terms used to refer to participation by the people in their government on both sides of the Atlantic.[13] The link between heterodoxy and democratic principles has been well noted, and although Rational Dissent did not necessarily champion republicanism, they nevertheless saw themselves as 'friends of liberty' with most advocating basic democratic principles.[14] Price too rejected any automatic divine right of kings or hereditary succession and called for American representation in government but, unlike many of his Rational Dissenting contemporaries who sought an alternative ecclesiology and political philosophy on the grounds of an anti-Trinitarianism, his reasons for rejecting this model were grounded in a distinctly theological and Platonic conception of liberty, which, as he saw it, made participatory politics an essential part of moral government.

Price's *Observations of the Nature of Civil Liberty* identifies four different interrelated branches of liberty, and the discussion here sets out the idea of liberty that underpins all his political tracts. Physical liberty, the first branch, is defined as the power to act free from external duress. It is the most basic kind of liberty and entails that our actions are not the effect of anything external to ourselves. We can be said to have physical liberty if our actions are caused by our will, desires, reason or volition and are 'not effects of the operation of any foreign cause.'[15] Religious liberty, the second type of liberty, is described as the freedom of religious belief, and it involves 'making the decisions of our own consciences respecting religious truth.'[16] Price says little to expand his discussion of this branch of liberty, however, because he links it directly to moral liberty, the third type: the power of following our sense of right and wrong and 'acting in conformity to our reflecting and moral principles, without being controlled by any contrary principles.'[17] Establishing moral liberty, he thinks, automatically legitimates religious liberty. Moral liberty is absolutely crucial for Price, and it is the foundation for his conception of human freedom. Although physical liberty involves the absence of external impediments, genuine freedom, he insists, lies in moral liberty, also defined in terms of self-government or 'being guided by one's own will' – a concept that Price describes as running through all the types of liberty. A discussion of moral liberty leads Price to a definition of civil liberty, the fourth and final branch of liberty. Civil liberty is the power of a civil society or state to govern itself by means of fair representation, and this definition results in his insistence on the absolute importance of a participatory government as a means of establishing self-governance within civil society.[18] Price elsewhere makes a clear analogy between civil and moral liberty,[19] and understanding his conception of moral liberty is imperative for understanding his political ideology. It is in attempting to do just this that the Platonic nature of his thought becomes apparent.

Price's Platonic anthropology underpins his account of freedom. As explained in Chapter 2, his tripartite division of the soul into appetites, affections and reason gives reason pre-eminence. Reason is the supreme self-reflecting principle; it directs and determines the other elements of the soul, directs the passions to their proper objects, confines them to their proper functions and corrects 'whatever is amiss in the inward man, and inconsistent with its sound and healthful state.'[20] Here he borrows Plato's analogy between the healthy mind and the well-ordered state: both are marked by liberty, righteousness and peace in which every member keeps his proper station, and faithfully performs his proper duty.[21] Piety and virtue are thus defined as the 'just regulation of the passions.'[22] The point here is primarily a psychological (rather than political) one: moral goodness, or virtue, is defined as the passions and affections being kept in subjection to reason and God. The deiform nature of reason is crucial here. That reason is 'immortal and divine' grants it due authority over the other elements in the soul. In this scheme, individual freedom is maintained as long as reason is supreme within the soul, whereas a person governed by appetites is merely a slave. For Price, it is in the possession of reason, and its superiority over the passions and instincts, that a person's liberty is located: 'What tranquillity and bliss must that mind possess whose oppressors and tyrants lie vanquished; which has regained its health and liberty.'[23] Liberty is then defined in terms of self-government and is explained in terms of the government of the human soul and its passions by reason: 'He whose perceptions of moral obligation are controlled by his passions has lost his moral liberty, and the most common language applied to him is that he wants self-government.'[24]

Platonic freedom

At the heart of this psychology lies a Platonic account of human freedom, perhaps most articulately expressed by Plotinus but also Ralph Cudworth and Benjamin Whichcote. Cudworth's distinction between freewill and freedom is important here, much of which is indebted to Whichcote and Plotinus. For Whichcote, moral freedom is not the freedom to do wrong, because the person who is truly free (who has moral freedom) will do what is right: 'The *Government* of our Spirits is the greatest *Freedom*.'[25] Freedom is therefore intrinsically connected to rationality and virtue. In his later development of this position, Cudworth envisages *freewill* as a mixture of perfection and imperfection as it entails the capacity to choose wrongly. *Freedom*, however, is the capacity for preferring the 'spiritual' to the 'animal,'[26] and a perfect being does not have to choose the good life because he or she lives the good life by nature. Whereas sin enslaves, a truly free person is habitually 'fixed' in moral goodness, and will freely and easily 'comply with the law of the Divine life.' 'True liberty . . . is a state of virtue, holiness, and righteousness.'[27]

Cudworth's and Whichcote's philosophy owes much to Plotinus's account of freedom, or what he calls 'being in power' over oneself. *Ennead* 6.8 is devoted to an examination of what it might mean for someone to be 'free' and rests upon a psychology of reason, passions and will. Always acting according to our wishes (what Price would call physical freedom) cannot, for Plotinus (or later for Price), be genuine freedom, or we would be enslaved to our will and would have to call those under the influence of drugs or alcohol free. Instead, for Plotinus,

> we shall grant voluntary action to one whose doings depend on the activities of Intellect and who is free from bodily affections. We trace back what is in our power to the noblest principle, the activity of Intellect, and shall grant that the premises of action derived from this are truly free.

The gods who live in this way, he says, can truly be said to have 'self-determination.'[28]

In Cudworth's development of Plotinus's philosophy, freedom and rationality are entirely the same thing, which is why, for Cudworth, the 'faculty' of the human soul is freedom because 'the human soul is self-active being,' by which, he says, 'we mean a being who has a spring and foundation of activity within itself.'[29] The Gospel law of love, therefore,

> [puts] us into a condition of the most pure and perfect Liberty; and whosoever really entertaines this Law, he hath *thrust out Hagar* quite, he hath *cast out the Bondwoman and her Children*. . . Here is Gospelfreedome, when *the Law of the Spirit of life in Christ Jesus, hath made us free, from the Law of sinne and death*; when we have a liberty from sinne, and not a liberty to sinne.[30]

The key to genuine freedom for Plotinus and the Cambridge Platonists is the interior characteristic of freedom. For Plotinus, the principle of intellect is in the good, which means the intellect is governed internally when it is determined by the good. Slavery is that which is imposed externally. Plotinus thus defines the power of self-determination as action according to a right opinion together with knowledge of *why* the opinion is right.[31] The Cambridge Platonists develop this Plotinian insistence on reason as that part of us which resembles the divine, seen as the spring of free action. Liberty is therefore defined as 'an inward, living principle of virtue and activity, further heightened, and united, and informed with light and truth.'[32] Such a view of freedom explained why Cudworth could never have accepted Thomas Hobbes's mechanism in which freedom means merely the 'absence of the lets and hindrances of motion,' or the absences of physical impediments to action.[33] Voluntary human action, Hobbes believed, is caused by appetite, and the concept of will ought not to refer to a separate faculty in the soul, but merely to the last appetite before action is carried out.[34] Central to this is a conception of reason as primarily passive and unable to initiate human action. Cudworth maintained against Hobbes that the human soul is 'self-active,' having a 'spring and fountain' of activity within itself. The very nature of the human soul is therefore expressed by the name '*liberum arbitrium* or free will.'[35] The defence of active reason able to override passions and affections was, for the Cambridge Platonists, essential for the very possibility of freedom and morality, and it underpinned their commitment to freedom of conscience and toleration.

Price adopts this view in its entirety and he follows Whichcote and Cudworth in contrasting a negative freedom (freedom from external constraints) with positive freedom (freedom to follow what is good). There are similarities here with Isaiah Berlin's definitions of positive and negative liberty, in which positive freedom is the freedom 'to lead one prescribed form of life,'[36] but in Price, it is worked out in connection with the good. For Price, those who confuse indifference between two moral choices and genuine freedom have confused moral liberty with natural, or physical, liberty: the most perfect moral liberty takes place, Price suggests, where there is the strongest attachment to rectitude and *not* where there is indifference.[37] His concept of physical liberty is in essence Cudworth's idea of freewill: a freedom from external constraint upon action. Positive freedom, however, is a freedom *for* what is good. 'The absolute government of reason' he states, 'would be an absolute dominion over our resolutions and actions, and therefore would be absolute and perfect liberty.'[38] Central to Price's account, as well as Cudworth's, is an insistence that there is more to action than just the effect of desires and passions:

> The human mind would appear to have little order or consistency in it, were we to consider it as only a system of passions and affections, which are continually drawing us different ways, without any thing at the head of them to govern them, and the strongest of which for the time necessarily determines the conduct. But this is far from being its real state.[39]

Just as the negation of mechanism was important for Cudworth, so too was it essential for Price in his stance against Priestley's emergence account of human action. Priestley maintained that all actions have causes in the form of motives and that that these motives have prior causes just as all events have causes. For Price, however, this freedom is predetermined because every effect, including all human action, depends on a previous sufficient cause and, for him, this type of freedom was insufficient: 'All voluntary action is, *by the terms*, free, and implies the *physical possibility* of forbearing it.'[40] Human action, he insists cannot be initiated by a material, mechanical cause. Postulating the existence of the spirit, which is independent and able to move matter, enabled Price to take the same approach against Priestley that Cudworth had taken against Hobbes a century before.

This philosophy of freedom explains why for Price and for the Cambridge Platonists, there could be no perceived antagonism between freedom and determinism. Freedom is not indifference to what is good, nor is it merely the power of choosing – this is merely the condition of physical liberty – but it is the power of determining oneself by the idea of good; freedom increases according to each person's identification with, and knowledge of, the good.[41] This is the Platonic answer to the age-old problem of the freedom of the gods discussed by Plato in the *Euthyphro* and later by Plotinus:

> Now, where there is no compulsion to follow another, how can one speak of slavery? How could something borne towards the Good be under compulsion since its desire for the Good will be voluntary if it knows it is good and goes to it as good? For the involuntary is leading away from the good and towards the compulsory, if something is carried to that which is not good for it; and that is enslaved which is not master of its going to the Good.[42]

The Cambridge Platonists take up the same argument. John Smith, for example, suggests, 'If we should ask a good man, when he finds himself best at ease, when he finds himself most free; his answer would be, when he is under the most powerful constraints of divine love.'[43] The divine understanding, because it beholds all things clearly, has the greatest freedom and is not determined to any particular action as it has eternal light and truth to act by. This conception of freedom and goodness is what lies behind Cudworth's reference to Hagar and is why, for Price, we are under a state of slavery if our passions usurp conscience – the one just authority over our actions. Our actions are not as Hobbes and Hume believed, necessarily determined by whichever desire happens to be the strongest but are free when determined by what is just and right. Genuine freedom is therefore the ability of the self to determine itself by reason in accordance with the moral law.[44] For Price, along with Cudworth, John Smith and Whichcote, freedom involves the will's action in regard to the good, and it rests upon a Platonically influenced conception of reason, which distinguishes between ratiocination and the understanding: reason is not only the ability to make logical deductions but also involves an imaginative ability which unifies the whole person in the pursuit of truth. This is a state of perfect liberty, and it explains why, for Price in his political tracts, liberty is a religious and moral issue. The absolute governance of reason, he says, is absolute perfect liberty, essential for the very foundation of morality.[45] The governance of reason over the passions, suggested by the tripartite division of the soul, is thus the governance of human life by the good and the true.

Moral liberty in the political sphere

In his political pamphlets, Price develops this Platonic psychology and its corresponding account of freedom, and uses it to argue, as a matter of principle, for the importance of self-governance in all spheres, particularly the political. In order to do good, a person must have reason in command; in order to be enlightened and virtuous, he argued, a country must be free without tyrants or slavery.[46] There are two strands to his argument here, and he makes little effort to distinguish them or even to indicate that he is aware of this complexity. On the one hand, he seems to see self-governance as an intrinsic good, or metaphysical ideal, which means, for him, that it should, as a matter of ethical principle, be established on every level possible, from the physical to the civil. The state, therefore, quite literally becomes the soul writ large. 'Reason' in the individual is the 'will of the people' in the state. There is an alienation of the 'passions' in this scheme: they are seen as 'other' and their dominance is nothing short of slavery. Civil liberty is therefore the power of a state to govern itself

> by its own discretion or by laws of its own making, without being subject to the impositions of any power in appointing and directing which the collective body of the people have no concern and over which they have no control.[47]

Self-determination and self-government are contrasted with slavery of all kinds, whether a metaphorical slavery to sin or a more literal slavery to a dictatorial government.

On the other hand, Price often argues that there is a moral imperative to make nations self-governing because every society should make sure that the conditions for moral virtue on an individual level are protected. He suggests, furthermore, that this could only be done within a self-governed state: the analogy between the soul and the state still holds in this interpretation, but the argument becomes more practical than metaphysical.

> The dominion of passion . . . is a kind of brute force unsettling our resolutions, and shackling our wills. It is licentiousness in the mind which produces a like restraint upon liberty and the same kind of evils, with licentiousness in the state.[48]

Liberty on all levels (including moral and civil) is regarded as vital for the development of virtue and is called a 'sacred' blessing. Price states that wherever liberty is lacking, whether as physical, moral, religious, or civil liberty, 'there is a force which stands opposed to the agent's *own* will; and which as far as it operates, produces *servitude*.'[49] The danger then is an invasion of the rights of every member of the state. A society endowed with freedom he argues tends to exalt human nature because each member of a free state possesses a consciousness of dignity and feels incitements to improvement. This might seem somewhat overly optimistic, but there can be no doubt that Price's belief was based on a genuine commitment to the view that the dignity of all human beings entailed that our natural and proper state is one of freedom and virtue, and it was to the end that he thought all people should be progressing.

What is important to note is that in this move from moral liberty to civil liberty, Price is not all that far removed from a political philosophy informed by a particular reading of several of Plato's dialogues. In many ways, it may seem strange that a defender of democratic principles like Price could find Platonism so attractive, as Plato was hardly the most highly regarded philosopher in the Western canon at that time, especially with many of those who advocated aspects of liberal philosophy. After reading the *Republic* for himself, Thomas Jefferson (with whom Price corresponded about the American situation) was clearly alarmed at the implications. He wrote to John Adams, 'It is fortunate for us that Platonic republicanism has not obtained the same favour as Platonic Christianity; or we should now have been all living, men, women, and children, pell mell together, like beasts of the field or forest.'[50] Jefferson distinguishes between what he saw as a Platonic politics and a Christianised Platonic epistemology and metaphysics, and he foreshadows later concerns with Plato's supposed authoritarianism and totalitarianism.[51]

It is tempting to cleave apart the influence of Platonism on the epistemology of the *Review* from Price's political ideas, just as Jefferson would have done with Plato himself. The two may not necessarily, however, have to be separated in this way. The much-maligned incompatibility between Plato's politics and liberalism largely lies with Plato's perfectionist philosophy. He has an account of the 'good' for human nature towards which human life should be orientated. The major problem the *Republic* has with democracy is the lack (characteristic of contemporary liberalism) of any conception of the good. There is no place in a democracy for good habits or any strong conception of a good environment in which to educate children.[52] A lack too of any notion of what might be called 'rights' puts Plato a long way from contemporary liberalism and sees him subject to Berlin's concern that there is a danger of authoritarianism in positive liberty.[53]

A closer examination of Plato reveals, however, that he is not so far removed from some of the central ideas that Price was promoting. At the heart of what Price is saying lies an indirect perfectionism, which makes him in some important respects rather more Platonic (or at least Socratic) than liberal. Plato characterises democracy by the freedom it gives its citizens: freedom of speech and freedom to choose the life they wish to lead. The result of this is a community notable for its variety of characters and its equality. Important too is that although everyone has a right to participate in government, no one is obliged to. Although Plato's widely recognised idea of the ideal republic is a stark contrast to this, there is a case to be made that the ideal republic is not a state that Plato intended as a reality to be established in this life.[54] Plato doubts towards the end of the *Republic* whether the republic could ever exist on earth and goes as far as to assert that it does not matter anyway, as it is a pattern in heaven on which our souls should be modelled: 'He who wishes can see it and found it in his own heart.'[55] Only philosophy can determine what is good for a state and, as it stands in this life, the republic is a pattern to follow internally. Drew Hyland points out the problematic nature of the very idea of the philosopher-kings: Socrates is the wisest man in Athens, and yet even he knows nothing. The wisdom needed to be a philosopher king is had by the gods alone, and the *Phaedrus*' myth of the charioteer highlights the intractable gulf between the gods and mere mortals who have had only a glimpse of the good.[56] This distinction is apparent too in the *Symposium*'s description of humans 'in the middle' between the mortal and the divine, in between ignorance and wisdom.[57] Furthermore, even if it were possible to establish the republic, it would inevitably decay, as Plato insists that human reason will always be imperfect and will lead to bad judgement.[58] Plato might have argued that the philosopher king is not impossible in theory, but his assessment of human character suggests he thought it impossible in practice.

What then, might Plato's political philosophy be for a human society that cannot actualise what is ideal? Plato's scheme can be seen as one of individual (rather than communal) perfectionism: 'The emphasis at the end of the *Republic* is on the individual's choice of a way of life; this is a major theme, in fact, of the myth with which the dialogue concludes.'[59] The 'story' or 'theory' of the republic might then be interpreted along the lines of the myth or likely story of the *Phaedrus*. The purpose of creating the state 'in discourse' might then be 'to see the justice or injustice of the individual soul writ large.'[60] What is most important is the search for justice in the human soul and the search for justice in the individual's choice of life.

Adopting an understanding of human teleology as individual perfection (understood as assimilation to God) means that it makes sense to interpret Plato as arguing for a form of democracy as a second-best politic.[61] A republic of philosopher-kings might be unattainable, but a democracy is best for the life that wishes to follow philosophy, and democracy enables one to choose the life one wishes. This is why, for Plato, 'anyone engaged in founding a state . . . should perhaps be made to pay a visit to a democracy.'[62] Important here is the Socratic emphasis on ignorance and the Platonic insistence that the good is beyond being. No mortal can have any assurance that he or she possesses knowledge of the good, and so it is absolutely vital in politics to safeguard against the tyranny of the absolute but ignorant ruler.[63] Epistemic humility is a guiding principle. Although, therefore, it is easy to see why some interpretations of Platonism see a real danger of totalitarianism with the possibility that certain beings might be considered more 'rational' than others, the emphasis on epistemic humility means, in actual fact, there is a clear argument against such conclusions embedded within Plato's own works.

The Phaedrus emphasises, perhaps more than most other dialogues, the fallen nature of human beings. Plato's concern in the *Laws* too is that absolute power should not be entrusted to a mortal: 'Human nature . . . is never able to take complete control of all human affairs without being filled with arrogance and injustice.'[64] Absolute power is thus to be avoided as human leaders are ignorant and mortal, not divine. This is why democracy, although not ideal, is a good runner-up to the ideal republic. Any lawgiver, therefore, should frame laws with an eye for freedom, unity and wisdom,[65] and the freedom that democracy gives is essential for the possibility of dialectic and for philosophy itself. Any polity must be based on the nature of the soul, and this is a soul that needs to engage in philosophy in order to attain wisdom. It is within a democracy that Plato can philosophise through dialogue and entertain different intellectual ideas. What is important for Plato then is that any political system is underpinned by the recognition of our fallibility.[66] Hence the conclusion drawn at the end of the *Theaetetus*: if Theaetetus and Socrates are unable to discover what knowledge is, then Theaetetus will at least be more 'gentle' towards his fellows.[67]

Plato's advocacy of democracy as a second-best solution is therefore firmly rooted in his metaphysic of individual self-perfection with regard to the good, but it maintains a much firmer commitment to liberty and freedom than is commonly recognised. The ideal republic, with its governance by the philosopher-kings is a pattern for our souls, and democracy is the best possible state that will encourage the realisation of this, through enabling the philosophical search for wisdom. This goes some way to explaining how liberty can foster virtue and why a Platonic motivation for political liberty is a deeply moral one.

Price's rejection of Burke's organic model of the state, and the application of his model of liberty in espousing a form of democracy, is therefore not all that far removed from this political theme of the Platonic dialogues. Although Price argues for basic liberal principles, he does so very much on perfectionist grounds, which marks a divergence between his political philosophy and the idea of freedom most often associated with liberalism. For Price, freedom is important, but it is largely instrumental to the development of the human person.

Becoming like god and the importance of teleology

Price's metaphysical commitment to the idea of the good and the true grounds the possibility of freedom and virtue. The *telos* of human existence is for him a life lived with regard to goodness, and a life that strives to become divine in so far as is possible. As argued in Chapter 2, Price follows the middle Platonists' interpretation of Plato's doctrine of deiformity and conceives of the ultimate end of human striving as being that of becoming like God in a deeply moral sense (as opposed to the more mystical Neoplatonic interpretation). That we are the 'intellectual offspring' of God means that in order to strive for divine excellence, we must make ourselves partake of God's nature.'[68] Acquiring a 'likeness to God,' for Price, involves replicating the moral excellence of God, and doing this is the key to true freedom. Deiformity involves a change in the orientation of human will towards truth and reason. Both moral and civil liberty are important for Price because they are the necessary prerequisites to such an undertaking.

Despite the fact that Price has been seen to accept a Lockean understanding of liberty and freedom, the positive flavour of his idea of freedom (in that it is freedom *for* what is good, as opposed to *from* restraint) is substantially more Platonic than Lockean.[69] It is inseparable from the Platonic idea of assimilation to God, involving a regaining of the soul's moral vision once glimpsed and now forgotten. Kinship between the knower and the thing known means that ethics and philosophy are thus inseparable: one cannot know the good without being good. This is why, for Plato, assimilation to God is accomplished through the gaining of wisdom and the 'moral respect' for God and human beings.[70] As Chapter 2 argued, both Whichcote and Price interpreted deiformity in terms of our imitating what they call God's moral 'attributes' or 'perfections' of love of truth, holiness and justice. Governing one's own will is important here, and it should be governed in accordance with the principle of truth, justice and goodness. Moral liberty is a positive conception of freedom because we must be free in order to achieve our potential to become like God. This positive, and moral, understanding of freedom was not alien to Locke, and in fact, it is important in his writings. Missing from Locke's view of liberty and an essential part of both the Cambridge Platonists' and Price's view of it, however, is the articulation of the positive sense of this freedom in terms of us freeing ourselves, through reason, from our passions in order to achieve our *telos*.[71]

Being free, in this account, means being governed by reason, which entails becoming like God. This makes Price's political philosophy a clear example of indirect perfectionism. It is perfectionist in that, as he sees it, the purpose of politics is to establish human perfection, but it is indirect in that he believes the state should safeguard the environment under which human improvement is made possible, rather than directly attempting to change its members for the better by interference. Human improvement means, for him, to 'become like God,' and this can only happen if an individual is morally free and not coerced in thought or action. It is easy to see why Price came to be so misunderstood in his own day, accused as he was by Adam Ferguson of wanting to grant thieves and pickpockets the right to make their own laws in an anarchist state.[72] Although he accepts, however, that civil liberty is in an important sense 'a power in everyone to act as he likes without any restraint,' it must be understood in conjunction with moral liberty. *No one* who acts wickedly acts freely, and liberty is essential not because of an individualistic right to do whatever one pleases, but because of the importance of freedom for virtue.

This ethical and political scheme highlights the internalising of religion and the commitment to an epistemic humility that echoes the Cambridge Platonists attitude to religious belief. Religion restores a good person to a just power of self-governance and enables the overcoming of self-will and passions. It establishes within a given person a 'just empire over all those blind powers and passions.'[73] Henry More develops this further in terms of freedom of conscience, and he foreshadows the eighteenth-century call for religious freedom by insisting on the right of freedom in religion, which should not be compromised by any magistrate. Liberty in religion, therefore, becomes a basic principle.[74] Price's call for religious freedom is a natural development of this prioritising of reason and conscience: true religion for Price is an honest mind and deiformity is the 'good,' so for Price, human society should be ordered to reflect this.

The writings of the Cambridge Platonists contain little political philosophy but Cudworth adopts the analogy between the state and the soul writ large. Commonwealth is an idea proceeding from the unifying power and activity of the mind itself.[75] A perfectionist scheme also guides Cudworth's attitude to political power, which for him is founded on the common good as a force that underpins society, being more fundamental than the social contract or power of government. The good grounds all contracts and covenants because without natural justice, contracts are meaningless. The true head of any state is God, not leviathan, because God (the principle of goodness and justice) underpins the social contract. It is goodness that creates the obligation for sovereigns to seek the good of their subjects and for subjects to obey sovereigns.[76] Cudworth has no developed philosophy of democratic self-governance, but his defence of any authority of the sovereign is grounded on the priority of moral goodness. The commonwealth cannot be grounded on a Hobbesian contract or an appeal to tradition because such voluntarism would only serve to undermine the reality of immutable morality, which means 'conscience, and religious obligation to duty, is the only basis, and essential foundation, of a polity.'[77] This leads Benjamin Carter to conclude that Cudworth's political principles are in fact 'a powerful, almost democratic defence of a society based on equality and justice for all.'[78] Price's defence of the constitution and the Glorious Revolution of 1688 is based on exactly the same principles. Like many defenders of the colonists, he tended to see the British attitude to America as an attempt to challenge the restrictions on monarchical power imposed by 1688. In his political pamphlets, he blends Locke's rejection of the divine right of a minority to govern the majority without consent with a Platonic epistemology and metaphysics that privileged the good and the true, and envisaged freedom as an escape from the alien passions that would usurp human conscience.

Price's understanding of freedom gave him a reason why the interests of the whole should not override those of the individual; one of the problems Berlin identifies with positive liberty. As a Rational Dissenter living in the eighteenth century, he would never have proposed, unlike some advocates of positive freedom, that the colonists or a slave, for example, is free if he or she is content.[79] In fact, he actively opposed John Wesley's argument that the colonies have more liberty and are better off under British rule. It was not liberty per se that was important to Price (this would be akin to the mere physical liberty of choosing), but the 'moral' liberty of self-determination, or self-government. He insists that only when a country is governed by adequate and just representation is it free. Great Britain is therefore trying to rob North America of 'that liberty to which every member of society, and all civil communities, have a natural and unalienable title.'[80] Just as the individual should be governed by reason, it must be a representative of the people who governs them because it must be the will of the community that governs the community. Representation must be complete, which means that all parts of society must be represented. The representatives of a free state must be freely chosen (there must be no buying of votes or corruption), the representatives themselves must be free (they must not be subject to any external will) and they must be chosen for short terms and be accountable to their constituents.[81] Price insists that this is not necessarily the best form of government, but these points are prerequisites of liberty. In the same way, self-determination is not the whole of virtue but is necessary for it. Although Price's model of liberty, with the 'head' or reason ruling over the 'animal' (or bodily) parts, is in an important sense organic, it leads to a conclusion vastly divergent from that of Burke.

Price's conception of liberty must be said, therefore, to be in some important respects far more Platonic than liberal in a Lockean or Rawlsian sense.

His Platonism makes liberty a moral concept, essential for the possibility of deiformity. Justice is not, as Rawls would see it, based on consensus but on metaphysics.[82] If John Rawls is right that the absence of commitment to comprehensive moral ideals is essential to liberalism as a political doctrine, then Price cannot be said to be liberal in this sense. He must also be located at some considerable distance from utilitarianism and its denial of any perfectionist human ideals. What Price does have in common with liberalism, however, is a strong emphasis on epistemic humility with regard to the good. That he saw all forms of government as imperfect motivated his campaign for a division between church and state. True freedom (a freedom for the good) for him can only be made manifest in a society that allows its members the freedom to pursue different paths. Without this, it would be logically impossible for anyone to attain true godlikeness.

This account of Price's political thought has suggested that Price's account of liberty, which was so widely read in the eighteenth century in both Britain and America, has to be studied in connection with his Platonism and its corresponding metaphysics. Like Plato and many of the Cambridge Platonists, he adopts a form of perfectionism and, like them, it is indirect, shaped by an epistemic humility that is sceptical of any claim to have complete knowledge of the good (a good that is, in Platonic terms, 'beyond being'). Identifying the importance of the Platonic tradition for the development of this one particular strand of eighteenth-century political thought is important for its own sake, but it also highlights the paradox of Popper's association of Platonic politics with totalitarianism. Rather than envisaging Price as engaged in the project of crafting a novel conception of Enlightenment autonomy, it may be more accurate to portray him as developing several key insights of the Platonic tradition.

The politics discussed in this chapter has demonstrated that contemporary conflicts are not clashes between religious and secular beliefs but between differing conceptions of the human good. Contemporary critics of liberalism such as MacIntyre and Stanley Hauerwas tend to assume that liberal political and ethical theories try to create just societies without just people, but Price suggests an alternative political philosophy that embraces a commitment to individual freedom (and which endorses many of the practical conclusions of liberalism) while at the same time asserting a strong teleology and conception of the human good. The next chapter will trace the radical direction some of these ideas took when they were transformed in Mary Wollstonecraft's *Vindications*.

Notes

1 Richard Price, *The Correspondence of Richard Price*, ed. W. B. Peach and D. O. Thomas, vol. II (Cardiff: University of Wales Press, 1991), 265. The President and Fellows of Harvard College to Price, 3 March 1785.
2 W. B. Peach, "Preface," in *Richard Price and the Ethical Foundations of the American Revolution: Selections from His Pamphlets, with Appendices*, ed. W. B. Peach (Durham, NC: Duke University Press, 1979), 11.
3 Peach, "Preface," 9.

4 Richard Price, "Observations on the Nature of Civil Liberty, the Principles of Government, and the Justice and Policy of the War with America," in *Richard Price: Political Writings*, ed. D. O. Thomas (Cambridge: Cambridge University Press, 1991), 20.

5 Martha K. Zebrowski, "Richard Price: British Platonist of the Eighteenth Century," *Journal of the History of Ideas* 55, no. 1 (1994): 20.

6 Martha K. Zebrowski, "We May Venture to Say, That the Number of Platonic Readers Is Considerable: Richard Price, Joseph Priestley and the Platonic Strand in Eighteenth Century Thought," *Enlightenment and Dissent* 19 (2000): 213.

7 William T. Cavanaugh, "The City: Beyond Secular Parodies," in *Radical Orthodoxy: A New Theology*, ed. Graham Ward, John Milbank, and Catherine Pickstock (London: Routledge, 1998), 182.

8 Isaiah Berlin, *Four Essays on Liberty* (Oxford: Oxford University Press, 1969), 122.

9 John Milbank, *Theology and Social Theory: Beyond Secular Reason* (Oxford: Blackwell, 1993), 330.

10 Jonathan I. Israel, *Democratic Enlightenment: Philosophy, Revolution, and Human Rights 1750–1790* (Oxford: Oxford University Press, 2011), 12.

11 Richard Price, *A Review of the Principal Questions in Morals*, 3rd ed. (Oxford: Clarendon, 1948), 36–7.

12 A. M. C. Waterman, "The Nexus between Theology and Political Doctrine in Church and Dissent," in *Enlightenment and Religion: Rational Dissent in Eighteenth-Century Britain*, ed. Knud Haakonssen (Cambridge: Cambridge University Press, 1996), 203.

13 Gordon S. Wood, *The Creation of the American Republic 1776–1787* (Williamsburg, Virginia: University of North Carolina Press, 1969), 24.

14 Joseph Priestley, "Essay on the First Principles of Government," in *Works*, vol. xxii, 1817, 356–8.

15 Price, "Observations," 22.

16 Price, "Observations," 22.

17 Price, "Observations," 22.

18 Price, "Observations," 23–4.

19 Richard Price, *Sermons on Various Subjects*, ed. W. Morgan (London: Longman, 1816), 217.

20 Price, *Review*, 229.

21 Price, *Review*, 230n. Price draws particular attention to the end of the fourth and ninth books of Plato's Republic; Alcinous states that "on the analogy of the division of the soul, the state is also divided into three elements" in Alcinous, *The Handbook of Platonism*, trans. John Dillon (Oxford: Oxford University Press, 1993), §34 p. 46; Plato makes an analogy between the well-ordered state and the healthy soul in Plato, *The Republic*, trans. Desmond Lee, 2nd ed. (London: Penguin, 1987), Book 4, 435a – b and 441c – e; For a discussion of Plato's analogy, see Bernard Williams, "The Analogy of City and Soul in Plato's Republic," in *Plato 2: Ethics, Politics, Religion and the Soul*, ed. Gail Fine (Oxford: Oxford University Press, 1999), 297–308; and Jerome Neu, "Plato's Analogy of State and Individual: The Republic and the Organic Theory of the State," *Philosophy* 46 (1971): 238–54. Neu's account challenges Popper's assumption that Plato's 'organic' view of the state denies individual rights.

22 Price, *Review*, 229.

23 Price, *Review*, 229.

24 Price, "Observations," 22.

25 Benjamin Whichcote, *Moral and Religious Aphorisms* (London: Printed for J. Payne, 1753), §62.

26 Ralph Cudworth, "Manuscripts on Freedom of the Will," British Library, Additional manuscripts, No. 4082.

27 Ralph Cudworth, "A Treatise of Freewill," in *A Treatise Concerning Eternal and Immutable Morality with a Treatise of Freewill*, ed. Sarah Hutton (Cambridge: Cambridge University Press, 1996), 196–7.

28 Plotinus, *Enneads*, trans. A.H. Armstrong, Loeb Classical Library (London: Heinemann, 1966), VI.8.3–4, 235–7.

29 Cudworth, "Freedom of the Will," Add. Mss., No. 4981.

30 Ralph Cudworth, "A Sermon Preached before the House of Commons," in *The Cambridge Platonists*, ed. C.A. Patrides (Cambridge: Cambridge University Press, 1969), 125.

31 Plotinus, *Enneads*, VI.8.3 7–10, p. 235.

32 John Smith, *Select Discourses* (London: Printed by J. Flesher, for W. Morden, bookseller in Cambridge, 1660), 394.

33 Thomas Hobbes, "Philosophical Rudiments Concerning Government and Society," in *The English Works of Thomas Hobbes*, ed. William Molesworth, vol. ii (London: Routledge, 1992), 120.

34 Thomas Hobbes, "Of Liberty and Necessity," in *Hobbes and Bramhall on Liberty and Necessity*, ed. Vere Chappell (Cambridge: Cambridge University Press, 1999), 37.

35 Cudworth, "Freedom of the Will," Mss. Add., No. 4981.

36 Berlin, *Liberty*, 131.

37 Price, *Various Subjects*, 213.

38 Price, *Various Subjects*, 215.

39 Price, *Review*, 215n.

40 Price, *Review*, 244.

41 John H. Muirhead, *The Platonic Tradition in Anglo-Saxon Philosophy* (London: Macmillan, 1931), 30. The determinism Muirhead is referring to concerns the way in which the good is seen as determining human action. This is compatible with true freedom for the Cambridge Platonists and is opposed to the determinism of Hobbes. See also James Deotis Roberts, *From Puritanism to Platonism in Seventeenth Century England* (The Hague: Martinus Nijhoff, 1968), 224.

42 Plotinus, *Enneads*, VI.8.4 15–20, p. 237.

43 Smith, *Select Discourses*, 395.

44 Price, *Various Subjects*, 210, 213.

45 Price, *Various Subjects*, 215.

46 Price, "Observations," 26.

47 Price, "Observations," 22.

48 Price, *Various Subjects*, 211–12.

49 Price, "Observations," 22.

50 The Adams-Jefferson Letters, ed. Lester J Cappon, J to A July 5 1814 quoted in Charles L. Griswold, Jr., "Platonic Liberalism: Self-Perfection as a Foundation of Political Theory," in *Plato and Platonism*, ed. Johannes M. van Ophuijsen (Washington: University of America Press, 1999), 102n.

51 R. M. Hare declares that Plato was a political authoritarian who made no allowance for human fallibility: R.M. Hare, *Plato* (Oxford: Oxford University Press, 1982), 68; see also Karl Popper's well known critique of Plato as totalitarian in *The Open Society and Its Enemies* (London: Routledge, 2002), 98.

52 Plato, *Republic*, 557b – c.

53 Berlin, *Liberty*, 154.

54 An argument made by Griswold, Jr., "Platonic Liberalism"; David Roochnik argues for a very similar interpretation in David Roochnik, *Beautiful City: The Dialectical Character of Plato's 'Republic'* (London: Cornell University Press, 2003).

55 Plato, *Republic*, 592a – b. See also 472c-d where the ideal state is called a pattern, like the Forms, in which particulars partake.

56 Plato, *Phaedrus & Letters VII and VIII*, trans. Walter Hamilton (Harmondsworth: Penguin, 1973), 247–8.

57 Drew A. Hyland, "Plato's Three Waves and the Question of Utopia," *Interpretation* 18 (1990): 103 makes this point.

58 Plato, *The Laws*, trans. Trevor J. Saunders (London: Penguin, 1975), 713c.

59 Griswold, Jr., "Platonic Liberalism," 115. I follow much of Griswold's argument here.

60 Diskin Clay, "Reading the Republic," in *Platonic Writings: Platonic Readings*, ed. Charles L. Griswold (London: Routledge, 1998). C.f. Plato, *Republic*, 501e.

61 Griswold also identifies the second-best polis theme in the Laws and in The Statesman, Griswold, Jr., "Platonic Liberalism," 117. See also Plato, *Laws*, 712a.

62 Plato, *Republic*, 557d.

63 See, e.g., the Statesman, 301c: a tyrant is someone who pretends to act like the person with expert knowledge. For further discussion of the Statesman, see Griswold, Jr., "Platonic Liberalism," 121.

64 Plato, *Laws*, 713c.

65 Plato, *Laws*, 701d.

66 Griswold, Jr., "Platonic Liberalism," 121.

67 Gerald M. Mara, "Socrates and Liberal Toleration," *Political Theory* 16 (1988): 483. Plato, *Theaetetus*, trans. Robin A.H. Waterfield (London: Penguin, 1987), 210c.

68 Price, *Various Subjects*, 376, emphasis mine.

69 See also Ronald Hamowy, *The Political Sociology of Freedom: Adam Ferguson and F.A. Hayek* (Cheltenham: Edward Elgar, 2005), 167. John Rogers points out that a positive understanding of liberty can be traced at least as far back as Plato, and he suggests it is Platonic thinkers who give it the fullest expression, as it is a central feature of much Platonic ethics, G.A.J. Rogers, *Locke's Enlightenment: Aspects of the Origin, Nature and Impact of His Philosophy* (New York: Olms Verlog, 1998), 167.

70 Plato, *Theaetetus*, 176b.

71 Rogers makes this point in relation to Locke and the Cambridge Platonists. Locke, just as much as More, saw liberty as a moral concept, not just a lack of external restraint on our thoughts and action. Both Locke and More see liberty and religion as held together by the cement of reason, Rogers, *Locke's Enlightenment*, 139–42.

72 Price discusses this criticism in his "Additional Observations on the Nature and Value of Civil Liberty, and the War with America," in *Political Writings*, ed. D.O. Thomas (Cambridge: Cambridge University Press, 1991), 80. The criticism was raised against him by Adam Ferguson, *Remarks on a Pamphlet Lately Published by Richard Price* (London: T. Cadell, 1776).

73 Smith, *Select Discourses*, 397.

74 Henry More, *An Explanation of the Grand Mystery of Godliness* (London: Thoemmes Press, 1660), 520.

75 Ralph Cudworth, *A Treatise Concerning Eternal and Immutable Morality with a Treatise of Freewill*, ed. Sarah Hutton (Cambridge: Cambridge University Press, 1996), 593. A commonwealth, he says, is an artificial man, which is a company of many united together by consent or contract under one government.

76 Ralph Cudworth, *The True Intellectual System of the Universe. . . with a Treatise Concerning Eternal and Immutable Morality*, ed. John Harrison, vol. iii (London: Thomas Tegg, 1845), 509.

77 Cudworth, *TIS*, vol. ii, 636.

78 Benjamin Carter, 'The Little Commonwealth of Man': The Trinitarian Origins of the Ethical and Political Philosophy of Ralph Cudworth (Leuven: Peeters, 2011), 128.
79 Berlin, *Liberty*, 164.
80 Price, "Observations," 21.
81 Price, "Additional Observations," 78–9.
82 A positive conception of liberty, on the other hand, is precisely the view outlined earlier, that freedom should be freedom for a particular end. See, e.g., John Rawls, "Justice as Fairness: Political Not Metaphysical," *Philosophy and Public Affairs* 14 (1985): 223–51.

6 'Wrought in each flower, inscrib'd on ev'ry tree'

Wollstonecraft, reason and the contemplation of divinised nature

In 1784, 25-year-old Mary Wollstonecraft moved to Newington Green with her best friend Fanny Blood and sisters Eliza and Everina to open a school for girls. She picked an intellectually stimulating and socially dynamic location. The chapel had been founded by the Presbyterians in 1708 and had, since 1758, been ministered by Richard Price, who lived on the Green, and who was often at home to an eclectic range of guests including Joseph Priestley, David Hume, John Quincy Adams and Benjamin Franklin. The neighbours included Hannah Burgh, who had lived there with her husband James – the Whig politician who had founded a Dissenting academy on the Green – until his death in 1775. Hannah Burgh and Wollstonecraft had a close and nurturing friendship.[1] Although she considered herself Anglican at the time, Wollstonecraft attended Price's chapel, and their close proximity quickly gave rise to a firm and lasting bond.[2] It is evident he encouraged her intellectual endeavours as well as providing personal encouragement and support. A weekly supper club was the centre of the Green's social life, and these convivial occasions introduced Wollstonecraft to other notable radical Dissenting thinkers, including Joseph Johnson.[3]

The year Wollstonecraft took up her residence was a lively one for Price. It saw the publication of his *Observations on the Importance of the American Revolution*, which confirmed his place at the centre of an Anglo-American political storm. The companionship between Price and Wollstonecraft would have undoubtedly involved abundant discussion of politics, ethics and theology, and, years later, when Edmund Burke launched a stinging attack on Price's politics in the form of his *Reflections*, Wollstonecraft's response was lightening: her *Vindication of the Rights of Men* tore into Burke's ideology and offered a spirited defence of her erstwhile mentor.

A broad yet under-explored influence from Price on Wollstonecraft is acknowledged.[4] Barbara Taylor notes that Wollstonecraft's *Thoughts on the Education of Daughters* (1786) was thoroughly orthodox and envisaged significant dangers in rationalism and deism. *Mary, A Fiction* (written in 1787 and published the following year), however, is regarded as reflecting Wollstonecraft's change to becoming a 'typical Enlightenment intellectual' rejecting blind faith in favour of rational religion and toleration. Taylor parallels this with the move to Newington Green.[5] 'The cant of weak enthusiasts have made the consolations of Religion and the assistance of the Holy Spirit appear to the inconsiderate ridiculous,' she wrote to her sister in 1784, the year the school at Newington Green opened. In *Mary*, this stance developed into a rejection of all forms of religious fervour, and the novel charts a change in the protagonist's theological disposition from orthodoxy into what might be called an increasingly unorthodox panentheism (in which God is interrelated with the world yet not identical with it) because of its promotion of a more immanent view of God, who is not external to the world. Hers is not a pantheist theology because God is more, for her, than the totality of what exists in the world, but she moves towards the view that all is part of God, especially when she reports how she feels closest to God in the contemplation of 'the grand or solemn features of Nature' rather than in church.[6]

That Wollstonecraft moved towards an increasing rationalisation in this stage of her life does not necessarily imply an abrupt change from her earlier stance against rationalism and deism, however. This book has argued that the rationalism of Rational Dissent did not position itself against faith, and it should not be equated with the rationalism of the deists. At no point in Wollstonecraft's life does she embrace deism, and her rationalism does not hesitate to distance itself from the ratiocination that had also been spurned by Price. In fact, Wollstonecraft's concept of reason at the time of her writing *Mary* and the *Vindications* should be seen as having a distinctly Platonic-Pricean hue. This Platonising aspect means that the change in her theology by the time she wrote *A Short Residence in Sweden* in 1796 should be seen not as a complete about turn but more of a radical development of her earlier thought. Wollstonecraft was crucial for the emergence of later Romantic conceptions of the imagination and paying the development of her thought greater attention points towards the evolution of a theology of nature with a profound commitment to the contemplation of the natural world. Wollstonecraft was an original thinker, but she draws on her rationalist Platonic forebears to create a rich theology of nature that is at once both deeply political and unmistakeably ethical.

Imagination and reason in Wollstonecraft's early work

The novel *Mary* combines a rationalist rejection of enthusiasm with an openness to a religion of nature. It contains a natural theology that relies on the contemplation of nature and which is committed to a divinised cosmos. Whereas Price's natural theology exhibits a tension between the arguments to and from design as suggested in Chapter 4, much of Wollstonecraft's theology is characterised by its development of a theology of nature – what might be termed an argument to design – and it is sensitive to how our models of the cosmos shape our understanding of ourselves and our ethical and political values.

The year before she wrote *Mary*, Wollstonecraft left Newington Green for a position as governess to the Kingsborough family in Ireland. This assignment was short-lived, however, and in 1786, she moved back to London to work as a reader and translator – and later a reviewer – for Joseph Johnson's *Analytical Review*. In his memoirs of her life, William Godwin tells us that she attended Anglican services until this time, but after that, she no longer deemed it necessary to engage in the rituals of the religion. She was clearly drawn further and further away from sacramental Anglicanism – a move reflected in the character of Mary and her journey towards a new radical form of faith.

The young Mary in the novel is decisively orthodox and so committed to the Anglican Eucharist that we are told she is unable to sleep because of violent emotion the night before the consumption of her first holy sacrament at the age of 15.[7] The author expresses some disquiet, however, that Mary's 'ardent affections' lead her to forget that only an infinite being, as she puts it, can satisfy her soul. It is God, not religious ritual, who is necessary for religion. There is a warning contained within about the young Mary's enthusiastic tendencies and a link is suggested between enthusiasm and a highly sacramental Anglicanism. As the novel progresses, it becomes clear that religion cannot be a matter of affection alone.

Mary then travels to Portugal, shadowing an overseas venture undertaken by Wollstonecraft herself when she accompanied Fanny Blood and her husband to that country during her residence in Newington Green. Here the character Mary has what she terms 'a metaphysical turn.' This made her consider, we are told, every object she encountered, with the result that 'she had not any prejudices, for every opinion was examined before it was adopted.'[8] Her enthusiasm was replaced by the refusal to accept beliefs without subjecting them to the due consideration of reason. This was no passive mental consideration, however, in which the mind makes no contribution. Rather Mary's 'mind was not like a mirror, which receives every floating image, but does not retain them.' It was, instead, an active instrument.[9] The use of reason in religion is clearly not something purely deductive but contains in it something of the activity of mind. On entering a Roman Catholic Church with some deists she meets on her travels, she feels it is only right to 'examine the evidence on which her faith was built.' This entails for her the consideration of the arguments of those who embrace reason, including Butler's Analogy. Doing this 'made her a Christian from conviction.' With this she is able to see how 'apparently good and solid arguments might take their rise from different points of view' and those with whom she should not concur 'still have some reason on their side.'[10] Reason is clearly not decisive in its conclusions.

The story of *Mary* does not amount to a simple endorsement of evidentialism, however. Mary's character is filled with sentiment that gushes forth in the contemplation of nature: 'rhapsodies of praise' are the spontaneous result when she listens to the birds or pursues the deer. Early on in the novel, she gazes on the moon and listens to the sea and the 'wandering spirits, which she imagined inhabited every part of nature, were her constant friends and confidants.'[11] The 'enthusiastic sentiments of devotion' in which 'her Creator was almost apparent to her senses in his works' lead her to delight in contemplation of 'the waves rolling' and 'the voice that could still the tumultuous deep.'[12] Rational consideration is inconceivable for her outside of the context of the divinised cosmos. It is easy from this to see how Godwin could later claim that Wollstonecraft's mind constitutionally attached itself to the sublime and the amiable. She found, he tells us, 'an inexpressible delight in the beauties of nature, and in the splendid reveries of the imagination.'[13] It was through contemplation that the character of Mary 'began to consider the Great First Cause' and form just notions of God's attributes, reflecting in particular on God's wisdom and goodness.[14] For Mary, the conceptualisation of God is inconceivable without the prior contemplation of nature.

What is evident here is a model of imaginative reason that begins from the contemplation of nature, not the study of logical arguments. This process of reflection is motivated first and foremost by love, most notably a distinctly Platonic conception of it. We are told Mary's sensibility urges her to search for an object to love, but it was not to be found on earth.[15] During these early years, she has a glimpse of a truth which comes to light more fully as the years advance. Her metaphysical turn and rational examination of evidence must be set within this context. God is everywhere for Wollstonecraft and is not just a first temporal cause. God is the 'source of perfection' who never disregarded an almost broken heart. Like Wollstonecraft, Mary is alone with nature in her moments of darkest despair, yet is convinced she is not alone.[16] Such solitariness is hardly possible when Godwin reports that when his late wife 'walked amidst the wonders of nature, she was accustomed to converse with her God.'[17]

By the time she wrote *Mary*, it seems reasonable to assume, as Taylor does, that her form of faith originally in harmony with the dominant orthodoxy was giving way to a less orthodox form of faith and that Price's rationalism helps to shape this transition. At the same time, it is widely accepted that Wollstonecraft's account of reason was very different from that of the Rational Dissenters. Taylor suggests it was not the 'chilly deductive faculty' found in most Unitarian preachings but a more libidinised, imaginative drive toward the truth and the good derived from Rousseau and the Christian Platonist tradition in which *eros* lay at the core of the religious experience.[18] Taylor accounts for this influence partly through Price and Anna Barbauld (and possibly Hartley) but mostly through Milton and Rousseau.

Wollstonecraft was, however, fiercely critical of both Milton and Rousseau's ideas of gender and her conception of rationality is not all that far removed from Latitudinarianism and Rational Dissent. Both Milton and Rousseau are deserving of the label 'sensualist,' and Milton's description of Eve's 'docile blind obedience' is the inspiration for Rousseau's Sophie, with which Wollstonecraft takes decisive issue in her *Vindication of the Rights of Women*.[19] Furthermore, rationality is not opposed to sentimentality for Wollstonecraft. Mary in her travels meets Henry, a man of learning whose 'rational religious sentiments received warmth from his sensibility.'[20] It is clear that rational religion is more than capable of the warmth of sensibility. In writing to her nephew George Blood, she says she would rather he didn't read Price's sermons. This, however, constitutes more of a reproach of her own kin than Price: 'They would lead you into controversial disputes' she says, 'and your limited range of books would not afford you a clue.' What motivates her warning is the detection of an inherent danger in complex thought for the uneducated and uninitiated. Price's Dissertations, however, she unreservedly recommends. They have a warmth that connects with the sentiments: they 'contain useful truths – coming warm from the heart they find the direct road to it.'[21] Price's arguments of the Dissertations propose a rationalist natural theology but this does not mean that they are considered frigid. Likewise, his *Discourse on the Love of Our Country* (1789) 'breathes the animated sentiments of ardent virtue' with an eloquence that ensures 'the heart speaks to the heart in an unequivocal language.'[22] Through this, the understanding assents without being bewildered by sophistical arguments. What matters most, as will be discussed further in the next section, is whether a philosophical argument can grab the imagination and move the heart, as well as secure a conviction of belief.

Reason and the *Vindication of the Rights of Men*

It is in Wollstonecraft's two *Vindications* that the echoes of Price's Platonic account of reason and deiformity can be clearly detected. In these, she endorses an anti-voluntarism that puts her in harmony with Rational Dissent but furthermore ties this together with an anti-materialism that contrasts acutely with Priestley's metaphysics. It is worth pointing out, as Taylor does, that this anti-materialism was unusual in Wollstonecraft's circle of radicals, which included Godwin and Priestley but it was formative for Coleridge years later.[23] Important, too, is Wollstonecraft's account of freedom, which as Taylor points out, unlike Godwin's, is grounded in the immortality of the soul, and a theological account of perfectionism.[24]

Wollstonecraft's *Vindication of the Rights of Men* (1790) was penned in haste out of concern to critique Edmund Burke's attack, in the form of his *Reflections on the Revolution in France*, on Richard Price's celebration of liberty, rights and the American and French Revolutions explicit in his *Discourse on the Love of Our Country*. In her first *Vindication*, Wollstonecraft does not so much defend Price as attack Burke but much of the substance of Price's philosophy is apparent in her rejection of Burke's account of hierarchy, property and authority of tradition.

Burke's main conceptual target in his *Reflections* was voluntarism – a fact not without irony given this was the same target that motivated so much of

Price's writing. Price, as previous chapters have shown, took steps to defend a representative self-government because he saw any subjection of a people to an arbitrary government as analogous to a voluntarist ethic. Lockean voluntarism is opposed at all costs by a Platonic rationalism. Burke's worry, however, was that the people should not imagine that their will, any more than that of kings, is the standard of right and wrong.[25] For Burke, Price's representationalism was itself a threat to freedom and smacks of anarchy.

Burke was a Whig politician. Characterised, as they were, by their stance against arbitrary power, the Whigs saw themselves as the custodians of the true legacy of 1688. This dispute about the nature and extent of the royal prerogative not only gave rise to the quarrels between Whig and Tory ideology but also contributed towards the fracturing of the Whigs themselves.[26] The 1760s saw a significant shift in British politics. For the Whigs of this decade, George III was a tyrant in the making and cast in the mould of James II, something evident in his attempts to advance the power of the crown. He embarked on various measures to curb the influence of the Whigs, including the ending of the proscription of the Tories at court. The Whigs, although concerned to defend the crown because of its legitimacy enshrined in the events of 1688, were continuously on their guard against any temptation the monarchy might have to assert absolutist power.[27] Their worries about the crown, whether correctly perceived or not, grew worse as the late eighteenth century wore on.

When the Marquis of Rockingham became the leader of the Whigs, he introduced 'country' elements to the party due in part to the fact he was a major landowner. These were in distinct contrast to the previously dominant 'court' elements that had as their focus concern for the defence of the crown.[28] The Rockinghams became increasingly uneasy with what they saw as the absolutist tendencies of George III – a concern confirmed to them by the events of the years immediately after Rockingham's death in 1782 when Shelburne, who had succeeded Rockingham, was promptly ousted in 1783 by an alliance between Lord North and those Whigs who followed Charles James Fox. This alliance came to an end when George III encouraged the House of Lords to vote down the government's East India Bill. The king then dismissed this North-Fox alliance and replaced it in 1783 with William Pitt the Younger as the first lord of the Treasury. For many Whigs, this looked like the result of the undue influence of George III and an unconstitutional removal of the North-Fox coalition. It also reinforced their self-portrait as the party of aristocrats standing in between the people and the crown, and protecting each from the other.[29] They were the true protectors, they believed, of the constitution, for both the good of the monarchy and the good of the people.

Divisions between the Whigs became increasingly apparent as the Foxites became more radical in the late 1780s. They were thoroughly aristocratic and extending the franchise would have been out of the question, but in 1787, Fox took steps to counter the Test and Corporation Acts and took up the cause of the Rational Dissenters. The result was a new identity for the party.[30] Burke was one figure who was distinctly displeased with this more radical turn. When the Revolution occurred in France, Fox was far more sympathetic towards it than Burke could tolerate. Fox and Burke could not see eye to eye on the right of the populace to choose a government or on the hereditary principle and its associated respect for custom. Burke's coining of the terms 'new' and 'old' Whig was an attempt to claim for himself – a self-professed old Whig – the true Whig tradition and a more conservative interpretation of 1688.

For Burke then, an anti-voluntarist stance was essential to safeguard the true form of government. He had defended Rockingham's ideas in *Thoughts on the Cause of the Present Discontents* (1770) and was hardly an unreserved monarchist, but he believed the hereditary descent of the crown was absolute and could never be altered by the will of the people. He detected more than just a sniff of this in both the Foxites and in Price. Revolutionary government by will, he insisted, is entirely arbitrary and therefore unstable, dangerous and downright morally wrong. Price's *Discourse on the Love of Our Country* provided Burke's blue touch paper.

If an anti-voluntarism unites them, Burke and Price are worlds apart in their applications of this philosophy. In her defence of her friend, Wollstonecraft marshals Price's philosophy of self-governance to issue a scathing rebuttal of what she sees as the inevitable voluntarist consequence of Burke's politics: the subjection of any one person's will to another's. In Wollstonecraft's eyes, Burke ends up promoting the very voluntarist philosophy he claims to stand against. Her approach is one that is based on a psychology of the supposed supremacy of the faculty of reason over passion, essential to guarantee freedom and virtue. Price's division of the soul into reason, affections and passions was used not only to present an argument for liberty but also to reject an organic conception of the state. It is his politicising of this psychology and his theological underpinning for it that is evident in Wollstonecraft's appropriation of this model of ethical relations. Price's Platonic philosophy of freedom and self-governance, based on his analogy between the human individual and the state, thus formed the basis of the much more radical deconstruction of hegemony in Wollstonecraft's Vindications.

As described in Chapter 2, the tripartite division of the soul makes reason, for Price, the eye of the mind and that which perceives truth and gains knowledge. It is 'the power in the soul to which belongs . . . the apprehension of truth.'[31] This Platonic account in which truth is something everlasting and sensation only perceives what decays and changes, is echoed later in Wollstonecraft's epistemic concerns. The exercise of the understanding is the 'clear light' by which knowledge is gained and it must not be subject to every whim of the passions, as this would be akin to accepting all opinions on trust. Reason, she says, is opposed to the 'crutch of authority' and independence here means independence of thought from the passions seen in terms of arbitrary force:

> I submit to the moral laws which my reason deduces from. . . my dependence on [God]. – It is not his power that I fear – it is not to an arbitrary will, but to unerring reason I submit.[32]

This rational argument is the basis of her rejection of patriarchy and hegemony. Independence means independence of thought and reason, and it galvanises her to insist that 'this fear of God makes me reverence myself.' Unlike Price, she does not distinguish so explicitly between passions and affections, but she does refer to the 'blind impulse of unerring instinct' and contrasts it with affections which proceed from reason but are only 'reason at second-hand.'[33] Reason is undoubtedly the superior faculty of the mind.

The distinction between reasons and passions, and the association of reason with moral truth and goodness, results in Wollstonecraft adopting a distinctly Pricean, and Platonic, account of virtue as right order in the soul. As suggested earlier, Price's belief in the pre-eminence of reason envisages goodness and virtue as the discipline of keeping the passions and affections in subjection to reason. Reason is articulated as the rightful governor of the soul and that which should examine action, judge, decide and direct.[34] The argument of Price's philosophy, evident in the Cambridge Platonists, that an individual is free only if reason governs the soul is clear in Wollstonecraft's first *Vindication*. Reason is explicitly necessary for moral action. If we are subject to the whim of passions, we are neither good nor evil and have neither virtue nor wisdom.

Without reason and reflection, our action is merely instinctive and has no moral content. The cultivation of reason is contrasted with the 'impulse of passion.'[35] Passions themselves are neither good nor evil, but 'if virtue is to be acquired by experience, or taught by example, reason, perfected by reflection, must be the director of the whole host of passions.' The analogy of the ship is a popular one when illustrating this point about reason's natural superiority: reason, Wollstonecraft asserts, 'must hold the rudder' or the vessel will never advance smoothly to its destination.[36] This is foreshadowed by Price's appeal for 'reason' to be kept 'vigilant and immoveable at the helm' and before him Plato's vision of 'intelligence' sitting 'at the helm of the soul' in the *Phaedrus'* myth of the charioteer.[37] Reason, for Price, as for the Platonic tradition, is the natural governor of the soul because it is the part of us that can reflect morally and comprehend knowledge of what is good. The source of moral goodness is the governance of reason. Likewise, Wollstonecraft asks, 'Who will venture to assert that virtue would not be promoted by the more extensive cultivation of reason?'[38]

This ethic is a theological one, and it has firm roots in the Platonic tradition. The Cambridge Platonic unification of morality and God, the nature of God as the foundation of truth and goodness and the capacity of reason as the candle of the Lord apparent in Price's account of the good and the true as a divine unity, is there in Wollstonecraft's depiction of reason as the 'heaven-lighted spark.' To 'act according to the dictates of reason is [therefore] to conform to the law of God.'[39] What is of primary concern here is the nature of morality itself. Morality cannot depend on God's will or it would be akin to human passions and would thus lose its immutability.

Previous chapters have outlined Price's response to the threat of voluntarism and his insistence on a standard of rightness that is inherent in God's nature and the foundation of reason and wisdom. Morality cannot be dependent on God's will, but neither can it depend on human will. At the time the *Review* was composed, the threat to the eternal character of morality was most pressing in the voluntarism of Descartes, Hutcheson and Paley. By the time Wollstonecraft wrote her first *Vindication*, the spectre of voluntarism was still apparent, this time rearing its ugly head in the relativism and arbitrariness of Burke's appeal to authority and tradition. Through these concepts, Burke justified his affirmation of a political and gendered hierarchy, which made for Wollstonecraft's target in the first *Vindication*. She rebukes Burke: 'Had you been a Jew – you would have joined in the cry, crucify him, crucify him' unimpressed by his uncritical acceptance of established practices, habits and institutions.[40] The arbitrariness of voluntarism is manifest in what she sees as the arbitrariness of cultural institutions. Locating goodness in the divine reason was the antidote for the affliction of voluntarism just as it was for Price. Truth, she says, cannot be determined by 'arbitrary authority and dark traditions,' but must be determined by the verdict of reason.[41] The authority of reason is thus conjoined with the authority of God and contrasted with the subjection of one human will to another. One hierarchy – that of reason over the passions – is used to subvert another, the hierarchy of will over nature, and the rationale is a theologically powerful one: it lies in the nature of God.

This is the argument that underpins her *Vindication of the Rights of Woman*, and in this work, a rationalist Platonic influence is even more substantial.[42] The divinity of reason is reaffirmed:

> The nature of reason must be the same in all, if it be an emanation of divinity, the tie that connects the creature with the Creator; for, can that soul be stamped with the heavenly image, that is not perfected by the exercise of its own reason?[43]

She accepts Price's concern that if morality is not immutable and eternal, it is merely a custom. In this lies the origin of all tyranny and slavery: it is associated with the arbitrary nature of voluntarist morality against which only reason can offer the rightful authority. This epistemology provides the weight of her damning assessment of Rousseau's account of gender (itself nothing more than a product of custom).[44] Morality must rest on truth, not falsehood, because 'if any class of mankind be so created that it must necessarily be educated by rules not strictly deducible from truth, virtue is an affair of convention.' The truth on which morality rests is none other than God: the 'only solid foundation for morality' is the 'supreme Being.'[45]

Liberty, deiformity and vindication of the rights of woman

Price and Wollstonecraft's concern to refute voluntarism and relativism by grounding truth and goodness in divine reason gives rise to a shared account of liberty. For both, goodness is absolute not relative, and because it is reason that apprehends the good, true freedom can arise only from the rule of reason. Price's definition of slavery as the usurping of reason is apparent in Wollstonecraft's claim that the dependence of reason on the passions produces slavery. 'In what respect are we superior to the brute creation,' she asks, 'if intellect is not allowed to be the guide of passion?' Both make divine reason the locus for freedom and self-governance and the key to escaping slavery becomes 'the power of exercising our understanding'[46] which raises us above the 'brutes' (i.e. slaves defined as such precisely because they lack reason and are subject to the sway of their passions). This psychology is developed in the *Vindication of the Rights of Woman*. The passions for Wollstonecraft are not to be dispensed with, or overcome by elimination, but regulated so that they are always under the direction of reason: therein lies the secret of true autonomy in opposition to 'tyrants of every denomination, from the weak king to the weak father of a family; [who] . . . are all eager to crush reason.'[47]

For Wollstonecraft, as for Price, self-determination is politicised. Whereas Price had sought to defend the cause of the American colonists, Wollstonecraft had the demolition of patriarchy in her sights. The previous chapter outlined the way self-governance runs through the different branches of liberty identified by Price: physical liberty (freedom from any external duress), religious liberty (freedom to follow one's religious convictions), moral liberty (freedom to follow one's conscience) and civil liberty (the ability of a state to govern itself). This means they are interconnected and stand or fall together. Civil liberty on this scheme becomes a moral matter, and it must be safeguarded as a matter of moral principle. The community governed by a will that is external or alien is in need of civil liberty and is consequently in a position of servitude. Self-determination might not be the whole of virtue, but it is a necessary precondition for it; because without freedom, there can be no moral progress.

Wollstonecraft adopts this idea of self-determination at the individual, civil and religious levels. At the civil level, slavery is the usurping of reason by passions associated with prejudice and unthinking authority:

> When a man makes his spirit bend to any power but reason, his character is soon degraded, and his mind shackled by the very prejudices to which he submits with reluctance.[48]

This applies particularly to the authority of tradition, including hereditary honours. In the *Vindication of the Rights of Men*, this is played out in terms of a debate with Burke about subjection to the church. If truth is immutable and eternal, then all individuals who possess reason have the ability to come to know it, independently of dependence on the Church, the state or the will of any other person. She rejects entirely Burke's insistence of a close connection between the state and the church as 'the source and original archetype of all perfection' and as the fountain of social order.[49] Individuals must think for themselves in order to be good, not slavishly follow the dictates of others. Burke's conception of liberty is mocked: 'Is power and right the same in your creed? – How can he be a true friend to liberty if liberty means subjection to another's will?'[50] Natural equality, for Wollstonecraft as much as for Price, entails freedom from subjection to the will of another, both at the individual and the civil level.

Liberty as a principle of freedom from subjection to the will of others was not uncommon to Rational Dissenting thought, but Price's work shows a particularly thorough application to foreign affairs. The Rational Dissenters appreciated that the freedom of any community requires the ability of the people within it to make enlightened decisions, which includes not only freedom from direct coercion but also from political spin and a suffrage based on strength of personality.[51] This was, ironically, why Price, despite his concern for liberty, did not champion the cause of universal suffrage. He was astute enough to realise that a despotic government is dangerous not only for the threat of restricting the physical movement of its populous but also for its ability to shape the minds and consciences of those subject to it.[52] Wollstonecraft goes much further than Price, however, in recognising the power of cultural conditioning. This plays out most notably in her consideration of constructions of gender and hierarchy. Among the affections she names are not only affections for parents but also reverence for superiors or antiquity, worldly self-interest and notions of honour. These affections must be subject to scrutiny and rejected if found wanting. In the face of culturally imbibed hierarchy, reason is one available life raft. Granting supremacy to reason affords a way for her to challenge the perceived natural inequality between those who are servile and those who are superior, and to reject the authority of tradition and culturally based hierarchy.[53] Freedom for women comes from freedom from socially constructed gender expectations and the ensuing pressure to conform to them.

Wollstonecraft's rationalist rejection of tradition in her *Vindication of the Rights of Men* lays the foundation for the feminist arguments of the *Vindication of the Rights of Woman*. She appreciates that honouring tradition for its own sake makes for a package of values that includes the reverencing of hierarchy, the assumption of patriarchy and the rejection of autonomous thought. All must be deconstructed by refusing to accept a voluntaristic hierarchy of will and by thinking for oneself:

> To subjugate a rational being to the mere will of another, after he is of age to answer to society for his own conduct, is a most cruel and undue stretch of power; and, perhaps, as injurious to morality as those religious systems which do not allow right and wrong to have any existence, but in the Divine will.[54]

Burke cannot claim an automatic right of respect for hierarchy and tradition when it comes to church and state, and likewise patriarchy cannot demand unreflective allegiance. Wollstonecraft draws an important parallel between the sacred majesty of kings, the standing army, the blind submission to the opinions of religious leaders and the subjection of women.[55] All four are incompatible with her idea of freedom of the will because all four involve unthinking subjection of the will.

These particular examples of hegemony are crucially important because they reinforce the radical nature of Wollstonecraft's thought and uncover its less appreciated inherently political nature.[56] By linking these different types of subordination, she undermines the link between familial patriarchal authority and political authority, and explicitly challenges the very structure of her society. She was echoing a common sentiment when she stated that 'a man has been termed a microcosm; and every family might also be called a state'[57] as belief in the inseparability of patriarchal authority and political authority was commonplace in the eighteenth century. Patriarchal government was grounded in the 'natural' authority of the father and/or husband – an idea encapsulated neatly by William Paley: 'Government, at first, was either patriarchal or military; that of a parent over his family, or of a commander over his fellow-warriors.' He went on to insist that it is paternal authority, and the order of domestic life, that supplies the foundation of civil government and the origins of empire: 'The constitution of families not only assists the formation of civil government by the dispositions which it generates, but also furnishes the first steps of the process by which empires have been actually reared.'[58]

Wollstonecraft's psychology of the well-ordered soul and its Platonic associations with the well-ordered state thus stand in stark contrast with the widely accepted belief that the well-regulated and happy country is one based on subordination.[59] Liberty envisaged as self-government was radically different from the assumption that 'to do what we will is natural liberty; to do what we will, consistently with the interest of the community to which we belong, is civil liberty.'[60] For this more conventional view, the interests of the community meant upholding the social and political hegemonic order and obeying ones superiors was an inescapable part of one's Christian duty. In the face of the argument that 'subordination of ranks, and the relation of magistrates and subjects, are indispensably necessary in that state of society for which our Creator has evidently intended the human species,'[61] Wollstonecraft presents a radical re-interpretation of nature, providence and human teleology.

The implications of Wollstonecraft's politics were much more far-reaching than Locke's. As it was necessary, as Locke saw it, that rule should be placed somewhere, it should fall to man as the abler and stronger, and every wife therefore owes her husband subjection.[62] Locke insists that slaves cannot have liberty because they do not have property: liberty is not the freedom to do what one wishes but the freedom to dispose of one's person, action and property how one wishes according to law (those who do not have property are not part of civil society). Whereas Locke's liberty is one that protects the possession of property (and the power of the magistrate) by means of the principle of tacit and voluntary consent, for Wollstonecraft, the 'demon of property' has encroached on man's rights. She laments the fact that English liberty has been defined by 'security of property' and her re-interpretation of liberty as a moral principle of self-governance is one that places her at odds with Locke and with her Lockean contemporary Catherine Macaulay who advanced a view of liberty as primarily involving security of property.[63]

Even the mainstream Unitarian movement remained subject to cultural and social views that reinforced women's subordination. Priestley, for example, insists that every family is a little society within itself and asserts that this authority is more absolute than that of any civil government.[64] One could easily be a late eighteenth-century Tory, Whig or Rational Dissenter and still accept familial hegemony as sacrosanct. In the face of this, the *Vindications* insist that equality, and not subjection, is the natural and ideal state of human beings. The universe is not, for Wollstonecraft, a system with an essence of subordination (on which beauty and happiness depend) but one in which a natural equality of all members of a species is asserted. She appreciated the extent to which hierarchical social and political concerns were perpetuated through a particular understanding of nature. Soame Jenyns, for example, articulated the popular assumption that the good order of the whole and the happiness of it was believed to come from 'a proper subordination,'[65] which meant that challenges to prescription, and the hegemony that justified it, were viewed as a direct challenge to government, foreign policy and the contemporary social order. This helps to explain why Thomas Taylor's parody of Wollstonecraft, *A Vindication of the Rights of Brutes*, sarcastically retorted with the equality of all species. Wollstonecraft's adversaries recognised at the time how all the enshrined hierarchies where of a piece: lose one and the rest are history too. Hence they insisted on natural (and divinely ordained) inequalities within species, not just between them.

In challenging the natural order of patriarchy in all its forms, Wollstonecraft did not simply challenge the domination of men over women but the whole political order. With this, she turned the moral universe upside down, quite literally; coveting and being envious of those above you in the hierarchy was regarded as a vice. Even virtue itself was determined through the perpetration of hegemony. The moderately High Church George Pretyman was adamant about this in a sermon to the House of Lords: 'Our holy religion forbids. . . all those private vices which lead to dissoluteness of manners, and enjoins the strict observance of those moral virtues which are the best support of order and regularity.' Obedience, he insists, is the direct result of virtue, defined in terms of manners that shore up the current status quo. True religion, therefore, forbids rebellion and 'must necessarily strengthen the hands of the civil magistrate, and in the most effectual manner promote subjection to the higher powers.'[66] Political liberty, defined in terms of subjection, was crucial for the defence of this view. Freedom is linked with serving God, which meant, as it did for Burke, serving the established political and religious powers. That Wollstonecraft's second *Vindication* appears to be more concerned with manners than with rights should not, therefore, perplex contemporary feminists. Virtue, manners and political rights were theologically inseparable, and although Wollstonecraft's grounding of liberty and government on the interpretation of human nature was not in itself new,[67] her interpretation of human nature (as rational and therefore to be self-governed) was profoundly radical in its implications for social and political order.

Theology, providence and God

Wollstonecraft was not the first English feminist-theologian. It would be more accurate to place her in a tradition of emerging feminist thought, preceded by Mary Astell, who had made a Biblical case against female oppression. Barbara Taylor points to a change of atmosphere, however, that emerged in the 1730s and continued to the end of the eighteenth century. During this time, women's claims were marginalised, and they tended to be pushed to the edges of evangelicalism. So much so that it was common for sermons by the 1780s to expound Paul's teaching against the ecclesiastic leadership of women.[68] From around the mid-eighteenth century, women came to be associated with feminine sensibility so that whereas 'in man, Religion is generally the Effect of Reason' in women it is 'the Effect of Nature.'[69] Mainstream moralists at this time, states Taylor, 'were as likely to denounce women with independent religious views as they were to condemn the godless.'[70] In fact, the two were seen as synonymous. Even those who accepted the legitimacy of reasoning about religion tended to draw a line when women tried to do the reasoning. James Fordyce spoke against the idea of women exercising reason, as it was their task to be submissive, modest and attractive. (*Sermons to Young Women*, 1766). The inevitable result was that the very enterprise of thinking about God was out of bounds. In typical fashion, John Gregory's tome of advice to women warned them against the study of theology (*A Father's Legacy to his Daughters*, 1774).[71] Wollstonecraft's account of reason in the Vindications should, therefore, be appreciated as an affirmation of the validity of women engaging in the very practice of theology and philosophy.

The rejection of both customary authority and male-neutral reason enabled Wollstonecraft to offer a different paradigm of Biblical interpretation. When it comes to the Genesis story, very few people who have thought about it seriously 'ever supposed that Eve was, literally speaking, one of Adams ribs.' This leads the way for the development of a Biblical hermeneutics of suspicion. Interpreted differently, the story shows us not that God created woman to fulfil men's needs but that man 'from the remotest antiquity' promoted his interpretative 'invention' of this story to show that the whole of creation was created for his convenience or pleasure.[72] Such a hermeneutic was only possible with a rejection of the authority of tradition argued for by Latitudinarians such as Clarke and the later Rational Dissenters. The ramifications of this for male-female relations and for men's relation to the wider cosmos are not drawn out here, but their profundity would have been obvious to her readership. 'Truth' is shaken and unmasked, not as the objective gaze from nowhere but as male-neutral untruth. With this, her philosophising about religion not only leads to a naming, or calling out, of theological androcentrism but also clears a space in which to be theologically creative.

Reason imagined as the emanation of divinity therefore gives Wollstonecraft a theology of deiformity that, as Taylor describes, underpinned her ability to transcend a constructed image of gender that saw women pursue the ideal of coquettish dependent. Her account of reason and political ideals made it possible for her to think of women as acquiring what she proposed as gender-neutral divine virtues related to 'Supreme Being, Creator and Image' instead of the 'feminine virtues' of docility, patience and good-humour.[73] The image of God in human nature depicted in this way ensures self-respect and self-governance. Wollstonecraft was not uncritical of the traditional concept of God either. 'To her mind,' Godwin tells us, '[God] was pictured as not less amiable, generous and kind, than great, wise and exalted.'[74] The model of God as friend was not unheard of in the eighteenth century, particularly in Dissenting circles, and was present in the 1729 edition of Butler's *Fifteen Sermons*, but it was considered by most to be unorthodox and potentially dangerous: atheistic in fact. How could a friend who would be keen to forgive transgression ensure just punishment after death for earthly sins? As Lilly Butler points out in his Boyle Lecture of 1709, those who deny that God is an object of fear are branded atheists because the God who will not hurt a creature does not know justice.[75] Wollstonecraft for her part rejected the doctrine of future punishments, which as she saw it, left God as a 'divine bully.'[76] If Godwin is to be believed, there was never a time when she accepted the doctrine of future punishment and retribution.[77] On this matter she offers a substantially different theology from Price and the other Rational Dissenters, as well as from Anglican orthodoxy, and it is developed later on in Wollstonecraft's life into an explicitly panentheistic concept of God, as will be touched on later in this chapter.

Before that, it is worth noting that a commitment to God's goodness entails a theology of providence that is at odds with the mainstream theology of the age. The argument of the *Vindications of the Rights of Woman* insists that God must have made women such that they can attain deiformity, which means it must be unethical to deny women the chance to flourish in this way. It is not God's providence to make women subordinate. As Sireci argues, the theology of earthly trial and moral development is crucial for Wollstonecraft's vindication of women's rights,[78] but Wollstonecraft is even more radical than Sireci suggests: her theology necessitates a radically different concept of God's action. Providence is no longer seen to be manifest in the current situation (of the family or of the British Empire)[79] but results in the demand for liberty and self-determination. In arguing against the conventional doctrine of providence, Wollstonecraft advocates a very different way of interpreting divine law and the moral governance of the world. Providence, she argues, destines women to strive for virtue. This doctrine is important not only as a theodicy but also as a theology that necessitates women's freedom and self-governance.[80]

Wollstonecraft's account of liberty distinguishes her from other Unitarian feminist thinkers of her day. Her comparing of the situation of women to that of slaves is a more radical feminism than that of Priscilla Wakefield or Mary Hays, as Ruth Watts points out.[81] Her account of reason is a further departure and allows her to move away from essentialist arguments about gendered characteristics. The connection between familial relations and political relations were so thoroughly interconnected in Wollstonecraft's time that, although she does not explicitly concern herself with political rights for women, the political implications of her philosophy are clear. The assertion that women should, as a matter of morality, govern themselves and that they should determine their own interests makes a powerful statement about their political rights.

The profound resonances of this re-interpretation of providence were not lost on Wollstonecraft: she acknowledges that the cry of atheism might well be levelled against her simply because she claims that woman was not made purely for the sake of man.[82] The inequality of the sexes, together with the inequality of the foolish and the wise, and the idle and the industrious, was enshrined in divine law and the peace of the world was at risk with any challenge to this universal order.[83] In her critique of patriarchy, therefore, Wollstonecraft clearly uses Pricean language and concepts of liberty, but she deconstructs both liberal Lockean and Tory political ideology and proposes a paradigm shift in the dominant conception of authority and self-governance. In arguing in the way that she does, she links the civil with the moral far more profoundly than Price. Whereas Price remained ambiguous towards the balanced constitution (which reflects an ambiguous application of the principle of liberty), Wollstonecraft was unequivocal in her dismantling of the philosophy of hegemony. Her position places her in direct opposition to Rousseau (from whom she is more commonly thought to derive her Platonic influence), as she insists that women can judge for themselves and should not be subject to any authority save that of their own reason.[84]

Individual agency becomes important in this model of providence. Wollstonecraft's account of reason is centred on the conviction that it is the governance of the human individual by reason that constitutes perfect liberty. The result is a perfectionist ethic, articulated in terms of deiformity, which interprets human *telos* as imitation of the divine. Love of God, Wollstone-craft argues, produces virtue, because when we love someone, we long to be like him or her. The character of Mrs Mason in *Original Stories* teaches that one must learn not only to love God but also to mimic God in moral perfections.[85] The similarity here between Wollstonecraft's language and that of Price and earlier Cambridge Platonists must denote a shared theology. Wollstonecraft admired Price's sermons, which expound a theology of participation in the divine nature as the purpose of human life and it is likely they were formative for her conviction that resembling God entails doing good.[86] This ethic in turn is the basis for their commitment to religious and civil liberty, and its safeguarding of the freedom to become virtuous.

The individualism of this ethic contrasts with Burke's account of perfection and the role of the state in achieving it. Whereas for Burke, God institutes civil society without which perfection is impossible, for Wollstonecraft, it is commitment to moral truth discerned by individual reason that constitutes perfection, and the *polis* does not make up any part of this perfection. Broadly speaking, she follows Price's redefinition of patriotism by rejecting an understanding of it in terms of the quest for the public good. She rejects the more popular Burkean argument that precisely because human perfection is unattainable, virtue and happiness are to be found within the hierarchical establishment.[87] For her, in contrast, justice and perfection are not defined by, and do not arise from, the good of the *polis*. Wollstonecraft thus moves towards an individualistic idea of moral perfection defined in terms of the capacity for reason and the inner harmony of reason and affection.

This does not mean, however, that the ethical community is unimportant to her. If the way things have been in the past is no longer believed to be the way of providence, there is a new ethical imperative to undertake critical reflection on religion and political society. For both Wollstonecraft and for the Rational Dissenters, political activity and perfectionism is envisaged in terms of the pursuit of truth through reasoned debate, motivated by a conviction about the fallibility of knowledge (and this has a direct link to the common good). Subjugating one's will to that of another ignores the reality that power corrupts. Self-governance, therefore, requires independence from the potentially corrupt will of all others, and for this, freedom of speech and expression is essential.[88] Wollstonecraft also appeals to human frailty, especially when political power is concerned. Whereas Burke defends a societal power imbalance on the grounds of sacred ordination and reverence for antiquity, Wollstonecraft keenly feels the corruption and damage that this power has brought. She is all too aware of the human frailty that has led to the systematic abuse of women through subjection and patriarchy. Men will warp the truth and shape it to their own convenience, she states, unless that truth is envisaged as being in some way attainable by all.[89]

This belief in the fallibility of conscience leads to a conviction about the moral imperative of the ongoing search for truth through the ethical community. The Rational Dissenters expressed this through a belief in candour as a means of reaching towards truth. Wollstonecraft adopts an optimism similar to Price's that truth will emerge quite naturally, without being forced by the state, in any society blessed with civil and political freedom.[90] It is not only that freedom is required for individual virtue but also that the liberation of women is essential for the moral development of a society. Women's theological voices must be heard. Reason is, for her, the power of discerning truth. Consequently, the freedom of women is necessary for a truthful and virtuous state.[91] Philosophy is not the uncovering of a view from nowhere but is rather more like the search for an elusive truth that can only be approached from the act of learning from a multitude of different standpoints.

This leads Wollstonecraft to a belief in the vital importance of the community, and her background is crucial in appreciating this. The Dissenting community, of which Wollstonecraft was an active part – in Newington Green, and later on in London in the company of Johnson's circle – was an important influence on Wollstonecraft not only in terms of its philosophy of education and ecclesiology[92] but also in terms of its aim to be a community that practiced what it preached. The community of candour was one that ultimately fostered and encouraged Wollstonecraft's own rejection of gendered conceptions of femininity. Their discussion groups and literary circles formed a community that consciously intended to change the structure of society by practising the ideals of virtue and the pursuit of truth. Pamphlets and books were written and arguments exchanged in order to enlighten others and to challenge prevailing opinions, which helps to explain why so many Rational Dissenters engaged in direct political activity.[93]

Candour then was perceived to be necessary for working towards a true account of the world. Important here too is social activity. If society is not necessarily arranged providentially, there is much more of an incentive to change it for the better. It is against this background that Wollstonecraft's Vindications should be read. They were a contribution to candour, and they had the intent of provoking social transformation. Her endorsement for practical action is therefore even stronger than Sireci suggests:[94] it is not only that intellectual improvement is divinely sanctioned but also that it is required for moral development.

Education plays a vital role in her revised account of providence, and she shares the Dissenters' belief that it can enact social change. Education is to blame for the current situation of hegemony, but it is also the solution. This contrasts bluntly with writers such as Soame Jenyns, who penned a defence of the established hierarchy by arguing that 'through education, the philosopher and the peasant; the prince and the labourer are fitted for their respective situations.' These are situations of privilege and subordination that are determined by the 'gracious hand of providence.'[95] Wollstonecraft, meanwhile, responds to this theology by proposing an ethical imperative to promote education and to contribute to public debate.[96] Education is the first step in 'advancing gradually towards perfection' perceived in terms of self-determined ethical perfection.[97] This was no uncontroversial position:

ignorance was deemed to be the lot of the poor, willed by God. By challenging this, she was challenging the perceived wisdom of God and the conventional model of divine action. Her theology of liberty as self-governance, therefore, underpins a conviction to empower the socially and politically subordinate.

Revisioning philosophy and natural theology

Wollstonecraft's school for girls may have been short-lived because of financial difficulties but it was a concrete attempt to enact her theory of education as socially and morally effective. *The Female Reader*, published in 1789 the year before the *Vindication of the Rights of Men*, did likewise. It was a volume 'principally intended for the improvement of females,' which ultimately meant teaching them to learn to think.[98] It also discloses an insight into Wollstonecraft's opinion on the nature and purpose of philosophical argument.

Young minds are relatively immature and for this reason cannot engage easily with philosophy: 'Reasoning must be tedious and irksome to those whose passions have never led them to reason.'[99] It is clear that passions precede the use of rationality for Wollstonecraft. Susan Khin Zaw speculates about the influence of Plato's *Phaedrus* on her spiritualised account of passion and the imagination.[100] Whether it was Price who introduced her to this particular dialogue, as Zaw suggests, it is impossible to say, but the pedagogy of the *Phaedrus* is echoed in the method of Wollstonecraft's teaching aid. Young people, she argues, should be allowed to read amusing stories full of allegories in order to ensure they are kept engaged. This is why, in her own reader, she includes tales that are directly addressed to the imagination, because they 'tend to awaken the affections and fix good habits more firmly in the mind than cold arguments and mere declamation.'[101] Arguments are defined as 'cold' simply because they do not fire the imagination or inspire the passions. This does not mean they are not suitable for those who already cherish philosophical argumentation but they will be of no use to those who are not already receptive to philosophical reflection.

The danger with philosophy, then, is that it works in isolation from our affections. In Wollstonecraft's introduction *The Female Reader*, she quotes extensively and approvingly from Anna Laetitia Barbauld's preface to her *Devotional Pieces*. 'Philosophy' Barbauld argues 'represents the Deity in too abstracted a manner to engage our affections.'[102] This abstract God sounds very like the immutable, immovable God so familiar to classical theism: it is the God who is 'neither delighted with praises, nor moved by importunity' and is so far removed from us that any form of relationality becomes difficult nigh impossible.[103] What is important for Barbauld, and evidently for Wollstonecraft, to consider is the practical effect of a given model of God. A God of mercy, and affection – who is even 'open to the feelings of indignation' – is far more amenable to fostering a feeling of human relationality with the divine. It is the ethical implications of different models of God that Wollstonecraft is alert to.

Philosophers, as both women see it, are thus at fault in accommodating no room for relationality with God. They also 'dwell too much in generals' by reducing everything to the operation of general laws, trying to 'grasp the whole order of the universe' while rarely leaving 'room for those particular and personal mercies which are the food of gratitude.'[104] Their fault is that 'they trace the great outline of nature, but neglect the colouring which gives warmth and beauty to the piece.'[105] In other words, they overlook all that is beautiful and, in the process, they fail to inspire. The point of philosophy, for Wollstonecraft and Barbauld, is thus to move us: to change our attitude, not just our propositional belief. For both writers, the philosophers should take a leaf out of the poet's book: it is not vague and general description that touches the heart, but a few striking images strongly worked up.[106] Attention to detail is too often missed whereas the point of philosophy is to change us for the better. It cannot do this without firing the imagination.

Barbauld presents a vision, reiterated by Wollstonecraft in her reprinting of this poetry, of two types of natural theology: one that takes us towards the abstract and the general God by logical argument, and one that gains its inspiration from the contemplation of the particulars of the natural world:

> I read [God's] awful name, emblazon'd high
> With golden letters on th' illumin'd sky;
> Nor less the mystic characters I see
> Wrought in each flower, inscrib'd on ev'ry tree.[107]

The second type of theology presents a vision of a reconceived natural theology that changes not only the vision of nature itself but also the idea of God. An early commitment to panentheism is clearly apparent in *Mary: A Fiction* in Mary's gazing on the moon and listening to the sea. This theology becomes even more pronounced in her later works including *Letters Written in Sweden, Norway and Denmark* (1796), which were composed much later in her life and exhibit radical differences from the Wollstonecraft of the earlier Vindications. Taylor describes a drastic change in her earlier views, so much so that she endorsed the freethinking Norwegians, whom she saw as the 'least oppressed people of Europe.'[108] She should not, however, be thought of as being any closer to embracing deism. Her faith in God was still deeply personal: it was essentially a panentheism that had at its heart an 'animated nature'[109] in which the divinised universe leads to a much more immanent divine. Witnessing fishermen casting their nets with seagulls hovering overhead, she remarks,

> Every thing seemed to harmonise into tranquillity. I pause, again breathless, to trace, with renewed delight, sentiments which entranced me, when, turning my humid eyes from the expanse below to the vault

above, my sight pierced the fleecy clouds that softened the azure bright-ness; and, imperceptibly recalling the reveries of childhood, I bowed before the awful throne of my Creator, whilst I rested on its footstool.[110]

There were plenty who were shocked at her reveries of the divine. One com-mentator accuses her of having

discarded all faith in Christianity . . . From this period she adored [God] . . . not as one whose interposing power is ever silently at work on the grand theatre of human affairs, causing eventual good to spring from present evil, and permitting nothing but for wise and benevolent pur-poses; but merely as the first great cause and vital spring of existence.[111]

This says less about Wollstonecraft's own theology than about how fragile the more orthodox idea of providence was, however, especially in the light of human suffering. Either everything must be orientated towards a good purpose or, if it wasn't, the only other option left was deism: a God who is only first cause. What Wollstonecraft represents is an attempt to think outside of these parameters. Her more panentheistic God – one who might, as Ruth Page has suggested more recently, let creatures 'be' rather than de-termine the passage of providence with a heavy hand – was so inconceivable to many that it could be encountered as nothing but either atheism or deism.

What is substantially different in Wollstonecraft's later thought is the au-thority she gives to personal experience and feeling or subjectivity. In writing the aforementioned *Letters*, she 'determined to let my remarks and reflec-tions flow unrestrained,' not giving merely a description of what she sees but conveying the 'effect different objects had produced on my mind and feelings.' Poovey sees this as the beginning of a new aesthetic programme in which feelings become an integral part of the truths she wishes to convey.[112] This results in a maturing of her earlier ideas of the relationship between reason and the imagination in which reason loses its status as superior and often generates or gives way to the emotions.

This creative imagination is life affirming because it proves the creative power of the individual who contemplates and 'anchors the subject in the external world.'[113] The *Letters from Sweden* portray reason and the imagi-nation as playing an equal role in the individual's education. Every time she encounters a new situation or natural scene, Wollstonecraft has a spontane-ous emotion, but it is only after rational reflection has taken place that this emotion is generalised to all humanity. Only once she uses her imagination to project herself into a scene does she intuit her own integrity and value.[114] Through her contemplations, she links together her own individual progress and that of society. Both are improved together.

At the same time she penned the novel *The Wrongs of Woman, or Maria* (begun in 1796), Wollstonecraft also wrote the essay 'On Poetry.' This con-tains a clear philosophy of the erotic imagination leading to the sacred. 'Love to man leads to devotion,' she states, as 'grand and sublime images strike the imagination – God is seen in every floating cloud, and comes from the misty mountain to receive the noblest homage of an intelligent creature – praise.'[115] It is ultimately the wisdom and goodness of God that inspire the admiration of God, however. 'Affections and remembrances fade' and give way to the 'sublime admiration' that is inspired by God's goodness and wisdom.[116] These most primary attributes of God inspire the imagination when God 'is worshipped in a *temple not made with hands.*' In such worship, initiated by the contemplation of nature, 'the world seems to contain only the mind that formed, and the mind that contemplates it!' A contrast is made with the 'weak responses of ceremonial devotion.'[117] This is clearly not pantheism (God and nature are not identical in her theology) and clearly not deism. What it represents is a rejection of a religion of ceremonial rituals and rites in place of a contemplative theology of nature instigated by the creative imagination.

Chapter 4 drew attention to the distinction between arguments to and from design and the tensions that existed between them. For the eighteenth century physico-theological tradition of which Price was a part, however, the argument from design made no sense without a commitment to a divinised value-laden universe. The rationalism of these arguments must not therefore be detached from this theology. Whereas Priestley adopts a more Socinian rationality that sees him espouse rational argument on which he believes all should in principle agree, Price, as the previous chapters have shown, exhibits much more caution as to reason's reach. His natural theology rests on this epistemic humility. The ambiguity and tensions apparent in Price's natural theology and in that of the earlier Latitudinarians result from an appreciation of the need to bring together the experiential aspect of religion while at the same time holding this together with a commitment to truth. Their natural theology takes places within an account of a divinised cosmos in which God's existence is a lived experienced reality.

Wollstonecraft, for her part, inherits, but also re-imagines, a Platonic rationalist theology. Notwithstanding her refusal to downplay the importance of emotion and the sentiments, she was committed to a deiform conception of reason, epistemic fallibility and emphasis on a theology of nature, as radically conceived. Her appeal to reason represents a search for truth, and her earlier works do much to promote the application of reason to religion, but this arose out of the recognition of the partiality of the system within which she was situated. In his critique of Enlightenment thought, Buckley draws our attention to the fact that the god of religion cannot be affirmed or supported adequately without the unique reality that is religion.[118] Wollstonecraft points us towards the closer attention and critique needed, however, in conceiving of that 'reality' and what it should aspire to be.

Notes

1 G. T. Barker-Benfield, "Mary Wollstonecraft: Eighteenth Century Commonwealthwoman," *Journal of the History of Ideas* 50, no. 1 (1989): 100.

2 Claire Tomalin, *The Life and Death of Mary Wollstonecraft* (Middlesex: Penguin, 1974), 47; Janet Todd, *Mary Wollstonecraft: A Revolutionary Life* (London: Weidenfeld and Nicolson, 2000), 60; Ralph M. Wardle, *Mary Wollstonecraft: A Critical Biography* (London: The Richards Press Ltd., 1951), 35.

3 Todd, *Wollstonecraft*, 59.

4 Todd, *Wollstonecraft*, 60; Barker-Benfield, "Mary Wollstonecraft," 103; Tomalin, *Life and Death*, 61; Wardle, *Wollstonecraft*, 35; Fiore Sireci, "The Spiritual Vindications of Mary Wollstonecraft," *Enlightenment and Dissent* 26 (2010): 195–229; Saba Bahar, "Richard Price and the Moral Foundations of Mary Wollstonecraft's Feminism," *Enlightenment and Dissent* 18 (1999): 1–15.

5 Barbara Taylor, *Mary Wollstonecraft and the Feminist Imagination* (Cambridge: Cambridge University Press, 2003), 103.

6 Taylor, *Mary Wollstonecraft*, 102.

7 Mary Wollstonecraft, "Mary, A Fiction," in *The Works of Mary Wollstonecraft*, ed. Janet Todd and Marilyn Butler, vol. 1 (London: William Pickering, 1989), 17.

8 Wollstonecraft, "Mary," 29.

9 Taylor, *Mary Wollstonecraft*, 102.

10 Wollstonecraft, "Mary," all 29.

11 Wollstonecraft, "Mary," 11.

12 Wollstonecraft, "Mary," 16.

13 William Godwin, *Memoirs of the Author of A Vindication of the Rights of Woman, 1798* (Oxford: Woodstock Books, 1990), 33.

14 Wollstonecraft, "Mary," 11.

15 Wollstonecraft, "Mary," 11.

16 Letter to Joseph Johnson, 1795 in Mary Wollstonecraft, *Collected Letters of Mary Wollstonecraft*, ed. Ralph M. Wardle (London: Cornell University Press, 1979), 325; Wollstonecraft, "Mary," 49.

17 Godwin, *Memoirs*, 33–4.

18 Taylor, *Mary Wollstonecraft*, 108.

19 Mary Poovey, *The Proper Lady and the Woman Writer: Ideology as Style in the Works of Mary Wollstonecraft, Mary Shelley, and Jane Austin* (London: University of Chicago Press, 1984), 72; Mary Wollstonecraft, "A Vindication of the Rights of Woman," in *A Vindication of the Rights of Men and A Vindication of the Rights of Woman*, ed. Sylvana Tomaselli (Cambridge: Cambridge University Press, 1995), 87.

20 Wollstonecraft, "Mary," 33.

21 Wollstonecraft, *Letters*, 170. Letter to George Blood, January 1788.

22 "Analytic Review" December 1789, in Mary Wollstonecraft, *The Works of Mary Wollstonecraft*, ed. Janet Todd and Marilyn Butler, vol. 7 (London: William Pickering, 1989), 185.

23 Anya Taylor, "Coleridge, Wollstonecraft, and the Rights of Women," in *Coleridge's Visionary Languages: Essays in Honour of J. B. Beer*, ed. Tim Fulford and Morton D. Paley (Cambridge: D. S. Brewer, 1993), 85.

24 Taylor, "Coleridge," 92.

25 Edmund Burke, "Reflections on the Revolution in France," in *Revolutionary Writings*, ed. Iain Hampsher-Monk (Cambridge: Cambridge University Press, 2014), 98.

26 Stephen M. Lee, "Parliament, Parties and Elections (1760–1815)," in *A Companion to Eighteenth-Century Britain*, ed. H. T. Dickinson (Oxford: Blackwell, 2002), 73.

27 Lee, "Parliament," 73.

28 Lee, "Parliament," 74.

29 Lee, "Parliament," 75.

30 Jennifer Mori, *Britain in the Age of the French Revolution, 1785–1820* (Harlow, Essex: Pearson, 2000), 5.

31 Richard Price, *A Review of the Principal Questions in Morals*, 3rd ed. (Oxford: Clarendon, 1948), 38.

32 Mary Wollstonecraft, "A Vindication of the Rights of Men," in *A Vindication of the Rights of Men and A Vindication of the Rights of Woman*, ed. Sylvana Tomaselli (Cambridge: Cambridge University Press, 1995), 34, 20.

33 Wollstonecraft, "Rights of Men," 31, 34.

34 Price, *Review*, 214.

35 Wollstonecraft, "Rights of Men," 31.

36 Wollstonecraft, "Rights of Men," all 32.

37 Price, *Review*, 228; Plato, *Phaedrus*, trans. Walter Hamilton (Harmondsworth: Penguin, 1973), 247d.

38 Wollstonecraft, "Rights of Men," 33.

39 Wollstonecraft, "Rights of Men," 31, 54; C.f. Emma Rauschenbusch-Clough, *A Study of Mary Wollstonecraft* (London: Longmans, Green and Co., 1898), 54.

40 Wollstonecraft, "Rights of Men," 12; Kristin Waters, ed., *Women and Men Political Theorists: Enlightened Conversations* (Oxford: Blackwell, 2000), 127.

41 Wollstonecraft, "Rights of Men," 18.

42 Todd argues for this in Todd, *Wollstonecraft*, 178.

43 Wollstonecraft, "Rights of Woman," 127.

44 Wollstonecraft, "Rights of Men," 23.

45 Wollstonecraft, "Rights of Woman," 165, 118.

46 Wollstonecraft, "Rights of Men," 31, 33.

47 Wollstonecraft, "Rights of Woman," 89, 69.

48 Wollstonecraft, "Rights of Men," 39.

49 Burke, "Reflections," 102.

50 Wollstonecraft, "Rights of Men," 12.

51 Martin Fitzpatrick, "Heretical Religion and Radical Political Ideas in Late Eighteenth-Century England," in *The Transformation of Political Culture: England and Germany in the Late Eighteenth Century*, ed. Eckhart Hellmuth (Oxford: Oxford University Press, 1990), 355.

52 Richard Price, "Observations on the Nature of Civil Liberty, the Principles of Government, and the Justice and Policy of the War with America," in *Richard Price: Political Writings*, ed. D.O. Thomas (Cambridge: Cambridge University Press, 1991), 28; Richard Price, "Additional Observations on the Nature and Value of Civil Liberty, and the War with America," in *Political Writings*, ed. D.O. Thomas (Cambridge: Cambridge University Press, 1991), 85.

53 Wollstonecraft, "Rights of Men," 31, 39, 20.

54 Wollstonecraft, "Rights of Woman," 245.

55 Wollstonecraft, "Rights of Woman," 84.

56 Sarah Hutton, "The Ethical Background of the Rights of Women," in *Philosophical Theory and the Universal Declaration of Human Rights*, ed. William Sweet (Ottowa: University of Ottowa Press, 2003), 32.

57 Wollstonecraft, "Rights of Woman," 274.

58 William Paley, *The Principles of Moral and Political Philosophy*, vol. 2 (Dublin: Printed for Messrs. Exshaw, White, H. Whitestone, Byrne, Cash, Marchbank, and Mc.Kenzie, 1785), 399–400.

59 William Paley, *Reasons for Contentment Addressed to the Laboring Part of the British Public* (London: R. Faulder, 1793), 3–4.

60 Paley, *Principles*, 2:175.

61 George Pretyman, *A Sermon Preached before the Lords. . . in the Abbey Church of Westminster, on Friday, January 30, 1789* (London: T. Cadell, 1789), 16.

62 John Locke, *Two Treatises of Government Edited with an Introduction and Notes by Peter Laslett* (Cambridge: Cambridge University Press, 1988), II, §57, 306; II, §82, 321; I, §48, 174; II, §85, 323.

63 Wollstonecraft, "Rights of Men," 13; Bridget Hill, "The Links between Mary Wollstonecraft and Catharine Macaulay: New Evidence," *Women's History Review* 4, no. 2 (1995): 184.

64 Joseph Priestley, *A Serious Address to the Masters of Families* (London: Printed for J. Johnson, 1770), 2. See also Kathryn Gleadle, *Radical Unitarians and the Emergence of the Women's Rights Movement, 1831–51* (London: Macmillan, 1995), 21.

65 Soame Jenyns, "A Free Inquiry into the Nature and Origin of Evil. In Six Letters To –," in *Miscellaneous Pieces in Verse and Prose* (London: Printed for J. Dodsley, 1770), 72.

66 Pretyman, *Sermon*, 1789, 16–17.

67 J.C.D. Clark, *English Society 1660–1832: Religion, Ideology and Politics during the Ancien Regime* (Cambridge: Cambridge University Press, 2000), 260.

68 Taylor, *Mary Wollstonecraft*, 99.

69 John Brown, *On the Female Character and Education*, 1765 quoted in Taylor, *Mary Wollstonecraft*, 100.

70 Taylor, *Mary Wollstonecraft*, 101.

71 See Barbara Taylor, "The Religious Foundations of Mary Wollstonecraft's Feminism," in *The Cambridge Companion to Mary Wollstonecraft*, ed. Claudia L. Johnson (Cambridge: Cambridge University Press, 2002), 106.

72 All Wollstonecraft, "Rights of Woman," 95.

73 Taylor, *Mary Wollstonecraft*, 129.

74 Godwin, *Memoirs*, 32.

75 Lilly Butler, "Religion No Matter of Shame," in *A Defence of Natural and Revealed Religion: Being a Collection of the Sermons Preached at the Lecture Founded by the Honourable Robert Boyle Esq (from the Year 1691 to the Year 1732)*, ed. Gilbert Burnet, vol. 2 (London: Printed by S. Powell, 1739), 476.

76 Ann Loades, *Feminist Theology: Voices from the Past* (Cambridge: Polity Press, 2001), 12.

77 Godwin, *Memoirs*, 35.

78 Sireci, "Spiritual Vindications."

79 George Pretyman, *A Sermon Preached at the Cathedral Church of St. Paul, London before His Majesty and Both Houses of Parliament 1797* (London: T. Cadell, 1798), 8.

80 Bahar, "Richard Price"; Wollstonecraft, "Rights of Woman," 87–8.

81 Ruth Watts, *Gender, Power and the Unitarians in England 1760–1860* (Harlow, Essex: Longman, 1988), 32.

82 Wollstonecraft, "Rights of Woman," 157.

83 George Horne, "A Charge Intended to Have Been Delivered to the Clergy of Norwich," in *Works*, ed. William Jones (London: Printed for J. Johnson, 1818), 531.

84 Wollstonecraft, "Rights of Woman," 174.

85 See, e.g., Taylor, *Mary Wollstonecraft*, 102; Watts, *Gender*, 92.

86 Mary Wollstonecraft, "Original Stories," in *Works*, ed. Janet Todd and Marilyn Butler, vol. 4 (London: Pickering, 1989), 431; c.f. Richard Price, *Sermons on Various Subjects*, ed. W. Morgan (London: Longman, 1816), 366, 376.

87 William Coxe, *A Letter to the Rev. Richard Price, upon His 'Discourse on the Love of Our Country' Delivered November 4, 1789, to the Society for Commemorating the Revolution in Great Britain* (London: T. Cadell, 1790), 43.

88 Fitzpatrick, "Heretical Religion," 342, 352.

89 Wollstonecraft, "Rights of Woman," 124.

90 See Fitzpatrick, "Heretical Religion," 355 on the Rational Dissenters.

91 Wollstonecraft, "Rights of Woman," 127, 272.

92 Gleadle, *Radical Unitarians*, 21, 58.

93 Fitzpatrick, "Heretical Religion," 359.
94 Sireci, "Spiritual Vindications," 211.
95 Jenyns, "Free Inquiry," 34–5.
96 Wollstonecraft, "Rights of Woman," 74, 243; Fitzpatrick, "Heretical Religion," 364.
97 Wollstonecraft, "Rights of Woman," 127.
98 Mary Wollstonecraft, "The Female Reader," in *The Works of Mary Wollstonecraft*, ed. Janet Todd and Marilyn Butler, vol. 4 (London: William Pickering, 1989), 55–6.
99 Wollstonecraft, "Female Reader," 56.
100 Susan Khin Zaw, "The Reasonable Heart: Mary Wollstonecraft's View of the Relation between Reason and Feeling in Morality, Moral Psychology, and Moral Development," *Hypatia* 13, no. 1 (1998): 78–117.
101 Wollstonecraft, "Female Reader," 56.
102 Wollstonecraft, "Female Reader," 57.
103 Wollstonecraft, "Female Reader," 57.
104 Wollstonecraft, "Female Reader," 58.
105 Wollstonecraft, "Female Reader," 58.
106 Wollstonecraft, "Female Reader," 58.
107 Barbauld, Poems, reprinted in *The Female Reader* in Wollstonecraft, "Female Reader," 345.
108 Taylor, *Mary Wollstonecraft*, 95; Mary Wollstonecraft, "Letters Written in Sweden, Norway and Denmark," in *The Works of Mary Wollstonecraft*, ed. Janet Todd and Marilyn Butler, vol. 6 (London: William Pickering, 1989), 297.
109 Taylor, *Mary Wollstonecraft*, 127.
110 Wollstonecraft, "Letters Written in Sweden," 280.
111 *The Monthly Magazine and American Review* 1, no. 1 (1799), p. 331 quoted in Taylor, *Mary Wollstonecraft*, 127.
112 Poovey, *Proper Lady*, 84, 86.
113 Poovey, *Proper Lady*, 86.
114 Poovey, *Proper Lady*, 85.
115 Mary Wollstonecraft, "On Poetry," in *The Works of Mary Wollstonecraft*, ed. Janet Todd and Marilyn Butler, vol. 7 (London: William Pickering, 1989), 8; Taylor, *Mary Wollstonecraft*, 140.
116 Taylor, *Mary Wollstonecraft*, 140.
117 Wollstonecraft, "On Poetry," all 8.
118 Michael J. Buckley, *At the Origins of Modern Atheism* (Yale: Yale University Press, 1987), 362.

Conclusion

Jonathan Israel is right that ideas are important. They are not mere epi-phenomena but rather they shape our values and are at once both ethical and political.[1] Their effects are real and tangible. For this reason, as the preceding chapters have shown, the history of philosophy is important for determining the nature and future shape of the philosophy of religion. What becomes clear through the contextualising of the theological and philosoph-ical ideas of the late seventeenth and eighteenth centuries is that the contem-porary understanding of philosophy of religion as a-political, and a-ethical, has over-determined the dominant narrative of its history.

This dominant story, as Victoria Harrison points out, sees the philosophy of religion adopting its common form in the period of Enlightenment by arguing against perceived threats to religious belief.[2] The result has been an acceptance of the justification of belief as the primary object of the exercise, made possible through the methods of science. This in turn feeds into the conviction, adopted too by the most popular narratives of Enlightenment, that the English natural theologians were the zealots of reason who wanted to reconcile faith with a new secular rationality. It is assumed that their agenda was pretty much at one with that of the deists, whereby a religion of reason usurps revelation and any claim based on faith is found wanting. Furthermore, the dichotomy this sets up between reason and revelation re-sults in a perceived gulf between the secular and the theological, which often goes hand in hand with an assumption that the values of Enlightenment, including liberalism, are inherently anti-Christian.

The assumptions that have been made about analytic philosophy of re-ligion's past have resulted in a discipline that is inherently politically con-servative in that it understands itself as a-political, rarely challenging the status quo. Ethical and political concerns are assumed unimportant and largely irrelevant to the field. Giving due attention to the English natural theologians who have been the subject of this book, however, shows it is an oversimplification to see the purpose of eighteenth-century natural theology as principally apologetic, devoid of any appreciation for the centrality of ethical and political concerns. When Swinburne claims that what has been the main concern down the centuries is primarily whether the claim that

God exists is true or false, he relays only part of the picture, resulting in a misleading impression of what were in fact the significant issues for many seventeenth- and eighteenth-century English natural theologians. These philosophers of religion were certainly occupied with worries about atheism but not only about atheism and not principally in terms of propositional belief. The important issues stirring their minds were those concerned with the reality of truth and goodness, the ethical implications of belief and the prospective use and abuse of political power.

Appreciating more fully the ethico-political orientation of English seventeenth- and eighteenth-century philosophy of religion demands a reconception of the aims and objects of the contemporary discipline. It results in a vision of the philosophy of religion that centres on the primacy of the ethical and the contemplation of nature. Some promising recent attempts to do this can be seen in the works of John Cottingham, Stephen Clark, Grace Jantzen, Pamela Sue Anderson, Douglas Hedley and Mark Wynn. All these thinkers offer philosophical models that hinge on the ethical and present new imaginative ways of incorporating the ethical and aesthetic in our engagement with the world. A much broader conception of natural theology follows. Pamela Sue Anderson articulates the need for such an account when she contrasts the narrow analytic variety of natural theology with a richer, broader version consisting of critical thought about how human beings live and relate to the natural world. This involves utilising different ways of thinking about the nature of human life and how we relate to non-human life and the wider world. It reminds us that how we understand ourselves, including our conceptions of self, rationality and *telos* is innately political. There is a precedent for this deeper understanding in the natural theology of the seventeenth- and eighteenth-century thinkers outlined in this volume. They do not, in any straightforward sense, act as forerunners to an analytic philosophy of religion that argues on the basis of evidence – entirely separate from revelation – for God's existence based on features of the natural world.[3] The Cambridge Platonists and Latitudinarians together with Price and Wollstonecraft were engaged in advancing a particular way of looking at the world – an attitude that prioritised its intrinsic value and the immutable non-relative nature of this value. In this, they guide our concerns principally towards ethics and are part of a rich tradition of Platonic philosophical theology, containing insights that must be at the forefront of any natural theology aptly reconceived.

Ernst Cassirer regards Plotinus's *On Beauty* as the centrepiece of Cambridge Platonist theology, and it helps to illustrate the central concerns of a Platonic natural theology. For Plotinus, the position of the soul in the cosmos is not fixed in the sense that it has no defined place in the world. Instead, its being – its ethical and physical quality – depends on its attitude or behaviour and on the direction it takes.[4] This idea was formative for Nicholas of Cusa and Marsilio Ficino and later became a central tenet of English Platonism. This does not mean, however, that Platonism necessarily asserts two different realities. Hadley, for example, explains that for Plotinus, we are capable of looking at one reality in two different ways. In adopting this philosophy, it might be said that we can look at the world in a reductionist, materialistic or neo-liberal way (as nothing but its physical component parts or solely in terms of its market value), or we can strive for an understanding of reality that considers it as the bearer of innate value.[5] In other words, we can choose to follow Descartes's move towards a model of control of nature for human purpose,[6] or we can see it as a world full of value with an integrity of its own, worthy of contemplation.

The natural theology of the Cambridge Platonists, Price and Wollstonecraft appreciated that a universe arising purely by chance could contain no real moral value and could not harbour truth. As Stephen Clark puts it, imagining that 'God does not exist' amounts to denying there is discoverable truth, or any truth worth discovering.[7] These English natural theologians should therefore be added to the company of the Platonist philosophers identified by Clark who realised before Darwin that if the immutable archetypes of beauty and value are replaced by materialistic chance events, then there is no real beauty in the world. They recognised that without eternal and immutable truth and goodness, science itself would be impossible.

The arguments of this broader type of natural theology are thus first and foremost about ethics rather than about proving the hypothesis of the existence of God, and any reconceived natural theology must be orientated around this insight. Central to its concerns is the promotion of a particular model of the cosmos in which the value of the natural world is more than what is projected onto it by human beings. If morality is eternal and immutable, it is more than a matter of will. Wollstonecraft's proposal that the mind is active and not merely a passive mirror reflecting back what is perceived echoes Pico della Mirandola's point that we do not accept our surroundings passively but give them our own form. In this Platonic philosophy, the prioritising of mind above matter is, as Douglas Hedley puts it, an ethical doctrine. The world does not consist of 'neutral' facts, nor is it solely what we make it.[8] Our ways of thinking cannot escape their ethical colouring. What Wollstonecraft perceives when she contemplates the natural world is a world replete with divine ethical value. It is the imagination that perceives this – a power not opposed to reason, but one that works with a type of reason far removed from ratiocination. As Plotinus put it intellect cannot be reduced to cognition: it is also a divinely inspired drunkenness.[9]

This approach to nature and to natural theology shapes the Cambridge Platonic attitude towards the purpose and scope of rational argument. The Cambridge Platonists did not advance the liberal theology of Hooker or Chillingworth, and they did not embrace the kind of tense tolerance brought about by having to live with differences of opinion. They instead believed in the necessity of such differences because, as they saw it, diversity of opinion is not something that should be endured but something that is 'the instrument of religious knowledge itself.'[10] Their thinking on this point was coloured by the

Renaissance Platonists. For Nicholas of Cusa, the existence of a variety of religious judgements does not demand tolerance for those who disagree, but is in fact something positive. It guides us towards a theology that affirms multiple viewpoints because no single stance can be said to possess the truth.[11] In the hands of the Cambridge Platonists, the demand to engage in a spirit of sincerity with the standpoints of others guards against 'false zeal': 'I *may* be mistaken. I *must* not be dogmatical and confident, peremptory and imperious. I *will* not break the certain laws of charity, for a doubtful doctrine or uncertain truth.'[12] It was for this reason Whichcote was able to argue against Tuckney that the good will of a heathen is godlier than the angry zeal of a Christian. As Cassirer states, these words express not only a contrast in atmosphere but also a decisive transformation of the idea of God.[13] It is just this philosophy that is taken up into Price's idea of candour. The 'honest mind' should therefore be regarded as one that accepts its own partiality and maintains a ceaseless search towards truth in its less partial form. The search is founded on the unwavering commitment to the unity of goodness and truth.

It is worth noting that talk of 'truth' cannot be used without caution. Harriet Harris quite rightly points out that feminists working in theology and philosophy have been suspicious of truth claims and of the quest for truth because such an enterprise has so often been repressive.[14] Talk of the immutability of truth might be interpreted as suggesting a hegemonic account of truth imposed on those who fail to 'see' it from a supposed universal perspective. A commitment to truth that is immutable and objective does not necessarily mean, however, that human perception of it has to be considered impartial or unmediated. A commitment to the reality of truth and value can be maintained alongside recognition of the need to guard against false zeal and to appreciate the impossibility of capturing truth in any one opinion. The primary concern of the Platonic tradition, as inherited by Price, is that there are better and worse ways of seeing the world and that truth and goodness are not determined by human will. The reality of truth is essential for this position, and it should ground the reimagined philosophy of religion. As Harris points out, without a commitment to truth, there can be no imperative to embark on the struggle for truth or to engage in the spiritual task of recognising falsehood and moments of truth, or to develop our understanding of truth as we attempt to disclose it. The insight is at the heart of Plato's *Euthyphro* and is central to the anti-voluntarist stance that truth is more than will, more than the whim of the gods and more than human assertion.

It is just such a concern for the primacy of goodness with its capacity for at least partial understanding by human beings that takes precedence for the thinkers considered in this book. Spellman is right to suggest that we misrepresent the late seventeenth-century divines if we fail to see 'that their insistence on the reasonableness of Christianity was not an iron grip on a deistic future' but was in fact something borrowed from the past.[15] The Calvinistic creed, as the Cambridge divines saw it, was flawed when it elevated God's will above reason, and Hobbes too was a danger when he declared that the law of the land absorbs human intellect and will.[16] The good mind has to be one that refuses the supremacy of will in favour of the struggle for truth. The natural theology of the eighteenth-century Latitudinarians is underpinned by just such an attitude, and it was an insight that was more than apparent to many of the Rational Dissenters whose daily lives brought home the extent to which truth claims can oppress. History was, as Seed states, a 'nightmare from which Rational Dissenters, more than most, were trying to awake.'[17] The study of those deemed heterodox, in this case the Rational Dissenters, does much to affirm some recent concerns that the appropriateness of a term such as 'orthodox' is itself an implicit claim to truth and authority, and is in danger of becoming merely a claim to power.[18]

In summary, natural theology should have two main aims as Pamela Sue Anderson proposes: a commitment to the reality of truth and goodness and the capacity to subject our models of self, nature and divinity to reflective scrutiny. Both of these aims are present to some extent in the philosophy of religion of the natural theologians discussed in this study, and they highlight how essential it is that analytic philosophy of religion and its resultant natural theology be reconceived. The thinkers discussed in this volume are part of a tradition that strives for truth and goodness with an acknowledgement of epistemic humility, and they display awareness that models of God, nature and the self have inescapable ethical and political implications. When these thinkers utilised the rational tools of abstraction, objectivity and coherence, they were concerned first and foremost with questions of an ethical and political nature: with the question of 'how should we live?' in the context of 'what is going on?' There is some historical precedent, therefore, for the Anderson's suggestion that these tools would be better used to try to answer the what, how, when and who of knowledge than be restricted to the justification of propositional belief. Not all of us might wish to go as far as Nietzsche in seeing the philosopher as 'a terrible explosive that is a danger to everything,'[19] but living a bit more dangerously is an imperative for philosophers of religion. It is vital that the philosophy of religion reclaim its self-consciousness as a discipline at once both ethical and political, and the history of philosophy, as this book has shown, is indispensable for the task.

Notes

1 Jonathan I. Israel, *Enlightenment Contested: Philosophy, Modernity, and the Emancipation of Man, 1670–1752* (Oxford: Oxford University Press, 2006), 23.
2 Victoria S. Harrison, "What's the Use of Philosophy of Religion?" in *God, Goodness and Philosophy*, ed. Harriet A. Harris (Farnham: Ashgate, 2011), 31.
3 Pamela Sue Anderson, "Feminist Perspectives on Natural Theology," in *The Oxford Handbook of Natural Theology*, ed. Russell Re-Manning, John Hedley Brooke, and Fraser Watts (Oxford: Oxford University Press, 2013), 354.
4 Ernst Cassirer, *The Platonic Renaissance in England*, trans. James P. Pettegrove (New York: Nelson, 1953), 27–8; c.f. Plotinus, *Enneads*, trans. A. H. Armstrong, Loeb Classical Library (London: Heinemann, 1966), I.6.8–9.

5   Douglas Hadley, "A Variation on the Dog and His Bone: The Unity of the World in Plotinian Philosophy," 1998, https://www.bu.edu/wcp/Papers/Meta/MetaHadl.htm. Last accessed 24/04/16.

6   John Cottingham, "Plato's Sun and Descartes's Stove: Contemplation and Control in Cartesian Philosophy," in *Rationalism, Platonism and God*, ed. Michael Ayers (Oxford: Oxford University Press, 2007), 37.

7   Stephen R. L. Clark, *Biology and Christian Ethics* (Cambridge: Cambridge University Press, 2000), 310, 66, 311.

8   Douglas Hedley, "Imagination and Natural Theology," in *The Oxford Handbook of Natural Theology*, ed. Russell Re-Manning, John Hedley Brooke, and Fraser Watts (Oxford: Oxford University Press, 2013), 549.

9   Stephen R. L. Clark, "What Has Plotinus' One to Do with God?" in *Philosophers and God: At the Frontiers of Faith and Reason*, ed. John Cornwell and Michael McGhee (London: Continuum, 2009), 34.

10 Cassirer, *Platonic Renaissance*, 36.

11 Ernst Cassirer, "Giovanni Pico Della Mirandola: A Study in the History of Renaissance Ideas," *Journal of the History of Ideas* 3, no. 2 (1942): 125.

12 Benjamin Whichcote, *Moral and Religious Aphorisms* (London: Printed for J. Payne, 1753), §130.

13 Cassirer, *Platonic Renaissance*, 73.

14 Harriet A. Harris, "A Theological Approach," in *Feminist Philosophy of Religion: Critical Readings*, ed. Pamela Sue Anderson and Beverley Clack (London: Routledge, 2004), 73.

15 W. M. Spellman, *The Latitudinarians and the Church of England, 1660–1700* (Athens, Georgia: University of Georgia Press, 1993), 77.

16 Deniz Coskun, "Religious Skepticism, Cambridge Platonism, and Disestablishment," *University of Detroit Mercy Law Review* 579 (2006): 595.

17 John Seed, "'A Set of Men Powerful Enough in Many Things': Rational Dissent and Political Opposition in England, 1770–1790," in *Enlightenment and Religion: Rational Dissent in Eighteenth-Century Britain*, ed. Knud Haakonssen (Cambridge: Cambridge University Press, 1996), 157.

18 James Hanvey, "Conclusion: Continuing the Conversation," in *Radical Orthodoxy: A Catholic Enquiry?* ed. Laurence Paul Hemming (Aldershot: Ashgate, 2000), 167.

19 Friedrich Nietzsche, "Ecce Homo," in *Nietzsche: The Anti-Christ, Ecce Homo, Twilight of the Idols: And Other Writings*, ed. Aaron Ridley and Judith Norman (Cambridge: Cambridge University Press, 2005), 115.

Bibliography

Alcinous. *The Handbook of Platonism*. Translated by John Dillon. Oxford: Oxford University Press, 1993.

Anderson, Pamela Sue. *A Feminist Philosophy of Religion*. Oxford: Blackwell, 1998.

———. "An Epistemological-Ethical Approach." In *Feminist Philosophy of Religion: Critical Readings*, edited by Pamela Sue Anderson and Beverley Clack, 87–102. London: Routledge, 2004.

———. "Feminist Perspectives on Natural Theology." In *The Oxford Handbook of Natural Theology*, edited by Russell Re-Manning, John Hedley Brooke, and Fraser Watts, 354–69. Oxford: Oxford University Press, 2013.

Annas, Julia. *Platonic Ethics, Old and New*. London: Cornell University Press, 1999.

———. "What Are Plato's 'Middle' Dialogues in the Middle Of?" In *New Perspectives on Plato, Modern and Ancient*, edited by Julia Annas and Christopher J. Rowe, 1–23. Harvard: Harvard University Press, 2003.

Aquinas, Thomas. *Summa Contra Gentiles*. Translated by English Dominican Fathers. Vol. 1. London: Burns, Oates & Washbourne, 1923.

Asad, Talal. *Genealogies of Religion: Discipline and Reasons of Power in Christianity and Islam*. London: John Hopkins University Press, 1993.

Ashcraft, Richard. "Latitudinarianism and Toleration: Historical Myth versus Political History." In *Philosophy, Science and Religion in England, 1640–1700*, edited by Richard Kroll, Richard Ashcraft, and Perez Zagorin, 151–77. Cambridge: Cambridge University Press, 1992.

Aston, Nigel. "Horne and Heterodoxy: The Defence of Anglican Beliefs in the Late Enlightenment." *English Historical Review* 108, no. 429 (1993): 895–919.

Ayers, Michael. "Analytical Philosophy and the History of Philosophy." In *Philosophy and Its Past*, edited by Jonathan Rée, Michael Ayers, and Adam Westoby, 41–66. Hassocks, Sussex: The Harvester Press, 1978.

Baggett, David and Jerry L. Walls. *Good God: The Theistic Foundations of Morality*. Oxford: Oxford University Press, 2011.

Bahar, Saba. "Richard Price and the Moral Foundations of Mary Wollstonecraft's Feminism." *Enlightenment and Dissent* 18 (1999): 1–15.

Barker-Benfield, G. T. "Mary Wollstonecraft: Eighteenth Century Commonwealth-woman." *Journal of the History of Ideas* 50, no. 1 (1989): 95–115.

Barne, Miles. *The Authority of Church-Guides Asserted in a Sermon Prech'd before Our Late Gracious Sovereign King Charles II at Whitehall, Oct 17th 1675*. London: Printed for Richard Green, 1685.

Barr, James. *Biblical Faith and Natural Theology*. Oxford: Clarendon, 1993.

Beaumont, Joseph. *Some Observations upon the Apologie of Dr Henry More for His Mystery of Godliness*. Cambridge: Printed by John Field, 1665.

Beiser, Frederick C. *The Sovereignty of Reason: The Defense of Rationality in the Early English Enlightenment*. Princeton: Princeton University Press, 1996.

Berlin, Isaiah. *Four Essays on Liberty*. Oxford: Oxford University Press, 1969.

———. *The Age of Enlightenment: The Eighteenth-Century Philosophers*. Oxford: Oxford University Press, 1979.

Blackburne, Francis. *Proposals for an Application to Parliament for Relief the Matter of Subscription to the Liturgy and Thirty-Nine Articles of the Established Church of England*. London: Sold by B. White, 1771.

Bombaro, John J. *Jonathan Edwards's Vision of Reality: The Relationship of God to the World, Redemption, History and the Reprobate*. Oregon: Wipf and Stock, 2011.

Bradley, James E. *Religion, Revolution, and English Radicalism: Nonconformity in Eighteenth-Century Politics and Society*. Cambridge: Cambridge University Press, 1990.

Bramhall, John. *The Works of the Most Reverend Father in God, John Bramhall*. Edited by A.W. Haddan. Vol. 4. 5 vols. Oxford: John Henry Parker, 1844.

Buckley, Michael J. *At the Origins of Modern Atheism*. Yale: Yale University Press, 1987.

Burke, Edmund. "Reflections on the Revolution in France." In *Revolutionary Writings*, edited by Iain Hampsher-Monk, 1–250. Cambridge: Cambridge University Press, 2014.

Burtt, Edwin Arthur. *The Metaphysical Foundations of Modern Physical Science: A Historical and Critical Essay*. London: Kegan Paul, Trench, Trubner & Co., 1925.

Butler, Joseph. *Several Letters to the Reverend Dr. Clark from a Gentleman in Gloucestershire, Relating to the First Volume of the Sermons Preached at Mr. Boyle's Lecture; with the Dr's Answers Thereunto*. London: James Knapton, 1716.

———. *The Analogy of Religion, Natural and Revealed, to the Constitution and Course of Nature*. London: Printed for John and Paul Knapton, 1736.

———. *Fifteen Sermons Preached at the Rolls Chapel. . . to Which Are Added, Six Sermons Preached on Publick Occasions*. London: Printed for John and Paul Knapton, 1749.

Butler, Lilly. "Religion No Matter of Shame." In *A Defence of Natural and Revealed Religion: Being a Collection of the Sermons Preached at the Lecture Founded by the Honourable Robert Boyle Esq (from the Year 1691 to the Year 1732)*, edited by Gilbert Burnet, Vol. 2. London: Printed for Arthur Bettesworth and Charles Hitch, 1739.

Cady, Linell E. "Foundation vs. Scaffolding." *Union Seminary Quarterly* 41 (1987): 45–62.

Cantor, Geoffrey. "Revelation and the Cyclical Cosmos of John Hutchinson." In *Images of the Earth: Essays in the History of the Environmental Sciences*, edited by Ludmilla Jordanova and Roy Porter, 17–35. Oxford: British Society for the History of Science, 1997.

Carter, Benjamin. *'The Little Commonwealth of Man': The Trinitarian Origins of the Ethical and Political Philosophy of Ralph Cudworth*. Leuven: Peeters, 2011.

Cassirer, Ernst. "Giovanni Pico Della Mirandola: A Study in the History of Renaissance Ideas." *Journal of the History of Ideas* 3, no. 2 (1942): 123–44.

———. *The Platonic Renaissance in England*. Translated by James P. Pettegrove. New York: Nelson, 1953.

Caton, Hiram. *The Politics of Progress: The Origins and Development of the Commercial Republic, 1600–1835*. Gainesville: University of Florida Press, 1988.

Cavanaugh, William T. "The City: Beyond Secular Parodies." In *Radical Orthodoxy: A New Theology*, edited by Graham Ward, John Milbank, and Catherine Pickstock, 182–200. London: Routledge, 1998.

Champion, J. A. I. *The Pillars of Priestcraft Shaken: The Church of England and Its Enemies*. Cambridge: Cambridge University Press, 1992.

Chandler, Jake and Victoria S. Harrison, eds. *Probability in the Philosophy of Religion*. Oxford: Oxford University Press, 2012.

Clack, Beverley. "Radical Orthodoxy and Feminist Philosophy of Religion." In *Interpreting the Postmodern: Responses to Radical Orthodoxy*, edited by Rosemary Radford Ruether and Marion Grau, 215–29. London: T&T Clark, 2006.

Clark, J. C. D. *English Society 1660–1832: Religion, Ideology and Politics during the Ancien Régime*. Cambridge: Cambridge University Press, 2000.

Clark, John Ruskin. *Joseph Priestley, a Comet in the System*. San Diego: Torch Publications, 1990.

Clark, Stephen R. L. *Biology and Christian Ethics*. Cambridge: Cambridge University Press, 2000.

———. "What Has Plotinus' One to Do with God?" In *Philosophers and God: At the Frontiers of Faith and Reason*, edited by John Cornwell and Michael McGhee, 21–37. London: Continuum, 2009.

Clarke, Samuel. *The Works of Samuel Clarke*. 4 vols. London: Printed for John and Paul Knapton, 1738.

Clay, Diskin. "Reading the Republic." In *Platonic Writings: Platonic Readings*, edited by Charles L. Griswold, 19–33. London: Routledge, 1998.

Coakley, Sarah. "Feminism and Analytic Philosophy of Religion." In *The Oxford Handbook of Philosophy of Religion*, edited by William J. Wainwright, 494–525. Oxford: Oxford University Press, 2005.

Collins, Jeffrey R. "The Restoration Bishops and the Royal Supremacy." *Church History* 68, no. 3 (1999): 549–80.

Cone, Carl B. *Torchbearer of Freedom: The Influence of Richard Price on Eighteenth Century Thought*. Lexington: University of Kentucky Press, 1952.

Cornwall, Robert D. and William Gibson. "Introduction." In *Religion, Politics and Dissent 1660–1832: Essays in Honour of James E. Bradley*, edited by Robert D. Cornwall and William Gibson, 1–14. Farnham: Ashgate, 2010.

Corrigan, Kevin. " 'Solitary' Mysticism in Plotinus, Proclus, Gregory of Nyssa, and Pseudo-Dionysius." *The Journal of Religion* 76, no. 1 (1996): 28–42.

Coskun, Deniz. "Religious Skepticism, Cambridge Platonism, and Disestablishment." *University of Detroit Mercy Law Review* 579 (2006): 579–99.

Cottingham, John. *The Spiritual Dimension*. Cambridge: Cambridge University Press, 2005.

———. "Plato's Sun and Descartes's Stove: Contemplation and Control in Cartesian Philosophy." In *Rationalism, Platonism and God*, edited by Michael Ayers, 15–44. Oxford: Oxford University Press, 2007.

Coxe, William. *A Letter to the Rev. Richard Price, upon His 'Discourse on the Love of Our Country' Delivered November 4, 1789, to the Society for Commemorating the Revolution in Great Britain*. London: T. Cadell, 1790.

Craig, William Lane. "Objections so Bad I Couldn't Have Made Them up (or, the World's 10 Worst Objections to the Kalam Cosmological Argument." In *Come Let Us Reason: New Essays in Christian Apologetics*, edited by Paul Copan and William Lane Craig, 51–65. Nashville: B&H Publishing Group, 2012.

Crowder, Colin. "Berkeley, Price and the Limitations of the Design Argument." *Enlightenment and Dissent* 8 (1989): 3–24.

Cudworth, Ralph. *The True Intellectual System of the Universe. . . with a Treatise Concerning Eternal and Immutable Morality*. Edited by John Harrison. 3 vols. London: Thomas Tegg, 1845.

———. "The Digression Concerning the Plastick Life of Nature, or an Artificial, Orderly and Methodical Nature." In *The Cambridge Platonists*, edited by C. A. Patrides, 288–325. Cambridge: Cambridge University Press, 1969.

———. "A Sermon Preached before the House of Commons." In *The Cambridge Platonists*, edited by C. A. Patrides, 90–127. Cambridge: Cambridge University Press, 1969.

———. *A Treatise Concerning Eternal and Immutable Morality with a Treatise of Freewill*. Edited by Sarah Hutton. Cambridge: Cambridge University Press, 1996.

———. "Manuscripts on Freedom of the Will." British Library, Additional manuscripts, nos. 4978–82.

Disney, John. *Sermons*. 2 vols. Cambridge: Printed for T. Payne; T. Cadell; J. Woodyer, 1771.

Ditchfield, G. M. "Joseph Priestley and the Complexities of Latitudinarianism in the 1770s." In *Joseph Priestley, Scientist, Philosopher and Theologian*, edited by Isabel Rivers and David L. Wykes, 144–71. Oxford: Oxford University Press, 2008.

Dobbs, Betty Jo Teeter. *The Janus Faces of Genius: The Role of Alchemy in Newton's Thought*. Cambridge: Cambridge University Press, 1991.

Dybikowski, James. "Joseph Priestley, Metaphysician and Philosopher of Religion." In *Joseph Priestley, Scientist, Philosopher and Theologian*, edited by Isabel Rivers and David L. Wykes, 80–112. Oxford: Oxford University Press, 2008.

Eagleton, Terry. *Culture and the Death of God*. London: Yale University Press, 2014.

Evans, C. Stephen. *Natural Signs and Knowledge of God: A New Look at Theistic Arguments*. Oxford: Oxford University Press, 2010.

Fara, Patricia. "Marginalized Practices." In *The Cambridge History of Science, Volume 4: The Eighteenth Century*, edited by Roy Porter, 485–508. Cambridge: Cambridge University Press, 2003.

Ferguson, Adam. *Remarks on a Pamphlet Lately Published by Richard Price*. London: T. Cadell, 1776.

Fitzpatrick, Martin. "Toleration and Truth." *Enlightenment and Dissent* 1 (1982): 3–31.

———. "Rational Dissent and the Enlightenment." *Faith and Freedom* 38, no. 2 (1985): 83–101.

———. "Heretical Religion and Radical Political Ideas in Late Eighteenth-Century England." In *The Transformation of Political Culture: England and Germany in the Late Eighteenth Century*, edited by Eckhart Hellmuth, 339–74. Oxford: Oxford University Press, 1990.

————. "Latitudinarianism at the Parting of the Ways: A Suggestion." In *The Church of England c.1689–c.1833: From Toleration to Tractarianism*, edited by John Walsh, Colin Haydon, and Stephen Taylor, 209–27. Cambridge: Cambridge University Press, 1993.

————. "Enlightenment, Dissent and Toleration." *Enlightenment and Dissent* 28 (2012): 42–72.

Force, James E. "Samuel Clarke's Four Categories of Deism, Isaac Newton and the Bible." In *Scepticism in the History of Philosophy*, edited by Richard H. Popkin, 53–74. London: Kluwer Academic Publishers, 1996.

Fowler, Edward. *The Design of Christianity; or, a Plain Demonstration and Improvement of This Proposition, Viz. That the Enduing Men with Inward Real Righteousness or True Holiness, Was the Ultimate End of Our Saviour's Coming into the World and Is the Great Intendment of His Blessed Gospel.* London: Printed by E. Tyler and R. Holt, 1670.

————. *The Principles and Practices of Certain Moderate Divines of the Church of England.* London: Printed for Lodowick Lloyd, 1670.

Fruchtman Jr, Jack. "Late Latitudinarianism: The Case of David Hartley." *Enlightenment and Dissent* 11 (1992): 3–22.

Garrett, Don. "Philosophy and History in the History of Modern Philosophy." In *The Future for Philosophy*, edited by Brian Leiter, 44–73. Oxford: Clarendon, 2004.

Gascoigne, John. *Cambridge in the Age of Enlightenment: Science, Religion and Politics from the Restoration to the French Revolution.* Cambridge: Cambridge University Press, 1989.

————. "Anglican Latitudinarianism, Rational Dissent and Political Radicalism in the Late Eighteenth Century." In *Enlightenment and Religion: Rational Dissent in Eighteenth-Century Britain*, edited by Knud Haakonssen, 219–40. Cambridge: Cambridge University Press, 1996.

Gay, Peter. *The Enlightenment: An Interpretation: The Rise of Modern Paganism.* London: Weidenfeld and Nicolson, 1967.

Gerrish, B. A. "Natural and Revealed Religion." In *The Cambridge History of Eighteenth-Century Philosophy*, edited by Knud Haakonssen, vol. 1, 641–65. Cambridge: Cambridge University Press, 2006.

Gerson, L. P. "What Is Platonism?" *Journal of the History of Philosophy* 43 (2005): 253–76.

————. *From Plato to Platonism.* London: Cornell University Press, 2013.

Gibbs, F. W. *Joseph Priestley: Adventurer in Science and Champion of Truth.* London: Thomas Nelson & Sons, 1965.

Gibson, William. *The Church of England 1688–1832: Unity and Accord.* London: Routledge, 2001.

————. "Dissenters, Anglicans and Elections after the Toleration Act, 1689–1710." In *Religion, Politics and Dissent 1660–1832: Essays in Honour of James E. Bradley*, edited by Robert D. Cornwall and William Gibson, 129–46. Farnham: Ashgate, 2010.

Gill, Michael B. "The Religious Rationalism of Benjamin Whichcote." *Journal of the History of Philosophy* 37 (1999): 271–300.

Gillespie, Neal C. "Divine Design and the Industrial Revolution: William Paley's Abortive Reform of Natural Theology." *Isis* 81, no. 2 (1990): 214–29.

Gleadle, Kathryn. *Radical Unitarians and the Emergence of the Women's Rights Movement, 1831–51*. London: Macmillan, 1995.

Godwin, William. *Memoirs of the Author of a Vindication of the Rights of Woman, 1798*. Oxford: Woodstock Books, 1990.

Goldie, Mark. "Cambridge Platonists (act. 1630s-1680s)." In *Oxford Dictionary of National Biography Online*, edited by Lawrence Goldman. Oxford: Oxford University Press, 2015. http://www.oxforddnb.com/view/theme/94274. Last accessed 01/05/16.

Goldschmidt, Tyron, ed. *The Puzzle of Existence: Why Is There Something Rather Than Nothing?* London: Routledge, 2013.

Gregory, Jeremy. *Restoration, Reformation and Reform, 1660–1828: Archbishops of Canterbury and Their Diocese*. Oxford: Clarendon, 2000.

Griswold, Jr., Charles L. "Platonic Liberalism: Self-Perfection as a Foundation of Political Theory." In *Plato and Platonism*, edited by Johannes M. van Ophuijsen, 102–34. Washington: University of America Press, 1999.

Grove, Robert. *A Vindication of the Conforming Clergy from the Unjust Aspersions of Heresie*. London: Printed for Walter Kettilby, 1676.

Gunton, Colin. *Enlightenment and Alienation: An Essay toward Trinitarian Theology*. Basingstoke: Marshall Morgan and Scott, 1985.

Haakonssen, Knud. "Enlightened Dissent: An Introduction." In *Enlightenment and Religion: Rational Dissent in Eighteenth-Century Britain*, edited by Knud Haaksonssen, 1–11. Cambridge: Cambridge University Press, 1996.

———. *Enlightenment and Religion: Rational Dissent in Eighteenth-Century Britain*. Cambridge: Cambridge University Press, 1996.

Hadley, Douglas. "A Variation on the Dog and His Bone: The Unity of the World in Plotinian Philosophy," 1998. https://www.bu.edu/wcp/Papers/Meta/MetaHadl.htm. Last accessed 24/04/16.

Hamowy, Ronald. *The Political Sociology of Freedom: Adam Ferguson and F. A. Hayek*. Cheltenham: Edward Elgar, 2005.

Hankey, Wayne J. and Douglas Hedley. "Introduction." In *Deconstructing Radical Orthodoxy: Postmodern Theology, Rhetoric and Truth*, edited by Wayne J. Hankey and Douglas Hedley, xiii–xviii. Aldershot: Ashgate, 2005.

Hanvey, James. "Conclusion: Continuing the Conversation." In *Radical Orthodoxy: A Catholic Enquiry?* edited by Laurence Paul Hemming, 149–72. Aldershot: Ashgate, 2000.

Hare, R. M. *Plato*. Oxford: Oxford University Press, 1982.

Harris, Harriet A. "Struggling for Truth." *Feminist Theology* 28 (2001): 40–56.

———. "A Theological Approach." In *Feminist Philosophy of Religion: Critical Readings*, edited by Pamela Sue Anderson and Beverley Clack, 73–86. London: Routledge, 2004.

Harris, James A. "Joseph Priestley and 'The Proper Doctrine of Philosophical Necessity'." *Enlightenment and Dissent* 20 (2001): 23–44.

Harrison, Peter. "Was Newton a Voluntarist?" In *Newton and Newtonianism: New Studies*, edited by James E. Force and Sarah Hutton, 39–63. London: Kluwer Academic Publishers, 2004.

Harrison, Victoria S. "What's the Use of Philosophy of Religion?" In *God, Goodness and Philosophy*, edited by Harriet A. Harris, 29–43. Farnham: Ashgate, 2011.

Hartley, David. *Observations on Man, His Frame, His Duty, and His Expectations*. London: T. Tegg and son, 1834.

Heathcote, Ralph. *The Use of Reason Asserted in Matters of Religion: Or, Natural Religion the Foundation of Revealed*. London: Printed for Thomas Payne, 1756.

Hedley, Douglas. "Should Divinity Overcome Metaphysics? Reflections on John Milbank's Theology beyond Secular Reason and Confessions of a Cambridge Platonist." *The Journal of Religion* 80, no. 2 (2000): 271–98.

———. "Real Atheism and Cambridge Platonism: Men of Latitude, Polemics, and the Great Dead Philosophers." In *Platonisms: Ancient, Modern, and Postmodern*, edited by Kevin Corrigan and John D. Turner, 155–73. Leiden: Brill, 2007.

———. "Imagination and Natural Theology." In *The Oxford Handbook of Natural Theology*, edited by Russell Re-Manning, John Hedley Brooke, and Fraser Watts, 539–50. Oxford: Oxford University Press, 2013.

Hill, Bridget. "The Links between Mary Wollstonecraft and Catharine Macaulay: New Evidence." *Women's History Review* 4, no. 2 (1995): 177–92.

Hoadly, Benjamin. *A Preservative against the Principles and Practices of the Non-Jurors Both in Church and State.* Dublin: Printed by A. Rhames, for E. Dobson, 1716.

Hobbes, Thomas. *The English Works of Thomas Hobbes.* Edited by William Molesworth. 11 vols. London: Routledge, 1992.

———. "Of Liberty and Necessity." In *Hobbes and Bramhall on Liberty and Necessity*, edited by Vere Chappell, 15–42. Cambridge: Cambridge University Press, 1999.

Hoecker, James J. "Joseph Priestley and the Reification of Religion." *Price Priestley Newsletter* 2 (1978): 44–75.

Hoffmeyer, John F. "Charitable Interpretation." In *Interpreting the Postmodern: Responses to Radical Orthodoxy*, edited by Rosemary Radford Ruether and Marion Grau, 3–17. London: T&T Clark, 2006.

Holmes, Geoffrey. *The Trial of Doctor Sacheverell.* London: Eyre Methuen, 1973.

Horkheimer, Max and Theodor W. Adorno. *Dialectic of Enlightenment: Philosophical Fragments.* Translated by Edmund Jephcott. Stanford: Stanford University Press, 2002.

Horne, George. *The Works of George Horne: to which are prefixed memoirs of his life, studies and writings by William Jones.* London: Printed for J. Johnson, 1818.

Hutchinson, John. *The Philosophical and Theological Works of John Hutchinson.* Edited by Robert Spearman and Julius Bate. 12 vols. London: Printed for J. Hodges, 1748–9.

Hutton, Sarah. "Introduction." In *A Treatise Concerning Eternal and Immutable Morality with a Treatise of Freewill*, edited by Sarah Hutton, ix–xxx. Cambridge: Cambridge University Press, 1996.

———. "Lord Herbert of Cherbury and the Cambridge Platonists." In *British Philosophy and the Age of Enlightenment*, edited by Stuart Brown, 20–42. London: Routledge, 1996.

———. "The Ethical Background of the Rights of Women." In *Philosophical Theory and the Universal Declaration of Human Rights*, edited by William Sweet, 27–40. Ottawa: University of Ottawa Press, 2003.

———. "A Radical Review of the Cambridge Platonists." In *Varieties of Seventeenth- and Early Eighteenth Century English Radicalism in Context*, edited by Ariel Hessayon and David Finnegan, 161–82. Farnham: Ashgate, 2011.

Hyland, Drew A. "Plato's Three Waves and the Question of Utopia." *Interpretation* 18 (1990): 91–109.

Israel, Jonathan I. *Radical Enlightenment: Philosophy and the Making of Modernity, 1650–1750.* Oxford: Oxford University Press, 2001.

———. *Enlightenment Contested: Philosophy, Modernity, and the Emancipation of Man, 1670–1752.* Oxford: Oxford University Press, 2006.

———. "Enlightenment! Which Enlightenment?" *Journal of the History of Ideas* 67, no. 3 (2006): 523–45.

———. *A Revolution of the Mind: Radical Enlightenment and the Intellectual Origins of Modern Democracy*. Princeton: Princeton University Press, 2010.

———. *Democratic Enlightenment: Philosophy, Revolution, and Human Rights 1750–1790*. Oxford: Oxford University Press, 2011.

Jackson, John. *Three Letters to Dr Clarke, from a Clergyman of the Church of England; Concerning His Scripture-Doctrine of the Trinity. With the Doctor's Replies*. London: Printed for John Baker, 1714.

———. *The Grounds of Civil and Ecclesiastical Government Briefly Considered*. London: Printed by A. Rhames, for E. Dobson, 1718.

Jacob, Margaret C. *The Newtonians and the English Revolution, 1689–1720*. Hassocks, Sussex: The Harvester Press, 1976.

———. "The Crisis of the European Mind: Hazard Revisited." In *Politics and Culture in Early Modern Europe: Essays in Honor of H. G. Koenigsberger*, edited by Phyllis Mack and Margaret C. Jacob, 251–71. Cambridge: Cambridge University Press, 1987.

Jammer, Max. *Concepts of Space: The History of Theories of Space in Physics*. Cambridge, MA: Harvard University Press, 1954.

Jantzen, Grace M. *Becoming Divine: Towards a Feminist Philosophy of Religion*. Bloomington, IN: Indiana University Press, 1999.

———. "Feminist Philosophy of Religion: Open Discussion with Pamela Anderson." *Feminist Theology* 26 (2001): 102–9.

Jebb, John. *The Works, Theological, Medical, Political, and Miscellaneous of John Jebb with Memoirs of the Life of the Author by John Disney*. Vol. II. 3 vols. London: Printed for T. Cadell, 1787.

Jenyns, Soame. "A Free Inquiry into the Nature and Origin of Evil: In Six Letters to -. " In *Miscellaneous Pieces in Verse and Prose*, 221–370. London: Printed for J. Dodsley, 1770.

Jones, William. *An Essay on the Church*. London: Printed by R. Raikes, 1787.

———. "Preface." In *The Works of the Right Rev. George Horne*, Vol. 1, ix–xxx. London: Printed for J. Johnson, 1818.

———. "The Life of Bishop Horne." In *The Theological and Miscellaneous Works of the Rev. William Jones*, Vol. 6, 1–172. London: Printed for C. and J. Rivington, 1826.

———. *The Theological and Miscellaneous Works of the Rev. William Jones*. London: Printed for C. and J. Rivington, 1826.

Kassler, Jamie C. *Seeking Truth: Roger North's Notes on Newton and Correspondence with Samuel Clarke c.1704–1713*. Farnham: Ashgate, 2014.

Kemp Smith, Norman. "Is Divine Existence Credible?" In *Religion and Understanding*, edited by D. Z. Phillips, 105–25. Oxford: Basil Blackwell, 1967.

Knight, Kelvin, ed. *The MacIntyre Reader*. Cambridge: Polity Press, 1998.

Kubrin, David. "Newton's Inside Out! Magic, Class Struggle, and the Rise of Mechanism in the West." In *The Analytic Spirit: Essays in the History of Science*, edited by Harry Woolf, 96–121. London: Cornell University Press, 1981.

Kuhn, Albert J. "Glory or Gravity: Hutchinson vs. Newton." *Journal of the History of Ideas* 22 (1961): 303–22.

Laboucheix, Henri. "Chemistry, Materialism and Theology in the Work of Joseph Priestley." *Price Priestley Newsletter* 1 (1977): 31–48.

Lee, Stephen M. "Parliament, Parties and Elections (1760–1815)." In *A Companion to Eighteenth-Century Britain*, edited by H. T. Dickinson, 69–80. Oxford: Blackwell, 2002.

Leech, David. *The Hammer of the Cartesian: Henry More's Philosophy of Spirit and the Origins of Modern Atheism*. Leuven: Peters, 2013.

Leighton, C. D. A. " 'Knowledge of Divine Things': A Study of Hutchinsonianism." *History of European Ideas* 26, no. 3–4 (2000): 159–75.

Lloyd, Genevieve. *The Man of Reason: 'Male' and 'Female' in Western Philosophy*. London: Methuen, 1984.

Loades, Ann. *Feminist Theology: Voices from the Past*. Cambridge: Polity Press, 2001.

Locke, John. *An Essay Concerning Human Understanding*. 2 vols. Dublin: Printed for H. Saunders, W. Sleater, D. Chamberlaine and J. Potts, 1777.

———. *Two Treatises of Government Edited with an Introduction and Notes by Peter Laslett*. Cambridge: Cambridge University Press, 1988.

Lucci, Diego. "William Wollaston's Religion of Nature." In *Atheism and Deism Revalued: Heterodox Religious Identities in Britain, 1650–1800*, edited by Wayne Hudson, Diego Lucci, and Jeffrey R. Wigelsworth, 119–38. Farnham: Ashgate, 2014.

Lund, Roger D. "Introduction." In *The Margins of Orthodoxy: Heterodox Writing and Cultural Response, 1660–1750*, edited by Roger D. Lund, 1–29. Cambridge: Cambridge University Press, 1995.

Macaulay, Catharine. *Observations on the Reflections of the Right Hon. Edmund Burke on the Revolution in France, in a Letter to the Right Hon. the Earl of Stanhope*. London: C. Dilly, 1790.

MacIntyre, Alasdair. *A Short History of Ethics: A History of Moral Philosophy from the Homeric Age to the Twentieth Century*. London: Routledge, 1967.

———. *After Virtue: A Study in Moral Theory*. 2nd ed. London: Duckworth, 1985.

Manuel, Frank E. *The Religion of Isaac Newton: The Fremantle Lectures 1973*. Oxford: Clarendon, 1974.

Mara, Gerald M. "Socrates and Liberal Toleration." *Political Theory* 16 (1988): 468–95.

McEvoy, J. G. and J. E. McGuire. "God and Nature: Priestley's Way of Rational Dissent." *Historical Studies in the Physical Sciences* 6 (1975): 325–404.

McGrath, Alister. *The Renewal of Anglicanism*. London: SPCK, 1993.

McGuire, J. E. "Predicates of Pure Existence: Newton on God's Space and Time." In *Philosophical Perspectives on Newtonian Science*, edited by Phillip Bricker and R. I. G. Hughes, 91–108. Cambridge, MA: MIT Press, 1990.

———. "The Fate of the Date: The Theology of Newton's 'Principia' Revisited." In *Rethinking the Scientific Revolution*, edited by Margaret J. Osler, 271–95. Cambridge: Cambridge University Press, 2000.

Meister, Chad, ed. *The Philosophy of Religion Reader*. London: Routledge, 2008.

———. *Philosophy of Religion*. Basingstoke: Palgrave Macmillan, 2014.

Milbank, John. *Theology and Social Theory: Beyond Secular Reason*. Oxford: Blackwell, 1993.

———. *Being Reconciled: Ontology and Pardon*. London: Routledge, 2003.

Milbank, John, Graham Ward, and Catherine Pickstock. "Introduction: Suspending the Material: The Turn of Radical Orthodoxy." In *Radical Orthodoxy: A New Theology*, edited by John Milbank, Catherine Pickstock, and Graham Ward, 1–20. London: Routledge, 1999.

Miller, Corey and Paul Gould, eds. *Is Faith in God Reasonable? Debates in Philosophy, Science, and Rhetoric.* London: Routledge, 2014.

Mills, Simon. "Scripture and Heresy in the Biblical Studies of Nathaniel Lardner, Joseph Priestley, and Thomas Belsham." In *Dissent and the Bible in Britain, c.1650–1950*, edited by Scott Mandelbrote and Michael Ledger-Lomas, 85–112. Oxford: Oxford University Press, 2013.

Mintz, Samuel I. *The Hunting of Leviathan: Seventeenth Century Reactions to the Materialism and Moral Philosophy of Thomas Hobbes.* Cambridge: Cambridge University Press, 1970.

Money, John. "Joseph Priestley in Cultural Context: Philosophic Spectacle, Popular Belief and Popular Politics in Eighteenth-Century Birmingham." *Enlightenment and Dissent* 8 (1989): 69–89.

More, Henry. *An Antidote against Atheism: Or, an Appeal to the Naturall Faculties of the Minde of Man.* Edited by G. A. J. Rogers. Bristol: Thoemmes Press, 1655.

———. *An Explanation of the Grand Mystery of Godliness.* London: Thoemmes Press, 1660.

———. *An Account of Virtue: Or, Dr. Henry More's Abridgement of Morals.* London: Printed for Benjamin Tooke, 1690.

———. "Conjectura Cabbalistica." In *A Collection of Several Philosophical Writings of Dr. Henry More.* London: Printed by Joseph Downing, 1712.

———. *Henry More's Manual of Metaphysics: A Translation of the Enchiridium Metaphysicum* (1679), translated by Alexander Jacob. Hildesheim: G. Olms Verlag, 1995.

Mori, Jennifer. *Britain in the Age of the French Revolution, 1785–1820.* Harlow, Essex: Pearson, 2000.

Muirhead, John H. *The Platonic Tradition in Anglo-Saxon Philosophy.* London: Macmillan, 1931.

Muller, Richard A. "Philip Doddridge and the Formulation of Calvinistic Theology in an Era of Rationalism and Deconfessionalization." In *Religion, Politics and Dissent 1660–1832: Essays in Honour of James E. Bradley*, edited by Robert D. Cornwall and William Gibson, 65–84. Farnham: Ashgate, 2010.

Nagasawa, Yujin. *Scientific Approaches to the Philosophy of Religion.* Basingstoke: Palgrave Macmillan, 2012.

Neu, Jerome. "Plato's Analogy of State and Individual: The Republic and the Organic Theory of the State." *Philosophy* 46 (1971): 238–54.

Newton, Isaac. "General Scholium." In *Mathematical Principles of Natural Philosophy*, Vol. 2. London: Benjamin Motte, 1729. www.newtonproject.ox.ac.uk/view/texts/normalized/NATP00056. Last accessed 01/02/17.

———. "De Gravitatione et Aequipondio Fluidorum." In *Unpublished Scientific Papers of Isaac Newton*, edited by A. Rupert Hall and Marie Boas Hall, 89–156. Cambridge: Cambridge University Press, 1962.

Nietzsche, Friedrich. "Ecce Homo." In *Nietzsche: The Anti-Christ, Ecce Homo, Twilight of the Idols: And Other Writings*, edited by Aaron Ridley and Judith Norman, 69–152. Cambridge: Cambridge University Press, 2005.

Pagden, Anthony. *The Enlightenment and Why It Still Matters.* Oxford: Oxford University Press, 2013.

Page, Anthony. "The Enlightenment and a 'Second Reformation': The Religion and Philosophy of John Jebb (1736–86)." *Enlightenment and Dissent* 17 (1998): 48–82.

———. *John Jebb and the Enlightenment Origins of British Radicalism*. London: Praeger, 2003.

Pailin, David. "Reconciling Theory and Fact: The Problem of 'Other Faiths' in Lord Herbert and the Cambridge Platonists." In *Platonism at the Origins of Modernity: Studies on Platonism and Early Modern Philosophy*, edited by Douglas Hedley and Sarah Hutton, 93–112. Dordrecht: Springer, 2008.

Paley, William. *The Principles of Moral and Political Philosophy*. 2 vols. Dublin: Printed for Messrs. Exshaw, White, H. Whitestone, Byrne, Cash, Marchbank, and Mc.Kenzie, 1785.

———. *Reasons for Contentment Addressed to the Laboring Part of the British Public*. London: R. Faulder, 1793.

Patrick, Simon. *A Brief Account of the New Sect of Latitude-Men Together with Some Reflections upon the New Philosophy*. London, 1662.

Patrides, C. A., ed. *The Cambridge Platonists*. Cambridge: Cambridge University Press, 1969.

———. "'The High and Aiery Hills of Platonisme': An Introduction to the Cambridge Platonists." In *The Cambridge Platonists*, edited by C. A. Patrides, 1–41. Cambridge: Cambridge University Press, 1969.

Peach, W. B. "The Ethics of Richard Price." PhD, Cambridge, MA, 1951.

———. "Preface." In *Richard Price and the Ethical Foundations of the American Revolution: Selections from His Pamphlets, with Appendices*, edited by B. W. Peach, 9–12. Durham, NC: Duke University Press, 1979.

Pfizenmaier, Thomas C. "Why the Third Fell Out: Trinitarian Dissent." In *Religion, Politics and Dissent 1660–1832: Essays in Honour of James E. Bradley*, edited by Robert D. Cornwall and William Gibson, 17–33. Farnham: Ashgate, 2010.

Philp, Mark. "Rational Religion and Political Radicalism in the 1790s." *Enlightenment and Dissent* 4 (1985): 35–46.

———. *Godwin's Political Justice*. London: Duckworth, 1986.

Plato. *Protagoras*. Translated by W. K. C. Guthrie. London: Penguin, 1956.

———. "The Apology." In *The Last Days of Socrates*, translated by Hugh Tredennick, 45–76. London: Penguin, 1959.

———. "Euthyphro." In *The Last Days of Socrates*, translated by Hugh Tredennick, 19–41. London: Penguin, 1959.

———. *Phaedrus & Letters VII and VIII*. Translated by Walter Hamilton. Harmondsworth: Penguin, 1973.

———. *The Laws*. Translated by Trevor J. Saunders. London: Penguin, 1975.

———. *Timaeus*. Translated by Desmond Lee. London: Penguin, 1977.

———. *The Republic*. Translated by Desmond Lee. 2nd ed. London: Penguin, 1987.

———. *Theaetetus*. Translated by Robin A. H. Waterfield. London: Penguin, 1987.

———. *Phaedo*. Translated by David Gallop. Oxford: Oxford University Press, 1999.

Plotinus. *Enneads*. Translated by A. H. Armstrong. Loeb Classical Library. London: Heinemann, 1966–88.

Pocock, J. G. A. "Post-Puritan England and the Problem of the Enlightenment." In *Culture and Politics from Puritanism to the Enlightenment*, edited by Perez Zagorin, 91–111. London: University of California Press, 1980.

———. "Conservative Enlightenment and Democratic Revolutions: The American and French Cases in British Perspective." *Government and Opposition* 24 (1989): 81–105.

———. *The Varieties of British Political Thought 1500–1800*. Cambridge: Cambridge University Press, 1993.

Poovey, Mary. *The Proper Lady and the Woman Writer: Ideology as Style in the Works of Mary Wollstonecraft, Mary Shelley, and Jane Austin*. London: University of Chicago Press, 1984.

Popkin, Richard H. "The Crisis of Polytheism and the Answers of Vollius, Cudworth, and Newton." In *Essays on the Context, Nature, and Influence of Isaac Newton's Theology*, edited by James Force and Richard H. Popkin, 9–25. London: Kluwer Academic Publishers, 1990.

Popper, Karl. *The Open Society and Its Enemies*. London: Routledge, 2002.

Porter, Roy. *The Enlightenment*. Basingstoke: Palgrave Macmillan, 1990.

Powicke, Frederick J. *The Cambridge Platonists: A Study*. London: J. M. Dent, 1926.

Pretyman, George. *A Sermon Preached before the Lords. . . in the Abbey Church of Westminster, on Friday, January 30, 1789*. London: T. Cadell, 1789.

———. *A Sermon Preached at the Cathedral Church of St. Paul, London before His Majesty and Both Houses of Parliament 1797*. London: T. Cadell, 1798.

Price, Richard. *The Nature and Dignity of the Human Soul: A Sermon Preached at St. Thomas', January the Fifth, 1766*. London: A. Millar, 1766.

———. *Sermons on the Christian Doctrine*. London: Printed for T. Cadell, 1787.

———. *Thoughts on the Progress of Socinianism; with an Enquiry into the Cause and the Cure. In a Letter Humbly Addressed to Learned, Orthodox, and Candid Ministers of All Denominations: With a Particular View to the Writing of Dr. Priestley: To Which Is Added, a Letter to Dr. Price, on His Late Sermons on the Christian Doctrine*. London: J. Buckland and J. Johnson, 1787.

———. *Sermons on Various Subjects*. Edited by W. Morgan. London: Longman, 1816.

———. "A Dissertation on the Being and Attributes of the Deity." In *A Review of the Principal Questions in Morals*, edited by D. Daiches Raphael, 285–96. Oxford: Clarendon, 1948.

———. *A Review of the Principal Questions in Morals*. 3rd ed. Oxford: Clarendon, 1948.

———. *The Correspondence of Richard Price*. Edited by W. B. Peach and D. O. Thomas. 3 vols. Durham NC: Duke University Press, 1983.

———. *Political Writings*. Edited by D. O. Thomas. Cambridge: Cambridge University Press, 1991.

Priestley, Joseph. *A Serious Address to the Masters of Families*. London: Printed for J. Johnson, 1770.

———. *A Free Discussion of the Doctrines of Materialism and Philosophical Necessity. In a Correspondence between Dr. Price and Dr. Priestley: To Which Are Added, by Dr. Priestley, An Introduction, Explaining the Nature of the Controversy, and Letters to Several Writers Who Have Animadverted on His Disquisitions Relating to Matter and Spirit or His Treatise on Necessity*. London: T. Cadell, 1778.

———. *The Theological and Miscellaneous Works of Joseph Priestley*. Edited by John Towill Rutt. 24 vols. London: Printed by George Smallfield, 1817–31.

Raphael, D. Daiches. "Introduction." In *A Review of the Principal Questions in Morals*, edited by D. Daiches Raphael, ix–xlvii. Oxford: Clarendon, 1948.

Rauschenbusch-Clough, Emma. *A Study of Mary Wollstonecraft*. London: Longmans, Green and Co., 1898.

Rawls, John. "Justice as Fairness: Political Not Metaphysical." *Philosophy and Public Affairs* 14 (1985): 223–51.

———. *A Theory of Justice*. Revised. Harvard: Harvard University Press, 1999.

Rea, Michael C. "Introduction." In *Analytic Theology: New Essays in the Philosophy of Theology*, edited by Oliver D. Crisp and Michael C. Rea, 1–30. Oxford: Oxford University Press, 2009.

Rea, Michael C. and Louis Pojman, eds. *Philosophy of Religion: An Anthology*. 7th ed. Stamford: Cengage, 2015.

Rée, Jonathan. "Philosophy and the History of Philosophy." In *Philosophy and Its Past*, edited by Jonathan Rée, Michael Ayers, and Adam Westoby, 1–39. Hassocks, Sussex: The Harvester Press, 1978.

Rivers, Isabel. " 'Galen's Muscles': Wilkins, Hume, and the Educational Use of the Argument from Design." *The Historical Journal* 36, no. 3 (1993): 577–9.

Rivers, Isabel and David L. Wykes. "Introduction." In *Joseph Priestley, Scientist, Philosopher and Theologian*, edited by Isabel Rivers and David L. Wykes, 1–19. Oxford: Oxford University Press, 2008.

Roberts, James Deotis. *From Puritanism to Platonism in Seventeenth Century England*. The Hague: Springer, 2012.

Rogers, G. A. J. *Locke's Enlightenment: Aspects of the Origin, Nature and Impact of His Philosophy*. New York: Olms Verlog, 1998.

———. "Locke, Plato and Platonism." In *Platonism at the Origins of Modernity: Studies on Platonism and Early Modern Philosophy*, edited by Douglas Hedley and Sarah Hutton, 193–205. Dordrecht: Springer, 2008.

Roochnik, David. *Beautiful City: The Dialectical Character of Plato's 'Republic'*. London: Cornell University Press, 2003.

Rorty, Richard, J. B. Schneewind, and Quentin Skinner. "Introduction." In *Philosophy in History: Essays on the Historiography of Philosophy*, edited by Richard Rorty, J. B. Schneewind, and Quentin Skinner, 1–14. Cambridge: Cambridge University Press, 1984.

Sapiro, Fiore. "The Spiritual Vindications of Mary Wollstonecraft." *Enlightenment and Dissent* 26 (2010): 195–229.

Saveson, J. E. "Differing Reactions to Descartes among the Cambridge Platonists." *Journal of the History of Ideas* 21 (1960): 560–7.

Schellenberg, John L. "Imagining the Future: How Scepticism Can Renew Philosophy of Religion." In *Contemporary Practice and Method in the Philosophy of Religion: New Essays*, edited by David Cheetham and Rolfe King, 15–31. London: Continuum, 2008.

Schofield, Robert E. *The Enlightenment of Joseph Priestley: A Study of His Life and Work from 1733 to 1773*. University Park, PA: Pennsylvania State University Press, 1997.

Scott, D. "Platonic Recollection and Cambridge Platonism." *Hermathena* 149 (1990): 73–97.

Sedley, David. "The Ideal of Godlikeness." In *Plato*, edited by Gail Fine, 791–810. Oxford: Oxford University Press, 2000.

Seed, John. " 'A Set of Men Powerful Enough in Many Things': Rational Dissent and Political Opposition in England, 1770–1790." In *Enlightenment and Religion: Rational Dissent in Eighteenth-Century Britain*, edited by Knud Haakonssen, 140–68. Cambridge: Cambridge University Press, 1996.

Sell, Alan P. F. "Samuel Clarke on the Existence of God." *Enlightenment and Dissent* 3 (1984): 65–75.

———. "Henry Grove: A Dissenter at the Parting of the Ways." *Enlightenment and Dissent* 4 (1985): 53–63.

Shakespeare, Steven. *Radical Orthodoxy: An Introduction*. London: SPCK, 2007.

Shapiro, B. J. "Latitudinarianism and Science and Seventeenth-Century England." *Past and Present* 40 (1968): 16–41.

Sireci, Fiore. "The Spiritual Vindications of Mary Wollstonecraft." *Enlightenment and Dissent* 26 (2010): 195–229.

Slowik, Edward. "Newton's Neo-Platonic Ontology of Space." *Foundations of Science* 18 (2013): 419–48.

Smith, James K. A. *Introducing Radical Orthodoxy: Mapping a Post-Secular Theology*. Grand Rapids, MI: Baker Academic, 2004.

Smith, John. *Select Discourses*. London: Printed by J. Flesher, for W. Morden, bookseller in Cambridge, 1660.

Smith, William Cantwell. *The Meaning and End of Religion: A Revolutionary Approach to the Great Religious Traditions*. London: SPCK, 1962.

Snobelen, Stephen D. "Isaac Newton, Heresy Laws and the Persecution of Dissent." *Enlightenment and Dissent* 25 (2009): 204–59.

Socinus, Faustus. *The Racovian Catechisme*. Amsterdam: Printed for Brooer Janz, 1652.

Solomon, Robert. *The Joy of Philosophy: Thinking Thin versus the Passionate Life*. Oxford: Oxford University Press, 1999.

Spellman, W. M. *The Latitudinarians and the Church of England, 1660–1700*. Athens, GA: University of Georgia Press, 1993.

Sprague, Elmer. "Hume, Henry More and the Design Argument." *Hume Studies* 14, no. 2 (1988): 305–27.

Spurr, John. "'Latitudinarianism' and the Restoration Church." *The Historical Journal* 31, no. 1 (1988): 61–82.

Standish, John. *A Sermon Preached before the King at White-Hal, September 26th 1675*. London: Printed by Henry Brome, 1676.

Stanlis, Peter J. *Edmund Burke: The Enlightenment and Revolution*. London: Transaction Publishers, 1991.

Stephen, Leslie. *History of English Thought in the Eighteenth Century*. 2 vols. London: Smith, Elder & Co., 1876.

Stewart, Larry. "Samuel Clarke, Newtonianism, and the Factions of Post-Revolutionary England." *Journal of the History of Ideas* 42, no. 1 (1981): 53–72.

Sullivan, Robert E. *John Toland and the Deist Controversy: A Study in Adaptations*. Cambridge, MA: Harvard University Press, 1982.

Swinburne, Richard. *The Existence of God*. Revised. Oxford: Clarendon, 1991.

———. *The Coherence of Theism*. Revised. Oxford: Clarendon, 1993.

———. "Intellectual Autobiography." In *Reason and the Christian Tradition: Essays in Honour of Richard Swinburne*, edited by Alan G. Padgett, 1–18. Oxford: Clarendon, 1994.

———. "Philosophical Theism." In *Philosophy of Religion in the 21st Century*, edited by D. Z. Phillips and Timothy Tessin, 3–20. Basingstoke: Palgrave Macmillan, 2001.

———. "The Value and Christian Roots of Analytical Philosophy of Religion." In *Faith and Philosophical Analysis: The Impact of Analytical Philosophy on the*

Philosophy of Religion, edited by Harriet A. Harris and Christopher J. Insole, 33–45. Aldershot: Ashgate, 2005.

Taliaferro, Charles. *Evidence and Faith: Philosophy and Religion since the Seventeenth Century.* Cambridge: Cambridge University Press, 2005.

Taliaferro, Charles and Alison Teply. "Introduction to Cambridge Platonism." In *Cambridge Platonist Spirituality*, edited by Charles Taliaferro and Alison Teply, 5–54. Mahwah, NJ: Paulist Press, 2004.

Taylor, Anya. "Coleridge, Wollstonecraft, and the Rights of Women." In *Coleridge's Visionary Languages: Essays in Honour of J. B. Beer*, edited by Tim Fulford and Morton D. Paley, 83–98. Cambridge: D. S. Brewer, 1993.

Taylor, Barbara. "The Religious Foundations of Mary Wollstonecraft's Feminism." In *The Cambridge Companion to Mary Wollstonecraft*, edited by Claudia L. Johnson, 99–118. Cambridge: Cambridge University Press, 2002.

———. *Mary Wollstonecraft and the Feminist Imagination.* Cambridge: Cambridge University Press, 2003.

Taylor, Charles. *A Secular Age.* Cambridge, MA: Belknap Press of Harvard University Press, 2007.

Tennant, Bob. *Conscience, Consciousness and Ethics in Joseph Butler's Philosophy and Ministry.* Woodbridge: The Boydell Press, 2011.

Thomas, D. O. *The Honest Mind: The Thought and Work of Richard Price.* Oxford: Clarendon, 1977.

Todd, Janet. *Mary Wollstonecraft: A Revolutionary Life.* London: Weidenfeld and Nicolson, 2000.

Toland, John. *Christianity Not Mysterious or, a Treatise Shewing, That There Is Nothing in the Gospel Contrate to Reason, nor above It: And That No Christian Doctrine Can Be Properly Call'd a Mystery.* London, 1702.

Tomalin, Claire. *The Life and Death of Mary Wollstonecraft.* Middlesex: Penguin, 1974.

Trakakis, Nick. *The End of Philosophy of Religion.* London: Continuum, 2008.

Versenyi, Laszlo G. "Plato and His Liberal Opponents." *Philosophy* 46 (1971): 222–37.

Wainwright, William J. "Philosophical Theology at the End of the Century." In *Philosophy of Religion in the 21st Century*, edited by D. Z. Phillips and Timothy Tessin, 21–30. Basingstoke: Palgrave Macmillan, 2001.

———, ed. *The Oxford Handbook of Philosophy of Religion.* Oxford: Oxford University Press, 2008.

Walsh, John and Stephen Taylor. "Introduction: The Church and Anglicanism in the 'Long' Eighteenth Century." In *The Church of England c.1689–c.1833: From Toleration to Tractarianism*, edited by John Walsh, Colin Haydon, and Stephen Taylor, 1–66. Cambridge: Cambridge University Press, 1993.

Wardle, Ralph M. *Mary Wollstonecraft: A Critical Biography.* London: The Richards Press Ltd., 1951.

Waterman, A. M. C. "The Nexus between Theology and Political Doctrine in Church and Dissent." In *Enlightenment and Religion: Rational Dissent in Eighteenth-Century Britain*, edited by Knud Haakonssen, 193–218. Cambridge: Cambridge University Press, 1996.

Waters, Kristin, ed. *Women and Men Political Theorists: Enlightened Conversations.* Oxford: Blackwell, 2000.

Watts, Ruth. *Gender, Power and the Unitarians in England 1760–1860.* Harlow, Essex: Longman, 1988.

————. "Introduction: Rational Dissenting Women and the Travel of Ideas." *Enlightenment and Dissent* 26 (2010): 1–27.

Webb, R. K. "The Emergence of Rational Dissent." In *Enlightenment and Religion: Rational Dissent in Eighteenth-Century Britain*, edited by Knud Haakonssen, 12–41. Cambridge: Cambridge University Press, 1996.

————. "Perspectives on David Hartley." *Enlightenment and Dissent* 17 (1998): 17–47.

Whichcote, Benjamin. *The Works of the Learned Benjamin Whichcote*. 4 vols. Aberdeen: Printed by J. Chalmers, for Alexander Thomson, 1751.

————. *Moral and Religious Aphorisms*. London: Printed for J. Payne, 1753.

Wilde, C. B. "Hutchinsonianism, Natural Philosophy and Religious Controversy in Eighteenth Century Britain." *History of Science* 18 (1980): 1–24.

Wilkins, John. *Of the Principles and Duties of Natural Religion*. London: Printed for R. Chiswell, 1710.

Williams, Bernard. "The Analogy of City and Soul in Plato's Republic." In *Plato 2: Ethics, Politics, Religion and the Soul*, edited by Gail Fine, 297–308. Oxford: Oxford University Press, 1999.

Wollstonecraft, Mary. *Collected Letters of Mary Wollstonecraft*. Edited by Ralph M. Wardle. London: Cornell University Press, 1979.

————. *A Short Residence in Sweden, Norway and Denmark and William Godwin Memoirs of the Author of the Rights of Woman. Edited with an Introduction and Notes by Richard Holmes*. Harmondsworth: Penguin, 1987.

————. *The Works of Mary Wollstonecraft*. Edited by Janet Todd and Marilyn Butler. 7 vols. London: William Pickering, 1989.

————. *A Vindication of the Rights of Men and a Vindication of the Rights of Woman*. Edited by Sylvana Tomaselli. Cambridge: Cambridge University Press, 1995.

Wood, Gordon S. *The Creation of the American Republic 1776–1787*. Williamsburg, VA: University of North Carolina Press, 1969.

————. "Classical Republicanism and the American Revolution." *Chicago-Kent Law Review* 66, no. 1 (1990): 13–38.

Wykes, David L. "The Contribution of the Dissenting Academy to the Emergence of Rational Dissent." In *Enlightenment and Religion: Rational Dissent in Eighteenth-Century Britain*, edited by Knud Haakonssen, 99–139. Cambridge: Cambridge University Press, 1996.

————. "Religious Dissent, the Church, and the Repeal of the Occasional Conformity and Schism Acts, 1714–19." In *Religion, Politics and Dissent 1660–1832: Essays in Honour of James E. Bradley*, edited by Robert D Cornwall and William Gibson, 165–83. Farnham: Ashgate, 2010.

Wynn, Mark R. *God and Goodness: A Natural Theological Perspective*. London: Routledge, 1999.

————. *Faith and Place: An Essay in Embodied Religious Epistemology*. Oxford: Oxford University Press, 2009.

Young, B. W. *Religion and Enlightenment in Eighteenth-Century England: Theological Debate from Locke to Burke*. Oxford: Clarendon, 1997.

Zaw, Susan Khin. "The Reasonable Heart: Mary Wollstonecraft's View of the Relation between Reason and Feeling in Morality, Moral Psychology, and Moral Development." *Hypatia* 13, no. 1 (1998): 78–117.

Zebrowski, Martha K. "Richard Price: British Platonist of the Eighteenth Century." *Journal of the History of Ideas* 55, no. 1 (1994): 17–35.

———. "Commanded of God, Because 'Tis Holy and Good': The Christian Platonism and Natural Law of Samuel Clarke." *Enlightenment and Dissent* 16 (1997): 3–28.

———. "We May Venture to Say, That the Number of Platonic Readers Is Considerable: Richard Price, Joseph Priestley and the Platonic Strand in Eighteenth Century Thought." *Enlightenment and Dissent* 19 (2000): 193–213.

———. "John William Thomson's 1728 Edition of Plato's 'Parmenides': A Calvinist Humanist from Königsberg Reads Platonic Theology in Oxford." *British Journal for Eighteenth Century Studies* 30, no. 1 (2007): 113–31.

Index